"THE HIGHER CHRISTIAN LIFE"

SOURCES FOR THE STUDY OF THE HOLINESS, PENTECOSTAL, AND KESWICK MOVEMENTS

A forty-eight-volume facsimile series reprinting extremely rare documents for the study of nineteenth-century religious and social history, the rise of feminism, and the history of the Pentecostal and Charismatic movements

Edited by

Donald W. Dayton
Northern Baptist Theological Seminary

Advisory Editors

D. William Faupel, *Asbury Theological Seminary*
Cecil M. Robeck, Jr., *Fuller Theological Seminary*
Gerald T. Sheppard, *Union Theological Seminary*

A GARLAND SERIES

THE DEVOTIONAL WRITINGS OF ROBERT PEARSALL SMITH AND HANNAH WHITALL SMITH

Garland Publishing, Inc.
New York & London
1984

For a complete list of the titles in this series
see the final pages of this volume.

Library of Congress Cataloging in Publication Data
Main entry under title:

THE DEVOTIONAL WRITINGS OF ROBERT PEARSALL SMITH
AND HANNAH WHITALL SMITH.

("The Higher Christian life")
Reprint (1st work). Originally published: Holiness
through faith / by R.P.S. Rev. ed. New York :
A.D.F. Randolph, 1870.
Reprint (2nd work). Originally published: The
Christian's secret of a happy life / by H.W.S. New ed.
rev. and enl. Boston : Christian Witness Co., c1885.
1. Holiness.   2. Devotional calendars.   I. Smith,
Robert Pearsall, 1827–1898. Holiness through faith.
1984.   II. Smith, Hannah Whitall, 1832–1911. Christian's
secret of a happy life. 1984   III. Series.
BT767.D45   1984   242   84-21117
ISBN 0-8240-6444-5 (alk. paper)

The volumes in this series are printed on
acid-free, 250-year-life paper.

Printed in the United States of America

CONTENTS

Holiness through Faith.

LIGHT ON THE WAY OF HOLINESS.

By R. P. S.

AUTHOR OF "THE SECRET OF VICTORY," "THY MAKER IS THY
HUSBAND," "IS THE VII. OF ROMANS TO BE THE CONTINUED
EXPERIENCE OF THE CHRISTIAN?" "THROUGH
DEATH TO LIFE," ETC., ETC.

"PURIFYING THEIR HEARTS BY FAITH."
Acts xv. 9.

REVISED EDITION.

NEW YORK:
ANSON D. F. RANDOLPH & CO.,
770 BROADWAY, COR. OF 9TH STREET.

These pages, written in America from week to week for a periodical, were collected by an English publisher and issued in book-form. They are now printed—with the Author's revision—for circulation in his native country.

THE PUBLISHER.

PREFACE.

"THE faith which was once delivered to the saints" was a faith which made them victorious over the world, the flesh, and the devil. By it Enoch walked with God three hundred years, having before his translation this testimony, "*that he pleased God.*" And yet God has "provided some better"—not an inferior—"thing for us" in this dispensation, which is noontide glory as compared with the twilight of revelation to the infancy of our race. The danger of the hour has been in occupying men's souls, not too much, but too exclusively, with their standing in Christ, while the standard of walk which should accompany it has been deemed as impracticable. Our privileges form the measure of our responsibility. The reception of the free and full remission of sins through Him " who his own self bare our sins in his own body on the tree," is incomplete, unless the expressed purpose of that sin-bearing be also accepted : " that we being dead to sins should live unto righteousness." Christ in mercy gave himself for us," but it was in order " that he might redeem us from all iniquity."

A work of faith allows of no apology, and requires but little explanation. Written with the simple and earnest desire to remove prejudice from honest hearts, and to lead fellow-believers into a perfect soul-union with Jesus, these papers are not intended to enter upon the range of systematic theology. As to their essential truth, I have proved it in my own experience, as have also many witnesses around me, and I do not shrink from the solemn responsibility before God of pressing the truth, which forms their subject, upon Christians everywhere. And yet, since every transmission of God's light is refracted by the medium through which it passes, I should not be surprised if advancing light should modify these statements upon some details and interpretations of passages, not affecting the essential truthfulness of the views here urged. We are not infallible. While enlightened, we are not inspired. While it is God's own light, His glorious light, in which we walk, yet we are not yet able to gaze upon all its fullness. May our spiritual vision be made clear, by a full deliverance from sinning, to behold the glory of God in the face of Jesus Christ!

In the words of another, "There is within me an inward testimony to the truth, so deep that all the world cannot shake it. It is the work of God upon my heart. Who will dare limit the power of God? Who will say that God, whose love is infinite as it is free, cannot give such proofs of love as He pleases to His creatures? Has He not the right to love me as He does? Yes, He loves me, and His love is *infinite*. I do not doubt it. And He loves you too, dear M——, in the same manner. This is eternal love manifested,—the heart of God drawn out, expressed towards his creature.

"In this state we understand the mutual secrets of the Lover and the beloved. Who will so deny the truth of the Lord as to question this ? When I hold my Beloved in my arms, in vain does any one assert, 'It is not so; you are deceived.' I smile inwardly and say, '*My Beloved is mine and I am His.*' If we receive the witness of men, how much greater is the witness of God!"

CONTENTS.

ILLUSTRATIVE INCIDENTS.

THE circumstances narrated as illustrations in this work have all come under the Author's own personal experience or observation, and are given with the conviction of their literal truth in every particular.

HOLINESS THROUGH FAITH.

CHAPTER I.

INTRODUCTORY.

BELOVED READER, — Do you feel that
your expectations at conversion have been
practically realized as to the righteousness, peace,
and joy, in the Holy Ghost, which you then
read were the characteristics of the kingdom?
Is there not some terrible deficiency in your
experience, for which you are unable wholly
to account? Did you not expect to be kept
more perfectly than results have realized, and
had you not the warrant of the Word for
this? When you compare your own inward
experience with others who, like yourself, it may
be, have lived prayerfully, and in earnest devotedness of outward effort to God, do you not find the
same sad and God-dishonoring story of unsancti-

fied affections and wandering desires : a divided
heart, with, it may be, outward failure in temper,
or otherwise ; things that have, with fearful certainty, been the index of remaining inward corruption ?   Would you be willing, when you are
leading a sinner to Christ, for him to see all that
remains in your own heart of unbelief ?

When some certain form of sin, known to your
own soul, is presented to you, although you turn
from it, is there not a response down deep in the
soul, that contradicts the verdict that you have
given, and which says of the evil thing, in unmistakable tones, "I LOVE IT !" Ah ! there is the fatal thing
—you *love it* after all.   Now what a man *loves*, in
a certain sense, that man himself *is* in character.
His affections show the central powers of his
being.   Out of the same fountain come sweet
waters and bitter, and upon the same tree grow
grapes and thorns.

Leaving for the present the question whether
those who claim to have received Holiness through
Faith are in the right way, would it not be the
greatest blessing of your life, beyond all earthly
gifts, if there were some means of your receiving
and grasping the rest of soul, the full victory over

sin, and the hourly communion with the Lord, which these claim to have received by faith? As a young minister said lately to the writer, "I would give all the world to believe and feel as you do,—I would give up my property, my prospects, my all!" While he could not trust our way of faith, he saw that the end set forth contained blessings immeasurably beyond what he had, or expected to have, in this life, and blessings that the Word seemed in many passages to set before him.

So far, my brother, we agree together. We greatly long that you and we might "walk by the same rule, and mind the same thing," "having the same mind, being of one accord, of one mind." How much else is there also that we agree in perfectly; that we were ruined, hopeless, helpless sinners, going down to hell, when God, in his wondrous mercy, quickened us by his Spirit to see our lost condition, and then led us to the cross, to behold Jesus bearing "our sins in his own body on the tree." We together know that, being born of God, we received, in addition to the old nature (the flesh) a new nature, an actual existence begotten of God, of "incorruptible seed;" and that, believing in Jesus, we have eternal life. Together

we have turned to God from our old idols, " to serve
the living and true God ; and to wait for his Son
from heaven," as our hourly expectation. Together we are begotten " unto a lively hope by the
resurrection of Jesus Christ from the dead." It
may be that together we have learned from the
same pages by the same Spirit, to come out from
the world and be separate—refusing the well-
watered plains of Sodom, in order to dwell on the
mount with faithful Abraham, possessing nothing
—as to the spirit of our lives—but a tent for our
pilgrimage, and an altar for our sacrifice. We have
both, perhaps, in this path, parted with much or
most that men hold dear, as to ease or reputation.
And lastly, we both with equal honesty of purpose, I trust, desire to know the whole of God's
blessed truth, and knowing it, to walk in it.

In all this we have long been and are now with
you. During many long years of earnest service
for God, we were also with you in the disheartening
life of bondage, which you confess, to inward corruption ; the old or natural man continually
brought us "into captivity to the law of sin,
which was in our members." We verily looked
for a progressive, partial deliverance and were

sometimes cheered by the temporary withering of some particular branches of the corrupt tree ; but after long years, we found it still vigorous, and sending forth fresh shoots.

We have gone a step farther, and it may be with you, in that, in public, in private, and in print, we opposed a teaching which we verily believed to be a lowering of God's standard of holiness, joined to spiritual pride. Being blind to the light, we denied the evidence of those who had sight, and who said that the sun shone. We did not understand that what was claimed was not " absolute perfection," but that *up to the measure of to-day's consciousness* they were kept by faith, and that all the glory was given to Christ equally and in the same way with that of remission of sins. Like yourself, we were stumbled—just as sinners are by false professors—by seeing the counterfeits of this life in Christ. We did not remember that from an angel of light, down to the smallest things, Satan's plan always is to counterfeit God's work and truth ; and that wherever there was a counterfeit, there we were to look for a divine truth, carefully distinguishing between them.

Dear brother, in how many things have we

agreed together! And now may I in the fear of
God tell you how that, while thus one with you, I
have been compelled to go farther, step by step,
in much prayer, and with much close searching of
the divine word. Follow me prayerfully, for I
write in calm confidence that God will guide you
and me if we are willing, as little children, to be
led by the Spirit.

LIGHT ON JUSTIFICATION AND SANCTIFICATION.

First, however, permit me to relate two simple
incidents. Soon after my own conversion I sat
down beside a dear relative, an earnest man, and
a student of the Scriptures, to show him justification by faith, from the Word. We turned to passage after passage that were, to my own soul, as
luminous as day. After going through them all,
his reply was, " Well, by thus picking out passages
here and there through the Bible, you can make
up what looks like a doctrine of justification by
faith alone and without works, but take the whole
of the Scriptures together, and they never meant
any such doctrine." When he became a Christian
himself, he found justification by faith alone, in

letters of light, from cover to cover of the Bible!
A few months since I urged upon another dear
friend, a most devoted Christian, the principle of
sanctification by faith, and not by works or effort ;
and he gave a similar reply, verily believing that
the whole thing was misapprehension of Scripture
and spiritual pride.   Later, it pleased God to give
him a sight of his inward corruption and deep
need, and to show him how he could by faith enter
into the glorious liberty of those who know the
full practical power of resurrection life in their
souls, and to lead him into it by the Holy Ghost.
The doctrine of sanctification by faith, an immediate
work, now shines for him in letters of light upon
every page, as it were, of Scripture ; and he finds
that in living this life of sanctification he is, for the
first time, really sitting humbly at the feet of Jesus.
His real life of presumption and self-confidence, he
now sees, was lived by him while he refused sanctification by faith alone ; and that instead of being
a testimony to self, as he formerly supposed, the
way of holiness is a testimony to the power of the
blood of Jesus.   He no longer depends partly on
himself or his progress in knowledge, but in a direct way only on Christ, and finds what it is to be

indeed " redeemed from all iniquity," pure in heart, and " filled with the Spirit."

We could multiply instances, did space permit, among the most instructed, earnest, and devoted Christians whom we know ; for it is to the earnest and devout and not to the careless, that God shows this divine secret. These will illustrate the *possibility* of your seeing the whole subject at some future time in a wholly different light.

Dear brother, with such a practical experience of inward failure as you frankly confess to, and with the testimony within your hearing of numbers who have for years walked in the same path with yourself of outward devotedness, and confessed inward failure, are you willing to believe that there may be *some* way of victory provided by grace,— even if ours be not it,—that you have not yet found out : some way of becoming actually "dead to sins," and " living unto righteousness "?

We both would, of course, say in advance that, if there be such a way, it must present these characteristics :

1. It must be a way taught in the Bible.

2. It must be a way in Christ.

3. It must be a way hid from mere intellect,

and revealed by the Spirit to the soul hungering for righteousness.

4. It must exalt the atonement of our Lord.

5. It must make the soul victorious over inward as well as outward sin.

6. It is the fulfilling of the Law of this dispensation.

7. In exalting Christ, it must humble the believer.

Should you find a way with these characteristics, would you be willing to lay aside your preconceived notions, and receive with meekness this word of grace and power? Do you shrink from Jesus taking full possession of your soul, turning out all the money-changers, and making it a holy temple for the Lord? Since your privileges as a believer are no less than those of Paul, are you willing to receive such a power from on high as would enable you to say, " I am crucified with Christ ; nevertheless I live ; yet not I, but Christ liveth in me ;"—" To me to live is Christ ;"—" Ye are witnesses, and God also, how holily, justly, and unblameably, we behaved ourselves among you that believe."

2

> " The perfect way is hard to flesh ;
> It is not hard to love ;
> *If thou wert sick for want of God,*
> *How swiftly wouldst thou move !* "

I trust that you will allow me the privilege of again addressing you on this important subject, and meanwhile remain yours in the loving fellowship of the gospel.

CHAPTER II.

IF the way we are seeking to set forth is indeed God's highway of holiness, it will bear the most scrutinizing tests, and it will by them be only made more clear to the heart that is tender before the Lord, not contending for a preconceived system of doctrine, but crying to God to show,—whithersoever it may lead,—His own truth.

As before remarked, it will have several evangelical characteristics, in which, if it fail, both you and I, who hold so much of God's blessed truth in common, would unite in condemning it. First of all, I would ask you to come " to the law and to the testimony," and let us both seek to clear our minds of prejudice, so that, guided by the Spirit in the Word, we may be able to follow where it leads. As indicated in my last, the Scripture seems to me to have the doctrine and the life I have received upon every page, as it were ; but I will try to divest myself, if possible, of my own views while I write, that we may together look straight to the written Word.

Let us read together Paul's prayer in the Holy Ghost for the disciples, and for us among them : "Unto him that is able to do exceeding abundantly above all that we ask or think, according to the power that worketh in us." If we give rein to our yearnings, asking of God whatsoever things we desire, what would be our first instinctive cry ? That we might be holy, and pure, and conformed to the image of Jesus Christ. How often has this been our prayer ! But not being with faith, or the yielding of the soul fully to Jesus, it was not answered, nor indeed could be. Does not our Lord's gentle rebuke come to our souls : " O ye of little faith, WHY REASON YE among yourselves ?" Was it by reasoning or by faith that we thought it impossible to " awake to righteousness, and *sin not ;*" "*perfecting* holiness in the fear of God," and serving the Lord "*acceptably,* with reverence and godly fear ?"

Faith is above circumstances, surroundings, impossibilities, and above the devil himself ; and when we look away from these *directly to God,* who can limit His grace and power ?   Nay, my brother, when we have made our largest requests of God, He is still "able to do exceeding abundantly above all that we ask or think." I must freely own that this is my continuous experience. Day by day, as I walk in this way of faith and holiness, wonder and praise fill my heart for heavenly communion, inward purity, victory over the world, abounding peace, and the known presence of Jesus in my soul,—blessings that rise above my asking or even my largest thoughts.

We have together passed through the third of Romans, and have had our souls to ring with joy, as we found joined in the same sentence, "All have sinned, and come short of the glory of God," with, "Being justified freely by his grace through the redemption that is in Christ Jesus; whom God hath set forth to be a propitiation through faith in his blood:"—the complete ruin by works, and the complete justification by faith, together in one brief sentence. But, beloved brother, are we under any less obligation to receive, in the sixth chapter, in their plain and obvious import, the words, "How shall we that are dead to sin live any longer therein? . . . . We are buried with Him by baptism into death; that LIKE AS Christ

was raised from the dead by the glory of the
Father EVEN so we also should walk in newness
of life."

I exhaust my utmost powers of memory and
imagination to conceive how, as a constant student
of the Word, I could ever have understood God to
mean in this passage anything else than complete
victory over sin, by realized resurrection-life ; for
now the continuing in sin seems that monstrous
thing of which the soul exclaims in holy horror,
" How shall we that are dead to sin live any
longer therein ?"   " Our old man is crucified with
Him, that the body of sin might be destroyed, that
henceforth we should not serve sin." . I know
how to pervert such expressions, for I have often,
to my own shame and loss, turned the edge of
the Spirit's sword by the poor " tricks of the
intellect."

But, my brother, let us now be honest with this
passage. When are we not to serve sin ? Plainly
now. From what is this deduced ? From the fact
of the body of sin being destroyed ("rendered
inert, or ineffective, as in suspended life," might be
the more exact translation).   When destroyed ?
Plainly, previously to our not serving sin.   When

was the old man crucified with Christ? Evidently, previously to the destruction of the body of sin. "The way of holiness," death unto sin and life unto righteousness, fairly flash in letters of light through such passages. God give you eyes to see them!

We have together looked forward to the purity of heaven as among its chief joys ; we have seen, as it were, the priestly hand of Jesus extended in blessing over "the pure in heart," as they that "shall see God." Reading the possibilities of this life by the light of our own experience, rather than by that of the Word, we long looked for real purity of heart as a privilege reserved for another scene of existence. One of the most earnest laborers in the Lord's vineyard in these parts said to me lately, "If, when I preach, the sinners round me saw the remaining corruption of my own soul, the uncontrollable evil thoughts, the self-worship, and the frequent coldness of my heart, they would not listen to me. My heart is a cage of unclean birds!" I have no reason to believe this dear brother to be worse than many others. I have regarded him as devoted and faithful beyond most ; but he walked in the searching light of the Word of God, and

like Job he abhorred himself, yet without having
gone in faith to Jesus for the remedy.

I own with shame that, had earthly eyes seen me
through and through, as God saw me,—even while
regarded by some as almost a Nazarite in separation from the world,—I could not have preached
even among those who loved me best.   When the
light of the Word shines clearly and steadily into
the caverns of the heart, it shows many a revolting
reptile and loathsome insect, not discernible in the
darkness, or even in the twilight !   May God keep
us from shrinking from the piercing light of his
own heart-searching truth, for its reception is the
first step towards "purifying our hearts by faith."

I remember the time when I first saw with clear-
ness the claims of God on me, as one of his children, for purity of heart.   I often read of "them
that call on the Lord out of a pure heart ;" and
that the " end of the commandment is charity out
of a pure heart, and of a good conscience, and of
faith unfeigned, *from which some having swerved,*
have turned aside into vain jangling."   I often
read of "pure minds," " a pure conscience," and
that I was to be " found of Him in peace, without
spot and blameless."   Then I looked within.   Oh !

the agony of my soul as I remembered that I was
a child of God, and that this inward purity was
what God plainly looked for in His children. His
command, " As He which hath called you is holy,
so be ye holy in all manner of conversation," did
for a time seem to me " grievous." I quailed in
spirit as I reflected on what a fearful upturning
of my whole nature, what terrible conflicts, what
rendings of my soul, must come, before the unclean spirits should be wholly cast out. All my
past, even my outward devotedness and inward
effort, were seen to be so tainted with self and sin
that " there remained no strength in me ; for my
vigor was turned into corruption, and I retained
no strength." Then, in my despair, my eye rested
on the words " purifying their hearts by faith."
How my soul leaped at these words, as in a moment I saw the possibility of my deliverance " *by
faith.*" " If then," I exclaimed, " it is by faith, I
will trust Jesus for a pure heart, and *now!*" and
with the act of faith there distilled into my heart,
like the gentle dew, the sweet consciousness of the
cleansing blood and presence of Jesus ;—" Christ
formed in me " taking full possession of my soul,
so that with my whole heart I could sing—

> " Now to be Thine, yea, Thine *alone*,
>   O Lamb of God, I come !"

I know not how to describe it in my own words,
but I know that "*this* is the victory that overcometh the world, even our faith ;" and since then
to me to live has been Christ in a different sense
and power than I had ever known before.   Obedience,—full-hearted obedience,—became then, and
is now, the easy yoke that my Lord promised.

An inward realization of purified affections, a
blessing exceeding abundant above all that I had
been able to ask or to think, has made obedience
simple and natural ; so that I can receive that
word, " Seeing ye have purified your souls in obeying the truth, *through the Spirit*, unto unfeigned
love of the brethren, see that ye love one another
with *a pure heart* fervently."   Thus has come a
harmony into my existence,—a *re-adjustment* of the
whole nature, spirit, soul, and body, to Christ,—
that must be the wonderful reality of the words,
" Christ formed in you," " Christ in you," the being
"filled with the Spirit," the " not I, but Christ liveth in me,"—and, " the life which I now live in the
flesh, I live by the faith of the Son of God."

Temptation comes to me more fiercely than

ever before, at times for days together; but temptation is not sin, for my Lord was tempted. There is, moreover, now this difference—that temptation finds me within my armor, and behind the shield of faith, so that it is my privilege to quench—not some—but ALL the fiery darts of the wicked one. It seems as though temptation is now from without, rather than from my own heart, and the struggle not so much a wrestling " with flesh and blood," as against wicked spirits,—a contest for my position of being seated by faith with Christ in the heavenly places,—the Canaanite rather than the wilderness enemies. There is much land yet to be possessed, but trusting thus in Jesus, the song of victory precedes the contest, and day by day is known the power of those words, " Grow in *grace*, and in the knowledge of our Lord and Saviour Jesus Christ," and of all that " *He* is able to do."

Does this seem presumption, my brother? I would ask your *heart*,—not your system of doctrine,—*Can* we trust Jesus too fully for everything that his Word sets before us? Have we not often seen a trembling, anxious sinner put away from him the cup of a free salvation, lest it should be " presumption " to take it just as he was? Was

not the presumption in daring to refuse what God
had put to his very lips,—the waters of Life? Have
not we bent all the prayerful energies of our souls,
to teach him that what God *gave* him, it would be
presumption to reject because of his own unfit-
ness? Did we not specially press upon him that
remission of sins is received by *faith*, and that to
try to make himself worthy was to reject Christ
now, and to dare to attempt partly to meet the
claims of God's holiness himself?

You have done this, probably, scores of times,
and now, my brother, suffer me, though but a
"little one," to point your heart in the same way to
Scripture warrant for receiving by faith, not only
forgiveness of sins, but inward purity of soul.
Christ gave Himself for you, that He might redeem you from ALL iniquity, and *purify* you unto
Himself a peculiar person, zealous of good works.
When is this redemption? *Now.* From what?
ALL iniquity. What else does his sacrifice propose
to you? To *purify* you unto Himself. When
ought you to receive the redemption? Now. And
when this purification? Equally NOW! How? By
simple faith.

If my poor words present difficulties to your

heart, dear reader, I beg you to take some prayer
from God's Word, upon which the Holy Spirit has
flashed its light, as expressing the deep needs of
your soul. Let the theories of your head go, and
permit your heart to go out to God in faith, thus
guided by the Word. If you are mourning over
inward corruption, what can be more simple than
to pray, "Create *in me* a clean heart, O God, and
renew a right spirit within *me*." Can you doubt
that such a petition, originating in God and returning to Him in the cries of one of His needy children, *honestly* offered in the name of Jesus, would
be answered by the grace of a clean heart and a
right spirit?

A, CHRISTIAN PHYSICIAN.

A "beloved Physician," the story of whose work
of faith and labor of love is scarcely second to
that of George Muller in interest and power,
writes,—

"O how my heart once yearned to *know* this
'victory that overcometh the world!' I remember
a few years ago, in reading II. Thess. 2, I came to
the 13th verse, where Paul says, 'We are bound
to give thanks always to God for you, brethren,

beloved of the Lord, because God hath from the beginning chosen you to salvation, through *sanctification* of the Spirit and belief of the truth.' *Through sanctification of the Spirit.* Here I paused, and read it over and over again, praying that God would sanctify me wholly by the Spirit. This verse comforted me many, many days. I felt that it was blessed to my soul, but the fullness of its meaning was not yet revealed to me. The inward currents of my heart were not stayed. I could not '*stand fast* therefore in the liberty wherewith Christ hath made us free,' for I was 'entangled again' and again 'with the yoke of bondage.' I could not 'reckon' myself 'dead' to the perplexities and irritations of daily life, which a heart yearning for purity condemns as dishonoring. to God. More earnestly than ever, and many times a day, I prayed for strength to overcome, but found no rest to my soul, until I stopped praying for strength to overcome, and *gave myself wholly tc God to be kept.*

"At this time the Lord revealed to me in a wonderful manner, in all its majesty, the power of the prayer which He taught us to use, 'Our Father which art in Heaven : hallowed be Thy name.

Thy kingdom come. Thy will be done on earth, as it is in Heaven. Give us this day our daily bread ; And forgive us our debts, as we forgive our debtors. And lead us not into temptation, but *deliver us from evil* : For Thine is the kingdom, and the power, and the glory, for ever. Amen.' O how my soul was filled, as I realized for the first time that it was His power that was to keep me !— for 'Thine *is* the power.'

"The work was all done then,—no more striving, no more praying for *strength* to overcome, but simply day by day, 'Jesus *keep* me, for Thine is the *power* and the glory,' and there *I rest* and am *kept*.

"I give this little record of personal experience, hoping that many who desire, but who have not gained 'the victory which overcometh the world, even our faith,' as they pray, 'Lead us not into temptation, but deliver us from evil, for Thine is the power,' may realize in all its fullness that the *power* belongs to Him who says He is 'able to keep you from falling.' "

The Psalmist says, "Thy Word have I hid *in mine heart*, that I might not sin against Thee."

Let any Christian, instead of handling the promises of God as abstractions, take them as the divine seed,—"spirit" and "life," as our Lord terms
them ; let him select some one beatitude, command, or promise, that embodies his soul's special
need ; let him believe that it contains God's covenant to himself ; let him search out other sayings
of God corresponding with this text ; let him pray
over it continually, morning, noon, and night, and
even amid the busy scenes of his calling ; let him
continually raise his heart to God in supplication
and trust ; let him seek to exhaust the possibilities
of faith and prayer, concentrating all the divinely-
imparted energies of his soul on the particular truth
embodied in the text ; and let him not weary in
well-doing, fully trusting that in due season he will
reap if he faints not ;—and he then shall find the
power of Jehovah Himself pledged to the fruit-
bearing of the seed thus sown and watered by
faith and prayer.

"Forever, O Lord, Thy Word is settled in the
Heaven!" and sooner shall this vast universe fail
in its orbits and sink into remediless ruin, than a
single promise of the eternal God fail toward one
of his little ones, who has thus in faith committed

the keeping of his soul to Him in well-doing as unto a faithful Creator.

God grant that this interview upon paper may be to His glory, and that He may open your heart to attend to these things spoken by Paul, as He did that of Lydia.

I trust that your prayers may go up with my own to God for a blessing on this intercourse, that whatever be God's truth, we may both know and live it to his glory. In this aspiration, and hoping that you will " suffer the word of exhortation," I am, your brother in Jesus.

CHAPTER III.

TO all his other blessings our heavenly Father
has added this, that his gifts, calling, and
grace, are all "*in Christ Jesus,* who of God is made
unto us wisdom, and righteousness, and sanctification, and redemption ; that, according as it is
written, 'He that glorieth, let him glory in the
Lord.'"

Chalmers speaks finely of " the expulsive power
of a new affection ; " and that love is indeed expulsive in its character at first, all who have been
deeply moved, in whatever way, well know. But
they also know that when a new emotion has
a little spent its energies, there comes a reaction,
proportioned oftentimes to the greatness of the
emotion. In this way is explained, and correctly,
the condition of failure that follows the warmth
and earnestness of the "first love" of Christians.
Feeling a painful void at the time present, their
hearts turn *to the memory of an emotion,* and that
memory is cherished till it becomes a substitute for

present, living faith. Or if this snare be severed, they depend on new discoveries in the truth of God to maintain, by the light they inspire, the devotion of their souls. Alas! that men will put His gifts between themselves and the living, life-inspiring Christ.

The almost universal character of this experience shows plainly that there is something wanting in their knowledge of Christ, since the gospel itself is not a failure, to perfect the walk of believers.

I was asked to preach lately to a congregation where the deacon, in stating the needs of the members, remarked. "We have just enough religion among us to make us miserable." Nòr did I wonder at his homely expression ; for instead of casting themselves upon Christ to sanctify, as He had already justified them, they had been led to look for power for holiness of walk, too exclusively from the peace resulting from their knowledge of final salvation, from the responsive love that *ought* to spring up in their hearts, because of their known "judicial standing," and from the emotions which, were they unfallen beings, would continually fill their hearts with lively gratitude for infinite favors bestowed.

Well, indeed, might they feel "miserable," as they contrasted what they knew *ought* to be the love and devotedness of their hearts, with their actual wandering affections and palsied efforts to serve God. It is enough to make any one possessing any tenderness of conscience "miserable" to live in the unvarying sense of failure, his heart so often condemning him for sinning, and without the hope that he shall ever in this life really please God in his walk. Nor does the fact that there has been offered a divine atonement sufficient to meet all the future judgment of these failures, bring the relief that the soul needs, while it expects nothing else than to go on sinning all its days.

"Every breath I draw is sin," was the extreme statement made to me by a Christian professing full confidence in the sacrifice of Christ, and seeking to live in separation from the world. I fear he was right. Every breath *is* sin to him, if he has not faith to live without it; for "whatsoever is not of faith is sin." If sin be the inevitable, constant condition of the Christian, then is redemption "from all iniquity" transferred to the next life; abiding in Christ a hopeless attainment; to "sin not" a grievous command; and pleasing

God now, an impossibility. The very assurance of being begotten of God, and the prospect of an eternity in his presence, make the present condition of sinning "miserable," yea, agonizing, to a heart happily not entirely hardened by the continual sense of transgression. To believe in, and, in some degree, to love God, and yet to be among those who "cannot cease from sin," may well weigh the soul down with sorrow.

Some resource must be found to meet this. Like the wandering sheep, who, though set with his face homewards, will, as shepherds tell us, always choose a wrong path, if such can be found, rather than the one that leads to the fold ; so, instead of going directly to Christ, as my wisdom to guide, my practical power of righteousness to live by, my sanctification of spirit, soul, and body, and my blessed, present redemption from all iniquity, I formerly turned from Christ, who is *both "the Way" and the entrance into it,* to adopt a system which puts off all those blessed offices of Christ in their full virtue, as intended for another state of existence ; persuading myself that, "judicially," I was without spot and blameless, while in reality I was spotted all over like a leopard, and under

often recurring condemnation for inward, even
when not for outward, sins. The atonement of
my Lord became to me too much of a theological
doctrine, rather than the glorious effective reality
which I now find it to be, meeting fully every *present* need of my soul.

Were anything revealed to man as "the power
of God," we should expect it to overcome the world
and all the powerful things in it, inasmuch as it
would be the power of God in direct conflict with
the powers of the world, the flesh, and the devil.
None would deny the power thus revealed being
capable of overcoming all else. The only question
would be, whether God intended to do it in this
stage of existence for those who trusted Him for
it ; and this being granted, there would remain
but the question of the means and their use.

In the opening of Paul's first letter to the Corinthians, he states that the preaching of the cross
of Christ is "the power of God unto us which are
saved ;" and that, while a crucified Christ is to the
legalist a stumbling-block, and to the worldly wise
foolishness, to those who are called, Christ is "the
power of God and the wisdom of God." That
through Christ's death on the cross, and his resur-

rection-life in the soul, God has provided a power capable of conforming the children of the kingdom to the image of its Head, few will venture to deny. The difficulty seems to come in when any *confess* that, having by faith availed themselves of these resources in Christ, they find their hearts "purified by faith," cleansed " from all unrighteousness," and, in keeping his word, " the love of God perfected " in their souls, (1 John ii. 5,) to the limit of present consciousness.

Thomas Walsh testified, " The Lord gives me to drink of his love as out of a river. I lay down, but could not sleep, through a deep and comfortable sense of the love of Christ. His Spirit rested on me, and made my heart flame with love to my God and my all. It never entered into my heart to conceive of thus loving Him with all the heart till He revealed it unto me by his Spirit. The fire of divine love burned incessantly in my soul." President Edwards said of Abigail Hutchinson, " She had from day to day such a sense of the glory of Christ and of God in his various attributes, that it seemed to me she dwelt for days together in a kind of beatific vision, and seemed to have as immediate intercourse with Him as a child with a father."

*Has God provided any less privilege in Christ for you,
my brother?* Are *you* willing to put by everything else, including your preconceived opinions,
to receive this fullness of the blessing of the gospel of Christ?

I confess to a tender, sincere sympathy with
those who, beyond many around them, have been
devoted to God, who have been used by God in his
service in saving sinners or teaching saints, and
who yet are unable to find anything in their own
experience corresponding to what is confessed by
some. Reading such narratives in the light of their
own history, or by a system modified, it may be,
to meet the requirements of this consciousness of
continual sinning, these experiences seem to them
egotistical and boastful. Instead of getting "out
of self into Christ," they fear that their brethren
are getting out of Christ into self again. This
fear arises from not understanding that, in confessing themselves to be made " dead to sins and alive
unto righteousness," their brethren are confessing
simply that for which Christ bare their sins in His
own body on the tree, as being accomplished in
their souls. (See carefully 1 Pet. ii. 24, and 2.
Cor. v. 17, 18.) Surely the words, "Christ liveth

in me," and "For me to live is Christ," cannot mean *less* than the habitual victory over sin.

Suffer me, my brother, to recall your own experience in the remission of sins. Its distinctive feature was, that you trusted Christ for your present felt need of soul, and *what you trusted him for you received*. What your soul needed was remission of sins, and after having in vain sought it by efforts of your own, you found it in faith, apart from all effort, a simple receiving from God. The Holy Spirit quickened your soul to a sense of your need of pardon, and then satisfied the desires thus begotten in you, by showing you the sacrifice of Christ.

You must agree with us, that whatever the Holy Spirit makes us to yearn for, Christ came to give. Now substitute "purity of heart," "holiness," being "filled with the Spirit," whole-hearted "love to God and your neighbour," or "righteousness," for the pardon you once felt the need of; satisfy yourself that the Word sets either of these privileges before you as a gift for which the Holy Ghost is making you to hunger and thirst; then seek this blessing, not by efforts of your own, —not as a doctrine, not in imitating an experience

of another, not in an emotion, but *in the Lord
Jesus Christ through faith,*—and who then shall limit
the extent to which your desires shall be satisfied ?
And when " filled with the fruits of righteousness,
which are by Jesus Christ, unto the glory and praise
of God," who shall then hinder you from proclaiming what the Lord hath done for your soul?

In no way so effectually as by following the example of Paul, in freely declaring what Christ has
done for and in you, can you lead others to the
same all-powerful Saviour. " The husbandman
that laboureth must be first partaker of the fruits,"
and the Lord's witnesses must witness that they
themselves experience what they teach. Satan's
kingdom is not much disturbed by preaching
which tells men that they ought to " go up and
possess the land," while the preacher has to confess that he has not done so, thus giving " an evil
report of the land," and practically saying, " We
are not able to go up against the people ; for
they be stronger than we." God give us leaders
like Caleb, who say, " Let us go up at once to
possess it ; for we are well able to overcome it ; "
men of the faith of Paul, who " can do all things
through Christ strengthening " and who will at

God's command blow the ram's horn till the Canaanite walls fall down.

The British ambassador was a true man, though he told the incredulous Eastern despot, who had never been where water froze, that in his country they walked on hardened water, and though he was dismissed as a liar. Our testimony ought to be credited, at least by Christians, when we affirm that in the path where we tread, Christ is both able and willing to sustain us to the utmost limit of our faith, even though to the eye of sense, only unstable water be visible. None are so manifestly and pitiably weak as the "little children" of the kingdom, when without the presence of Christ ; but none so strong as they who, *without reserve abandon themselves perfectly to Christ to live in them,* perfecting his strength in their weakness.

I know your love for the Lord and his cause, my brother. I know the virtue—the earnest, manly effort—that you have added to your faith. I know, by my own former experience, the unsatisfactoriness of the *current* of your inward life, even though you have seasons of joy, when the Lord comes to you as one that tarrieth for a night, and abideth not. I know that God has given you

hungerings and thirstings after righteousness, so
that you might even speak of " gnawings of
hunger ; " and that they were not given to tan-
talize you, but that you might so receive Christ as
to have them satisfied.

Now, that you have not gone to him aright is
evident, or you would have been "filled." I will,
in true Christian love, use great plainness of
speech. *You* have failed,—*not Christ.* I feel confident that the point of your failure is in not
having committed unreservedly everything to
Christ, in perfect self-abandonment. If I do not
hold my ALL,—spirit, soul, and body,—committed
to Him, I am walking with heavy weights, and
miserable.   Sometimes, becoming conscious of a
weight, before unsuspected, I find it a sore effort
to part with it ; but my soul is in bondage till it
is laid aside.   Then it rises free before God.   Try
this, my brother, this laying aside *every* weight—
THE VERY LAST ONE, whether it be care, or transgression, and you will then rise into the cloudless
atmosphere where God's light can shine down
upon you unhindered, where you no longer frustrate the grace of God, and where you can know
" Christ formed in you."

Practical sanctification and purity of soul, with the consciousness of them, are as surely God's gift as is the forgiveness of sins ; but the method is faith. It is a calling, and *in Christ*. It is a grace, and this grace " came by Jesus Christ."

Apart from Christ, we are instruments of unrighteousness to sin, as my hand is a rotting piece of flesh apart from my heart and brain. But, joined to Christ, we become instruments of righteousness unto God, just as my hand is full of life by its connexion with my heart, and rightly guided by its connexion with my brain. The thickness of a piece of paper will sever my hand's connexion with heart and brain, and yet the union may be maintained through a lifetime without interruption. It is just in this way that all our life, our strength, our righteousness, is *in Christ*, not in ourselves, except as we are receiving from Christ. We are not only weak, and poor, and helpless, but we are *nothing*, absolutely nothing apart from Christ. Yet *in Him* we have all things. O ! blessed union, which joins us to the living heart and living Head, each one members in particular of the ONE body. O ! miracle of grace, which gives us life for death, and incorruptibleness for corruption. Since faith

is the channel of communicable life, O Lord, increase our faith !

> " If our faith were but more simple,
>   We should take Him at His word;
> And our lives would be all sunshine
>   In the sweetness of the Lord."

THE ACTRESS AND HOME MISSIONARY.

While addressing a company in one of the mis-
sion-houses in New York, I noticed a young woman
much affected.   I found after the meeting that she
was an actress who had been brought to the point
of turning her back on all her past life ; but she was
unable to believe that such a sinner as she was
could receive the grace that was set before her.
To my explanations of the divine sacrifice for sinners she only exclaimed,

"O yes, sir,—I know that it's all true, but I can't
believe that it is *for me.*"

It seemed too great "presumption" for her to
believe that all her sins were blotted out, and she
at once placed in the family of God.   I left her in
this condition of mind, longing for salvation, and
yet too faithless to believe that it was for her.

It was very instructive to see immediately afterward a striking illustration that upon whatever level we may be walking, the same failure of faith to take the grace intended for us may be found. *Lack of faith to receive from God, is the sin that doth so easily beset us, and lies at the root of every failure, all the way from the first quickening of the Spirit, onward to the highest altitudes of devotedness and service to God.*

Upon parting with the actress, I was introduced to a refined, matronly, Christian woman, who, I understood, was giving her life to this gospel work among the abandoned. Her whole heart was in her work with an energy and simplicity that I have never seen surpassed. Her joy was to spend her years in the midst of this moral leprosy, raising the cross among the dying souls around her. But even while thus laboring for Christ, she was feeling most deeply her need of some privilege greatly beyond her present experience. So in earnest was she that she had just passed a sleepless night of sorrow and of prayer, for the full and satisfying revelation of Christ, with the *complete* victory over her own will. She knew that her sins had been forgiven her, and that she truly loved Jesus. Work for Jesus was the most delightful thing in the world to her.

" Sacrifices " were to her only privileges ; but she mourned over the remaining evil of her own soul. She hungered for righteousness, and was not filled ; the fountain of her heart, which ought only to well up with sweet waters, sent forth both bitter and sweet. She knew that there was in the gospel a redemption "from *all* iniquity ;" but she had not found it. She knew that Christ bore her sins that she might become "dead to sin, and alive to righteousness," but she had not attained to it. If work, as some suppose, could bring a full blessing, surely it would have been found here. But her need was one which work could not supply.

The secret of this unsupplied need was soon found. ·Full of faith for God's work in others, and up to a certain point in herself, she needed to open the door of her heart yet more widely that the King of Glory might come in. This dear saint, who had so often taught the lesson, to anxious sinners, of faith, as the means of blessing, now saw that the very same lesson was to be learned by herself upon a different level. The very words that a few moments before had been said to the awakened actress,—*trust in Christ for what her soul felt the need of*,—were now to be applied to herself. She had prayed for inward holiness and full victory over sin, without faith to receive the immediate answer in Jesus.

Unbelief was the obstacle to the full answer, just as in the prayer for mercy from the awakened sinner. To sinner and saint alike, upon whatever level, unbelief is the bar, while faith is the channel of God's blessing. When Christians pray for full cleansing of soul and deadness to sin, the answer is unto them exactly according to their faith or their unbelief. Full faith gives the full deliverance ; partial faith the partial victory. So much faith, so much deliverance, no more, no less! *If we would live up to the gospel standard of holiness, we must believe up to the gospel standard of faith*. Every complaint of leanness, failure, or sinning, is but a confession of want of belief. The stream can ascend no higher than the passage that conveys its waters from the fountain. Faith is the channel. While the fountain is infinite in depth and in height, its flow is regulated by the channel opened for it.

Shortly after this interview, the actress found in Christ, through faith, pardon for all her sins, and the missionary upon her high level of Christian experience also *found in Christ, through faith,* cleans-

4

ing "from all unrighteousness." Faith in each
grasped the promise, " My God shall supply all
your need, according to his riches in glory *by
Christ Jesus.*"

May what is here written in prayer be also read
in prayer!   " We pray always for you that our
God would count you worthy of his calling, and
fulfill *all* the good pleasures of his goodness, and
the work of faith with power, that the name of our
Lord Jesus Christ may be glorified in you, and ye
in Him, according to the grace of our God, and
the Lord Jesus Christ."

CHAPTER IV.

A WAY HID FROM MERE INTELLECT, AND REVEALED BY
THE SPIRIT TO THE SOUL HUNGERING FOR RIGHT-
EOUSNESS.

THERE is a path which no fowl knoweth,
and which the vulture's eye hath not seen :
the lion's whelps have not trodden it, nor the
fierce lion passed by it. . . . . The gold and the
crystal cannot equal it. . . . . God understands
the way thereof, and He knoweth the place thereof."
Whatever may be the primary application of
these words, they well express the closing of the
way of holiness to every effort of the intellect.
The consciousness of almost the whole race,
sinners as well as "professors," is against it ; for
error is always with the many in these evil days ;
and however much men may differ about other
things, they are nearly all agreed as to the impossibility of living without sin. "Eye hath not
seen, nor ear heard, neither have entered into the
heart of man, the things which God hath prepared
for them that love Him. But God *hath* revealed

them unto us by his Spirit ; for the Spirit searcheth all things, yea, the deep things of God."

These things prepared by God are not all postponed to a future scene, but are even now spiritually discerned. We are neither surprised nor disappointed, much as we may be pained, when the testimony to the present fullness of blessing is rejected. To some the Sun of righteousness has already arisen with healing in his wings, in a sense never before known, albeit the mists of educational prejudice or doctrinal system may hide his rays from the vision of those around them. We therefore intreat you dispassionately, prayerfully, and humbly, to seek wisdom of God, whether these things be so.

" The blood " is the meritorious and only ground upon which any of God's blessings can reach us without frustrating the eternal justice of the Ruler of the universe, but the means selected by God are the indwelling and guidance of the Holy Spirit. First the blood, then the anointing oil,— forgiveness, and then cleansing. Were the merit and power of the blood more fully applied by faith, then would the power of the Holy Ghost in Christians be more known.

The perpetual prayer of the Church of England is, " Almighty God unto whom all hearts are open, all desires known, and from whom no secrets are hid ; cleanse the thoughts of our hearts by the inspiration of the Holy Spirit, *that we may perfectly love Thee*, and worthily magnify Thy holy name." Connect this with the soul-inspiring words of our blessed Lord in Mark xi. 22–24 : " Have the faith of God.   For verily I say unto you, That whoso-ever shall say unto this mountain, Be thou removed, and be thou cast into the sea ; and shall not doubt in his heart, but shall believe that those things which he saith shall come to pass ; he shall have whatsoever he saith.   Therefore I say unto you, What things soever ye desire, when ye pray, believe that ye receive them, and ye shall have them."   And again : " All things whatsoever ye ask in prayer, believing, ye shall receive."   After half a century of experience of the power of this promise, the apostle is enabled to add by the Holy Ghost : " And this is the confidence that we have in Him, that if we ask anything according to his will, He heareth us.   And if we know that He hear us, whatsoever we ask, we know that we have the petitions we desired of Him."   " And whatsoever we ask, we receive of Him because we keep his commandments, and do those things that are pleasing in his sight."

The only question would then seem to be, whether "the first and great commandment," as recited by the Lord Jesus—"Thou shalt love the Lord thy God with all thy heart, and with all thy soul, and with all thy mind"—is included in the "righteousness of the law," which is to be "fulfilled in us, who walk not after the flesh, but after the Spirit." How strange that we should ever have doubted it! We ask, then, according to God's will when we *believingly* pray, "Cleanse Thou our hearts by the inspiration of thy Holy Spirit, that we may perfectly love Thee, and worthily magnify thy holy name!" And when the petition is granted, who shall say that it is presumption to affirm that our prayers have been answered? The acknowledgment is "glorying in the Lord" as truly as the owning that we are saved from future wrath.

Is it not strange that God's children can mock their Father in heaven by asking for things that they do not expect to receive—shall we say hard'y really desire—in this life? and that, themselves

too faithless to be able to receive full answers to
their prayers, they should be grieved by those who
say that they have asked, and have received what
they prayed for. I confess to have been myself
once stumbled by a dear brother saying that he
did indeed love God with all his heart, soul, and
mind. Of his exterior holiness of life none could
doubt, for we have never known any one who
seemed so uniformly filled with the Spirit. It was
the testimony of an inmate of his family that his
whole life was consumed in praise, prayer, and
working for God. Measuring his faith and blessing by my own little measure, I thought that
there must be some self-delusion; but when it
pleased God, in answer to months of prayer, to
open in power to my soul that word, " He that
dwelleth in love dwelleth in God, and God in
him," I found to my own surprise and joy that it
was the Spirit's work so to fill my poor wavering
soul, that, *so far as I was conscious*, I did and do
now love God with my whole heart, soul, and
mind. I ask to be preserved from ever again
judging of the faith of others by my own smaller
measure. It is " *according to the riches of his
glory*," and not according to man's limits, that God

fills his trusting children " with might by his Spirit in the inner man."

Many a tender soul that loves the Lord finds its acutest suffering in the consciousness of a divided heart and wandering affection, so that it has often in substance exclaimed—

> " 'Tis worse than death my God to love,
> And not my God alone ! "

As in many congregations true lovers of God are kept bound hand and foot in grave-clothes by the teaching all around them, that it is presumption in any one that is not dying to be sure of going to heaven : so now are many precious and tender souls restrained by the grave-clothes of the doctrine that habitual sinning is the inevitable condition of God's own saved saints, and that the command to love the Lord with our whole heart, soul, and mind, can only be fulfilled through death,—that the bride may not *wholly* love her husband till her heart is about to be stilled in the grave. May the same divine voice which, in our death in trespasses and sins, said to us " Come forth ! " be also effectually heard saying, " *Loose him and let him go !* " Let the taste and atmosphere of a past death pass away with the bestowal of "life more abundantly." He who spake by a human voice to Lazarus is speaking through Christendom to his saints by his Spirit, and giving us by his divine power "all things that pertain to life and godliness, through the knowledge of Him who hath called us to glory and virtue," and making us "partakers of the divine nature, *having escaped the corruption that is in the world through lust.*"

There is one point in this subject which we find from letters received, is not understood, though repeatedly stated. When the Christian thus puts on the Lord Jesus Christ, or recognizes Him living in his heart, and reigning in victory over sin, he is not thereby made complete in understanding, or in judgment, or in doctrine. He simply is placed where he by faith receives from God power to act day by day up to the given measure of light upon his duty. It is the power of overcoming all *discerned* evil that is bestowed ; and as the Spirit enlightens the conscience (or *consciousness*) from time to time faith gives the victory. "Beloved, *if our hearts condemn us not,* then have we confidence toward God." This is all that is claimed.

To-morrow I may discern evil in things in

which to-day I am living without condemnation.
Were the sight of angels given us, we could
scarcely take one step in our mingled surroundings. It has not pleased God to reveal at once
either the whole measure of his grace and power,
or the whole nature of the evil things around us.
This principle is clearly stated by Paul. "Let us
therefore, *as many as be perfect*, be thus minded,
and if in anything ye be otherwise minded, God
shall reveal even this unto you. Nevertheless,
whereto we have already attained, let us walk by
the same rule ; let us mind the same thing." A
heathen converted last week may be now walking
up to the standard to which he has " already attained," and yet be in practices from which a further knowledge of God's will shall separate him.
Through all the steps of his advance he may,
through Christ, have no stain on his conscience
(or knowledge). Thank God! there *is* provided in
Christ, who lives in the heart by faith, power to
walk from day to day without blame before God in
love, in fulfilment of every duty as progressively
revealed.

The divine principle to a Christian is,—" Whatsoever is not of faith is sin," and conversely what-

soever is of faith is not sin.   "Without faith it is
impossible to please God," but with faith it is possible to please God.   I breathe to-day the atmosphere of the love of God, every past sin forgiven,
and through the blood of cleansing, without a
present sense of transgression,—not a cloud to
separate me from God ; but I may not be able to
walk to-morrow with a clear conscience in all the
paths I tread to-day.   Nevertheless I am to-day
walking in the light, having fellowship with God,
and knowing that the blood of Jesus Christ, His
Son, cleanseth me from all sin.   This might be
termed a Christian, not a Divine, nor an angelic
nor yet an Adamic "perfection ; " but those who
by faith enter into its privileges may overcome the
world, and be conscious that up to the present
capacity of the poor, weak vessel, they are filled
with the Spirit.

   The great practical question is—not the meta-
physics of sin,—but *what pleases God ;* and what
pleases Him should satisfy the believer's heart.
Enoch, in a dispensation that was scarcely as the
dawn to our own glorious day, " pleased God," and
surely our privileges in resurrection-life are not
below those of Enoch.   John was able to say,

" We keep his commandments, and do those things that are pleasing in his sight," and God is working in some hearts and lives " that which is well-pleasing in his sight, through Jesus Christ."

It follows from this that persons who have great light in the teaching of Scripture may be walking outwardly in advance of the sanctified but ignorant Christian, while yet the one is sinning and under a sense of condemnation, and the other, more ignorant but more trusting, walks with a conscience void of offence. The understanding of " all mysteries and all knowledge " would be but a poor equivalent for the simple faith that always takes Jesus for all that He reveals Himself, and so finds present victory.

To " be filled with the Spirit " is one of Christ's " commanding promises and promising commands." It is connected with the warning to the Ephesians not to allow themselves to be carried beyond their natural condition by the stimulus of wine, but rather to be filled with the Spirit, that psalms, hymns, and spiritual songs should fill their mouths, while they made melody in their hearts to the Lord. The apostles, when filled with the Spirit, had to defend themselves from the charge of drunkenness, and those who yield themselves up to be filled by the Spirit may, to an unbelieving world, or to cold-hearted, sinning professors, seem like men "filled with new wine," or appear to them as David did to Michal, when he danced before the ark, even though God hath given them the "Spirit of power, and of love, and of a sound mind."

The great hindrance to being "filled with the Spirit" is the pre-occupation of the heart with worldliness or sin, so that room is not left for the manifestation of the Spirit. God's Spirit is the Spirit of Holiness, and it cannot dwell with sin, or even with the love of the world. I tremble for "professors of religion" as I read these words, "If any man love the world, the love of the Father is not in him." "He that hath my commandments, *and keepeth them*, he it is that loveth Me ;" and "If any man love not the Lord Jesus Christ, let him be Anathema Maran-atha." I thank God that I have not to determine to whom they apply.

We are solemnly warned that " *they that are in the flesh* cannot please God ; " and the Word adds, "But ye are not in the flesh, but in the Spirit, if so be that the Spirit of God dwell in you. Now if any man have not the Spirit of Christ, he is none of his." And it adds the text, "*And if Christ be in you the body is dead because of sin;* but the Spirit is life because of righteousness." "For if ye live after the flesh, ye shall die; but if ye, through the Spirit, do mortify the deeds of the body, ye shall live." The words are God's, not ours. Shall we turn the edge of these solemn tests to professing Christians by vainly trying to conform them to some theological system? Or shall we receive them in their solemn and deeply searching lessons, rousing us from every sleep of false security?

When God by the Spirit leads any one into this humble and clean condition, where the whole power of the atonement is by faith received, then, emptied of all else, he can be filled with the Spirit. What is needed is this emptying of all self-merit, self-effort, self-worship, self-guidance, self-praying, and self-acting. As the air rushes into a vacuum, so the Spirit must fill the soul emptied of self. The great need of our time is Holy Ghost power in our ministry. There is many a professor as harmless to Satan's kingdom as the cannon-ball that the child rolls across the floor. But put the

power behind it, and it will fly like lightning on
its mission of destruction to the strongholds of the
devil. There is many a rusting locomotive, a
mere obstruction in the way. Apply but the steam
to it, and it would draw thousands heavenward.

Without the almighty power of the Holy Ghost,
preaching is but the sounding brass and tinkling
cymbal. Oh! my brother, what would you not
give to have this power of God that will make
you a flaming herald of the gospel, imparting to
your soul at all times the unction and power of
the Holy Ghost, so that God's purposes should be
always accomplished in and by you? God does
not so much ask you to give, as to *receive*. Do
not " frustrate the grace of God," which now
in this stream of full and present salvation is
flowing around you. Erect no barriers to its
waters,—hinder no drop of its fulness from covering your soul. Take Jesus *now* for all that He
presents Himself to you as able to do, yielding
yourself without the smallest reservation a living
sacrifice, made holy by the altar on which your
thank-offering is laid. When you have done this,
do not shrink from owning yourself among the
holy brethren, who lift up holy hands without

wrath *or doubting* to the holy God, from whom
you have that command—possible to faith only,
but to faith surely possible—"BE YE HOLY, FOR I
AM HOLY."

A MANUFACTURER,

a Christian who had for many years been preaching Christ a Saviour for sinners, while yet he
found himself living under a painful sense of
inward corruption, remarked, among the workmen
under his care, a few who seemed different from
the professors around them, in that they seemed
so filled with the Spirit, so much in prayer, and
bearing into the workshops such a uniform sweet
savour of Christ. These men, closely associated
with their employer in Gospel work, often pressed
upon him the privilege of a present, practical, full
sanctification in Christ. Against this doctrine he
had the strongest prejudice, constantly opposing
it by every argument as a dangerous heresy.

At the solicitation of one of these Christians he
set apart an evening to examine with him the
Scriptures upon the subject, and being versed in
theological argument he was able to silence the

explanations of the praying workman. Sometimes a different reading or translation seemed
to break the power of the text urged upon
him ; sometimes another meaning could be got
out of it ; and, sometimes, where there was no
other escape, it was interpreted in a forensic or
judicial sense, with a denial of its practical application. The pious workman, conscious, notwithstanding all the arguments, that Christ was
formed in his own soul, closed the interview
sadly, feeling that though overcome by argument,
no one could take from him the living, blessed
reality of faith that did overcome the world, the
flesh, and the devil.

Not long after, he one day said to his employer

" When in the morning I *entirely trust* my soul
to the keeping of Jesus, relying on Him *alone* to
be preserved from transgression through the day,
He always answers my faith and *does* keep me
from known sin."

This simple testimony from an honest God-
fearing Christian, went home to the heart of the
reasoner. Where argument failed, a faithful
witnessing prevailed. He had denied it as a
doctrine, but he could not gainsay so simple and

5

scriptural an *experience* of faith. "*Can it be true ?*" he said to himself. The clouds of a deficient theological system were pierced, and like a gleam of sunshine over his soul, came the blessed hope that his life might become a victory where it had been a failure, holy where it had been unholy, blameless where it had been sinful.

Prayer and the study of the Scriptures now seemed to open the very heavens to his soul. Instead of asking Christ to *help* him, he now handed everything over to his Saviour, to *do* for and in him. When temptation assailed him, as one would put a screen between his face and a scorching fire, just so by faith he uniformly placed Christ between him and the snare, and rejoiced in beholding his Saviour only, the temptation being shut out. His soul was filled with wonder as from day to day he thus found himself so fully delivered from his besetting sins.

The obstacle of unbelief, with its resulting transgressions, being thus taken away, there followed, some time after, while waiting upon his knees in silence before God, the wonderful baptism of the Spirit, in a power which he had never conceived possible in this life, and he became, and now remains, after several years, solemnly conscious of the fulfilment of that promise : "If a man love me, he will keep my words : and my Father will love him, and we will come unto him and make Our *abode* with him."

Thus, Christ, God's Way of holiness, hidden from his intellect, was revealed to his heart, even before he could clearly state the Scriptural doctrine as to "Holiness through Faith." Since then years have passed, bringing with them constantly enlarging blessings, both in the conversion of sinners and in the leading of saints into soul union with Christ,—tenfold beyond any ever known before. The Scriptures are now, from cover to cover, radiant with the doctrine of a present practical sanctification, as well as justification, *in Christ*. Both were received by the same simple faith.

> " How Thou canst share Thy life with us,
>   Yet be the God Thou art,
>   *Is darkness to my intellect,*
>   *But sunshine to my heart.*"

CHAPTER V.

IN this chapter, before writing which, I have waited for some weeks in special prayer for enlightenment and guidance on so solemn a subject, I desire to point out how greatly the atonement is exalted by trusting to it for a present salvation from sinning.

In the Epistle to the Hebrews, which deals so specially with the sacrificial aspect of our Lord's work, we find the various forms of the word "sanctify" more often than in all the other epistles combined. It was that Jesus "might *sanctify* the people with his own blood," that He "suffered without the gate." "For if the blood of bulls and of goats," the epistle argues, "and the ashes of an heifer sprinkling the unclean, sanctifieth to the purifying of the flesh; *how much more* shall the blood of Christ, who through the eternal Spirit offered Himself without spot to God, purge your conscience from dead works to serve the living God?" "Now once in the end of the world hath

(68)

He appeared to put away *sin* by the sacrifice of Himself."

Opening with the declaration of how Jesus takes his place as the fulfilment of every type, this epistle shows that the law made nothing perfect, but that there is *the bringing in of a better hope.* It further shows the continual sacrifices failing to "make the comers thereunto perfect," and then declares that we are, by the fulfilment of His will, "sanctified through the offering of the body of Jesus once for all." In harmony with all this we find the epistle concluding: "Now the God of peace, that brought again from the dead our Lord Jesus, that great Shepherd of the sheep, *through the blood of the everlasting covenant,* make you perfect in every good work to do his will, working in you that which is well pleasing in his sight, through Jesus Christ ; to whom be glory for ever and ever."

It is because this sanctification, to which we bear testimony, is through the blood of Jesus, that we feel confidence in casting ourselves unreservedly upon Christ, to receive its accomplishment. The gospel has been too much preached as though Jesus had said, "Be thou convalescent : try not to

sin," rather than, " Behold, thou art made whole :
sin no more." When the leper, kneeling, cried,
" If thou wilt, thou canst make me clean," the
compassionate reply followed at once, "I will ; *be
thou clean.*" It is the blood of Jesus Christ, applied to those who walk in the light, that now
" cleanseth us from all sin ;" and even should our
feet for a moment stumble, it does not follow that
we were not treading the highway of holiness ;
nor should we for a moment lose our confidence,
but see to it that the same flash of consciousness
which shows us our fall should also bring its confession, and, with the confession, the re-cleansing of
the soul "from all unrighteousness." Nor will
then the believing heart, even after so sad an
event as a transgression, doubt its sanctification or
fear its confession ; for it hears the command,
" What God hath cleansed, that call not thou common."

The subtlety of Satan is perhaps nowhere more
shown than in stopping the saints short at one
half the truth conveyed in passages of Scripture.
Half-texts rob God's children of half their
present joys and half their power of service, as
well as half their future crowns for service. I

preached for ten years on the words, ' Who his own self bare our sins in his own body on the tree," before I realized the expressed purpose of that sin-bearing to be, that we should become *actually*, and not as a mere figure of speech, " dead to sins and alive to righteousness." " Who gave Himself for us " was always a precious word ; but the other half of the text was not received into my heart,—" to redeem us from all iniquity ;" for such a *present* redemption was too much for my faith. However much I might rejoice in the atonement as washing away the stains made by sin, I had not learned to forego self confidence so entirely as to receive the blood as cleansing the fountain, the very source of evil thoughts, murders, and so on. I did not see that the reason that this fountain of the heart sent forth both sweet and bitter waters was, that the blood had not been allowed to manifest its full virtue in cleansing from all unrighteousness.

" The blood of Jesus Christ, his Son, cleanseth us from all sin " was probably more constantly on my lips than any single passage of Scripture for ten years, before I saw that its application was not primarily to cancelling the record of sin, but to the inward cleansing of the souls of those who " walk in the light as He is in the light." When a sinner is converted to God, he is brought to *Jesus the Light,* which shines upon and into him. If he then walks in the Light,—or in Jesus,—He shines through and through him, revealing hourly the things that are contrary to God and to holiness ; and as they are revealed by the light, they are cleansed by the blood. *A walk in the true Light always leads to the blood of cleansing.* Thus we find that if we walk in the light as He is in the light, God and ourselves have fellowship one with another, and then we realize that the blood of Jesus Christ cleanseth us inwardly from all sin.

" Whatsoever doth make manifest is light, and all things that are reproved are made manifest by the light." Happy child of God, who, as from day to day he walks in the light, shall bring. *everything* that is made manifest in his outward or inward life, to the fountain opened for sin and for uncleanness, and find himself thus hourly cleansed inwardly from all sin, and possessing a heart that, condemning him not, leaves him in confidence toward God.

Nothing short of this is walking in the light. It is solemn to remember that if any one *saith* that he has fellowship with God, and walks in darkness, he lies, and does not the truth. It is God that says so! Alas, how many around us are claiming to have fellowship with God, while yet they walk in darkness, with defiled consciences and stumbling steps! Would that I could say something to arouse them to the fact that *God must have realities.* "Awake to righteousness, *and sin not.*" Self-persuasion that we have fellowship in a simple recognition of the truth, is not a reality. The soul must yield itself up to the Holy Spirit, to be led in a walk in the light, where everything is given up to God, and everything received from God— where "all things are of God, who hath reconciled us to Himself by Jesus Christ. . . . For He hath made Him to be sin for us, who knew no sin, that we might be made the righteousness of God in Him."

In reply then to the question often asked us by dear brethren, who value the precious blood of Christ, and who feel a jealous fear lest it should be set aside or slighted, " If you are walking thus in the way of holiness, where is the need of blood?" we reply that we exalt the atonement far more than ever before. It is most blessed to bring the outward actions to the atonement for remission of sins, but is it not far more blessed to bring the inward being or soul to the cross, so that the body or root within us of all sinning may be kept continually in the place of death, and that putting on the new man, which after God is *created in righteousness and true holiness*, it alone may be alive and active?

Ah! beloved friends, there never was so much need of the blood as now, because it is only by that blood every moment applied that we can walk here. That blood was shed not only to wash away the stain which sins had left upon us, but to wash inwardly the sin itself away; and if I am not sinning at this moment, it is because the deep inbred sin of my nature, which would make it utterly impossible for me to please God, is being at this moment purged by the blood of Christ. And this seems to be the teaching in 1 John i. 7–10; ii. 1. We are told here that if we walk in the light, the blood of Jesus cleanseth from all sin, not only from the stains of sin, or the punishment of sin, but from sin itself. (1 John i. 7.)

This, however, must not make us think sin is eradicated otherwise than in our participation of

Christ. The angels themselves would instantly find corruption in their souls, were they separated from the great Source of life. We have no independent holiness. We are to be vividly alive to the fact, that it is only as we are every moment cleansed that we can at all walk in the light of God, who is of purer eyes than to behold iniquity (ver. 8). But this need not discourage us ; for if we confess our sins, He is faithful and just to forgive us our sins, and to cleanse us from all unrighteousness, and He does do it (ver. 9). As though a child by disobedience had fallen into the mire : the first thing is the confession, then the forgiveness, and then the stains are all washed out. And last of all, lest any from being thus cleansed should forget they had been sinners, we are again reminded of the sorrowful fact (ver. 10), but are at once told that these very things have been written to us "that we sin not." (ii. 1.)

Let us suppose that here is a spring of water which is poisoned in its very source, and which can of course therefore send forth none but poisoned waters. But a remedy is found which counteracts the poison, and makes the waters pure and sweet. That remedy is applied in the

very source of the spring itself, and the waters
flow out therefore pure and sweet. But they do
so only so long as it is applied. The moment
the remedy is stayed, that very moment the
poisonous waters flow out as foul as ever. Now,
this is what the blood of Christ does for us,—it
reaches the very spring itself, "purifying *our
hearts* by faith," cleansing us "from all filthiness
of the flesh and spirit," and enabling us by faith
to realize that wondrous statement that "every
man that hath this hope in Him purifieth himself,
even as He is pure." We purify ourselves, not
by effort, but by faith ; not by works, but by the
precious blood of Christ. This clean and humble
condition, however, is ours only while the blood
is applied by faith, for the very moment faith
ceases to apply it, corruption ensues, and the same
old bitter waters flow out.

It is mistaking the very meaning of the word
to suppose that the blood of Christ cleanses only
from the stains and guilt of sin, and that unless
sins are committed we do not need its present
application. We need it far more to *prevent* our
sinning, than even to wash it away when committed. We need it to purge our consciences, to

purify our hearts, to deliver us *from* our sins ; and we have a very faint conception of its infinite worth when we confine its power to cleanse, only to obliterating the record of our sins, and to washing away their stains.

The little stone by the road side receives dust from every passing wind. The shower has often cleansed it, but it has always become again soiled. Another stone of the same lustre lies near by, but within the brook. It is perpetually cleansed and kept clean by the flowing waters. Clouds of dust may pass over it, but they do not reach it, and it always reflects the clear rays of the sun. All its cleansing, all its purity is in the stream, not in itself.

There is no need, therefore, for continuing in sin in order that grace may abound ; for grace much more abounds in our being cleansed from sin, and hence obtaining a continual deliverance from it, since it is grace, and grace only, that does it all. And none know the worth of Jesus like those whose hearts have been opened to receive *all* the salvation He died to procure, even a salvation from sinning as well as a salvation from hell ;

nor can any sing with such a depth of meaning as
these the simple yet precious words—

> " I'm a poor sinner, and nothing at all ;
> But Jesus Christ is my All in all."

Oh, my brother, how shall you and I ever praise
God enough for such a wonderful salvation, so
manifested in the souls of those who will receive it
by faith, and triumph through Christ, amid all the
works of Satan, and in the presence of his apparently full victories in the world around us.   Let
us, therefore beware lest the atonement of our Lord
be dishonored by too much limiting its results to
the future world, thus making our Lord to accomplish in death what He is not willing to do in our
life.   Let us remember that whosoever confesses
Christ with the mouth unto salvation, should also
believe in his heart *unto righteousness*—practical
righteousness—and that when we call Him by his
name, the Lord Jesus Christ, we are supposed to
believe of him that for which He is so called—
King, Saviour, the Anointed.   He is thus named
because God sent Him to rule in his kingdom in
our hearts,—to save us from (not in) our sins, and
to purify unto Himself a holy priesthood.

I prayed long over that text, "They overcame him by the blood of the Lamb;" but, thank God, I know its meaning now by a blessed experience, that the blood of Christ cleanseth, not only the stream, but the fountain. I keep carefully to the word, "*cleanseth*," not *hath cleansed once for all*, but now cleanseth by the continual application of faith. From the cleansed heart, prepared for the manifestation of the Holy Ghost, must necessarily flow the fruits of the Spirit; for the blood of atonement and the oil of the Holy Spirit go together.

Were the life commencing in this walk of Christian holiness prolonged on earth a thousand years, and were it to progress indefinitely, each day learning and practising more perfectly the lessons of Christ, there would be realized at the close of such a life, yet more deeply than at its commencement, the need of the blood of Christ. We may build upon it, but never can we leave it behind, nor cease to need its merits as our only ground of confidence before God.

There is some fearful mistake when the same fountain is found to "send forth at the same place sweet water and bitter!"—when there come from the same heart love and hatred, joy and variance, peace and envying, longsuffering and wrath, gentleness and strife, faith and heresies, meekness and emulations; "out of the same mouth blessing and cursing." It is said of those "that are Christ's" that they *have* crucified the flesh, with its affections and lusts, not that these things continue alive.

The Lord grant you and me, if we "live in the Spirit," to "also walk in the Spirit," so continuously and entirely cleansed by the blood of Jesus, as that out of a perfect heart shall flow *only* rivers of living water, to the salvation and refreshment of many.

The Lord make you not faithless, but believing for larger blessing,—the "exceeding abundantly"—above all that you have ever asked or thought.

A PRESBYTERIAN MINISTER.

"I had been preaching with much joy one evening, during an awakening in a neighbouring church, on the text, 'The blood of Jesus Christ, His Son, cleanseth us from all sin,' and seeking to teach through it, to the sinners present, their privilege of immediate and full remission of sins, through the blood of Christ. On returning to my lodgings with a Christian brother, he spoke to me of his enjoyment of the address, and then went on to make some remarks on teaching half truths from half texts. He related how that for ten years he had constantly preached from the words, ' Who his own self bare our sins in his own body on the tree,' without ever teaching the complement in the last half of the verse : 'that we being *dead unto sins*, should live unto righteousness.' He had taught abiding in Christ, without its result of sinning not. He had often said ' Who gave himself for us,' without adding, 'that He might redeem us from *all* iniquity.' I was led to see that the text I had preached from was addressed to my own soul primarily, rather than to the sinners before me, and that it was myself who needed the lesson. The Holy Spirit opened to my understanding that if I, a Christian, would walk in the light, as God is in the light, I should have fellowship with Him in a sense little as yet conceived of, even amid all my earnestness ; that I should know inwardly, as a blessed reality, that ' the blood of Jesus Christ cleanseth us from all sin ; ' and that all my groanings for deliverance from my inward cor-

6

ruptions, should be met by the fountain opened for sin and uncleanness. I cannot define fully the effect upon my own soul of the words of my friend, but never had I been filled with such precious views of the purifying power of Christ.

"This blessed view of the cleansing blood opened up more and more on my soul for two years —a period of prayerful investigation, and yet of anxiety lest my friend were not in error in his understanding of these texts. All this time I was praying God to show me my full privileges in Christ, but to save me from heresy. I met my friend several times in the railway cars, when he always earnestly set before me the fulness of present privilege that was in Christ, and at our command through faith, illustrating his views by Christian experience.

"At a conference meeting of Presbytery, it was one evening proposed to consecrate ourselves more definitely and fully to God, and the act was accompanied by a wonderful baptism of the Spirit, which opened to my soul the hope of the near consummation of my soul-longings. Shortly after this, I invited the brother who had opened these things to me, to address the church under my care.

At the close of his address, on being ' dead to sin, and risen with Christ,' I spoke to the people of the power of Christ to save from their sins all those who would fully consecrate themselves, and trust Him.

"During that week I was led to see, as never before, the privilege of an *entire* soul-rest in Christ, and that it was to be entered into by faith. On the Lord's day, I preached twice on this subject, from a full soul, and after the evening service I proposed to a Christian manufacturer that a few Christians should meet together the next day to enter into rest. I did not say to seek rest, but, so confident was my faith, ' *to enter in.*' Ten earnest, godly men, mostly from his workshops, on the following day, knelt down in my friend's warehouse, among the boxes. We remained on our knees an hour and a quarter, in prayer, praise, and consecration. Of us, too, it might be said, ' And when they had prayed, the place was shaken where they were assembled together, and they were all filled with the Holy Ghost.'

"I have been conscious ever since that it was then and there that in a definite transaction with God, I entered into a complete soul-rest in Christ,

a rest, through the cleansing blood, which my soul
has never lost for one hour since. It was attended
by the satisfying certainty that whatever spiritual
blessings I thenceforth claimed in simple faith
should be mine.

"Since then I have received answers to my
prayers for holiness as never before. I have again
and again realized more growth in one day, than
before in a whole year. From that time my
soul has been filled with a wonderful divine consciousness of the actual, in-wrought reality of the
expression, 'I am crucified with Christ, nevertheless I live ; yet, not I, but Christ liveth in me.'
Instead of pining for rest, I am continually
praising God for realized rest, the deep, inward
Sabbath-keeping of my blood-cleansed soul. I can
now see no limit to the possibilities of the life of
Christ in my soul, since I have accepted the atonement in its full purposes, both of pardon and
holiness."

CHAPTER VI.

THERE is an experience, not universal, it may be, to all who profess the name of Jesus, but uniform, so far as my observation extends, in those who walk in the full, searching light of God, and who honestly bring their deeds to this light. The work of conversion has been unmistakable; the assurance of final salvation is unvarying; the apparent devotedness to God is exemplary; the joy in the study of the Word great; and the access to God in prayer at times soul-inspiring. This condition of soul may continue for years, and through watchfulness and prayer, outward sin may be mostly avoided. The heart finds, even though often overcome by inward evil, great happiness in working for Jesus. Though sometimes brought into sorrow for transgresssion, through sudden temptation, the sense of forgiveness is clear. And yet, through all these privileges, there is the continued and undefined yet

(85)

painful feeling, as though a cloud intervened between God and the soul,—a cloud which neither earnest, self-denying service, nor attainments, however large, in scriptural truth, are able wholly to dispel. Work is sometimes entered on, and even recommended, as a relief to this unrest. This uneasy sense of the lack of full, unhindered fellowship with God is the great sorrow of many, if not most Christian hearts.

But the plummet has not yet sounded to the depths of the soul: and to those who do not shrink from it, another step of faith is yet to be taken. Far down, deep below the current of the previous consciousness, while occupied with the intense activities of Christian life, there are the continual motions of *inward* sin. The spiritual vision now discovers a great sink of iniquity within, so that instead of "a pure heart," there is conscious inward impurity. The quickened and tender conscience is convicted by the Holy Spirit of a deep, in-wrought pollution, antecedent to any acts of sin. This, which had been a *doctrine* before, becomes now a soul-harrowing, conscious reality. Self-distrusting and self-renouncing before, the soul now becomes self-abhorring, and cries out "Create in me a *clean heart*, O God, and renew a *right spirit* within me!" It is not now so much a question of manifested sins, as of *sin* as their root, that the soul must grapple with. " Must I ever find within me an active fountain welling up bitter waters along with the sweet fruits of the Spirit? Am I to be for ever conscious of inward impurity? Is death alone to be my inward deliverer? Can I never call upon God out of a pure heart,—a heart *consciously* cleansed?" the soul now bitterly exclaims.

The Holy Spirit never creates hungerings and thirstings after righteousness but in order that Christ may fill the longing soul. These convictions of *inward* sin in a believer, so remarkable in their parallel to the work of conviction as to *outward* sins in an unbeliever, bring the saint a second time to the cross. Once it was forgiveness of sins for which the soul cried out; now it is cleansing— holiness. A holy intensity of desire to be indeed entirely the Lord's, and to find Christ formed within and reigning in resurrection-life over inward as well as outward sin, takes possession of the heart. Nothing can now satisfy it without the consciousness of having received that blessed result of the sin-bearing of Jesus, the "being *dead* to sins," and the *living* "unto righteousness" (see 2 Peter ii. 24)—inward and outward purity. The soul which before pleaded for the impossibility of ceasing from sin, and consoled its own consciousness of failure by the narratives of the failures of the saints, now rather uses them as warnings, and instinctively turns with indescribable longings to the highest standards of practical holiness that the Scriptures or the examples of saints present, and pleads THE BLOOD as the means of cleansing.

Glimpses of the possibilities of a different and a higher life burst through the clouds of sorrow for indwelling sin, that envelope the soul. All remnants of confidence in self-effort wither in the remembrance of past failure, and the awful sense of the holiness of God. The occasional soul-inspiring views of the scriptural standard of inward purity combine with the convictions of the Spirit of God, to bring the soul into an agony of self-despair, which finds vent in such language as " *Who* shall deliver me from the body of death ? "

This is the very place to which the Holy Spirit has led the soul, and He who to all its former prayers for holiness seemed to have " answered not a word," now finds that it has reached the

point of self-despair where these prayers for purity
can be answered. It is then that the heart, unable
to define its experience in the suddenness and the
joy of its discovery of the present power of Jesus
to save from sin, breaks out, "I thank God
through Jesus Christ our Lord!" And thus, in
the joyful sense that there is "now no condemnation to them that are in Christ Jesus," the soul
goes on to realize that " the law of the Spirit of life
in Christ Jesus hath made me free from the law of
sin and death. For what the law could not do,
in that it was weak through the flesh, God sending his own Son in the likeness of sinful flesh, and
for sin, condemned sin in the flesh : THAT THE
RIGHTEOUSNES OF THE LAW MIGHT BE FULFILLED IN
US, WHO WALK NOT AFTER THE FLESH, BUT AFTER
THE SPIRIT!"

Doth not the present heaven of privilege, in
putting off the old man, and putting on the new
man, *which after God is created in righteousness
and true holiness*, burst through these inspired
words, my brother, upon your soul ?

He who has *thus* taken Christ finds a sweetness
in communion never before experienced, and a
victory over inward and outward sins that he

never conceived of as possible for him in this life. The atonement becomes more intensely real than ever before, as the expression of the love of the Father. The solemn scene upon Calvary, God manifest in the flesh suffering for man, seems unveiled to faith as never before. Jesus is now realized answering the prayer—

> " Be of sin the double cure,
> Save from wrath and make me pure ! "

A new sense of oneness with Christ fills the heart. The Scriptures are radiant with promises of present sanctification,—a redemption from all iniquity,—studied a thousand times, but never understood till now. Prayers for holiness are now answered, and a holy joy, a divine peace, a rest in God, and the witnessing of the Holy Spirit to the work of Christ, *for* the soul and *in* the soul, ensue.

This experience, where enjoyed, is in most cases strongly marked, as a definite step of faith, which,—whatever may be the after-growth in grace,—practically brought the soul at a definite period into new and overwhelmingly lovely practical relationships to Christ,—relationships

which ought to have been ˙entered into at conversion, but which are, alas! mostly deferred till
after a long and God-dishonoring experience of
wilderness failure.   Sometimes, however, like the
time of justification, the exact period is less
defined, the blessed Word having distilled like the
dew into the Lydia-like worshipping heart.   But
whether the experience be the work of a moment or
of a year, it is the gracious operation of the Spirit,
taking of the glorious things of Christ and his
salvation, and showing them unto us.

Now we must inquire, What is the condition as
to indwelling sin into which the soul is thus by
faith brought? Is it, or is it not, an inward
cleansing from *all* unrighteousness? So glorious
is this revelation of Jesus as a Saviour from sin,
and so complete faith's present overcoming of the
world, that the consciousness cannot be trusted for
a reply.   We may well hesitate to accept the experience, even of our own hearts, if it be unsup-
ported by Scripture, as well as contrary to that of
others.   Consciousness does not so much take
note of the quiescent state of the soul, as of its
activities.   Whether because we do not feel the
inward motions of sin, for a longer or shorter
period, it is therefore purged, it is not in the range

of consciousness to determine. Where *we* dare not answer, the Scripture is very definite as to what is wrought in the soul, and if the Word, fairly rendered, corresponds with our consciousness, may we not trust our convictions, as the witnessing of the Spirit. We are told that the blood " cleanseth us from *all* sin," — " from *all* unrighteousness ;" that we are " made free from sin," as once we were " free from righteousness :" " free from the law of sin and death :" " light in the Lord :" and that " the truth as it is in Jesus," is the putting on " the new man which after God is created in righteousness and true holiness." The less we limit the intent of this large class of passages, and the more we cast ourselves upon Christ to have the real meaning accomplished in our souls, the better shall we understand them. Happy he who seeks prayerfully to raise his practical experience up to the level of God's word, rather than to lower God's word to the level of his own experience !

We know no one who interprets these terms in their absolute sense, as though the unconditioned holiness of God were ours. The Scripture addresses our *need* and our *consciousness*, carefully avoiding all metaphysical distinctions. My conviction is, that we do well to act on this scripture plan of not analyzing these things, but that we should simply receive them in their plain and obvious import. Care must be taken in our definitions of "sin" and "holiness." A condition necessarily imperfect in even the knowledge of what is evil, and which is capable of hourly progress in holiness, is scarcely, in the accepted meaning of words, to be therefore called sinful and unholy. We seek to use terms in the intuitive sense, comprehensible by the great mass of Christians to whom the sacred Scriptures are addressed.

God's commands are not grievous, and He does not set before his redeemed children a line of obedience through which the grace and truth that are by Jesus Christ cannot lead them. We could not say, as do some, that the injunctions of Jesus are like the law, given but to manifest the sin of believers, so as to cast them more entirely upon the atonement. Nay, my elder Brother would not leave me in so miserable a condition. He came to save His people *from* and not *in* their sins. To the flesh, or old nature, these commands are superlatively impossible, but to the Spirit-led disciple there must be far more possibility, in this dispensation, of having the testimony that we please God, than when Enoch walked with God for three hundred years.

AN AUTHOR.

Permit me to relate some simple incidents, illustrating the views here given. About three years since, I was earnestly pressed to visit a Presbyterian minister with whom I had labored in tent-preaching ten years before, He had for probably twenty years borne an eloquent and most clear testimony to justification by faith alone, both in his preaching and in his writings, issued by millions from the press on both sides of the Atlantic, and had lived a life of unusual practical devotedness to God. The Holy Spirit, however, had been leading him to a discovery of his inward corruption and deep needs, such as is referred to above.

After our first greetings, I inquired of him in substance—

" Have you, my brother, found Jesus a Saviour from this constant sinning ? "

"No," was the reply ; " and I feel my need of some power beyond what I have yet known."

" Do you," I asked, " believe it the will of Jesus to give you power uniformly to overcome the world ? "

" I do."

"And how only can such a victory come?" I again inquired.

"By faith alone," he replied.

"Are you willing to yield yourself," I said, "to trust the Lord to work in you, *to will* as well as to do, of his good pleasure? Are you willing to trust Christ to do all that *you* have failed in?"

"I am."

I only added as I looked him full in the face, "WHEN?"

There was a severe struggle and a pause. He had not expected to be brought so soon to the test of yielding the last remains of unbelief in the power of Jesus, of giving up the very last corner of his heart to Christ; but faith triumphed as he exclaimed—

"NOW!"

Immediately he was filled with a peace in the Lord, such as he had not known before since his conversion, and found a victory over sin, and a power in preaching Christ "with the Holy Ghost sent down from heaven," such as he had never before realized. Recent intercourse with him assures me that he would not for worlds exchange his present experience of victory over sin and communion with Jesus for the former life, eminently devoted and successful in winning souls as it was.

One more incident among many. In a large tent, where, in 1857-8-9, we preached to the non-church-going-masses, a young man, who came to mock, remained to pray, found Jesus, and went forth to proclaim His salvation with great success. For a while he took a charge as a Presbyterian minister, but his unusual abilities as a public speaker led him into other work, in which he travelled from Maine to California, reaching with his voice probably millions of his fellow-creatures, and with many seals to his ministry of the Word.

While earnestly laboring in an extensive field, he came to realize this need of inward holiness. After long prayer, I pressed him so earnestly to come and visit me, that, although the distance was near a hundred and fifty miles, and his engagements urgent, he dropped everything, and came. Other calls pressing upon me, our private interview was limited to about an hour. There, in the solemn searching light of God, he reviewed his life, inward and outward. The remedy for all sin and sinning was presented to him, and he saw, by the light of the Word, that it was indeed to be found in Jesus Christ. He could not, however, have faith for it. We knelt before God for the Spirit to show him the full power of Jesus, and to plead his sacrifice. His agony grew greater. He cried out, "Oh my unbelief! my unbelief!" so loudly, as to resound through the house. We could only wait upon God to show the cause of his not finding through Jesus the victory which he sought. It was then recalled to my memory that the brother had said that once he had, as he thought, cast himself upon Jesus for this victory over sin, and then immediately, to see if he were indeed able to overcome, had voluntarily placed himself in circumstances of temptation, and had failed as formerly. He wanted a *sign* before he would believe. He was now led to see that this was not faith, and that he must, as in attaining to a knowledge of remission of sins, *believe without a sign*, simply upon the word of Jesus. The last difficulty was removed, and his soul entered into a joy and communion with Jesus which he had not known since his first hours of faith in his tented birthplace.

Upon his return those in the Gospel laboring under his direction around him wondered at the heavenly change wrought in him, though they knew not the cause. A day lately spent with him, after the interval of a year, gave the additional assurance, were it needed, that this second coming to the cross was to him indeed the work of the Holy Spirit, opening the way to such victory over sin and self-abnegation as he had not before known.

Permit me, in closing this chapter, to remind you that I do not present this secret of the Lord as a doctrine to be discussed, but as a *life* to be enjoyed. I well know how little access it has to the hearts of professors, even while they lament their own backslidings, and how almost all, however they may differ in other things, unite in opposing it. I believe, however, that you are humbly and devoutly waiting upon God to open it to your understanding and heart, ready to follow wherever his truth may lead. And should I have the privilege of removing any difficulties, or of piercing the clouds to bring down a ray of hope for deliverance from this body of death, then my purpose in writing will be gained.

I know that the Holy Spirit *alone* can really unlock to your soul these treasures that are in Christ for every child of God who will hold out emptied hands to grasp them. I only add, *When Christ places them in your hand, grasp them ;* hold them firmly, watchfully, feverently to the end. And *so,* having in this sphere become a partaker of the divine nature, having escaped the corruption that is in the world through lust, an entrance shall be ministered to you *abundantly* into the everlasting kingdom of our Lord and Saviour Jesus Christ.

CHAPTER VII.

IT is remarkable how many dear Christians there are who would gladly go to the stake rather than deny their Lord, and yet who confessedly fail frequently, or even habitually, in the smaller acts of hourly obedience and consecration; and who live under a painful sense of their lack of love and obedience to God. It is remarkable, too, how many there are who appear to have given God the supreme place in their affections, who yet, —unconsciously in some cases,—retain for themselves, and for their idols, corners, hidden places as it were, in their hearts. Strange is it, too, how great the shrinking is from the thorough searching of the soul, and from yielding these last outposts after the general surrender has been made to God: —when so much of the heart has been cleansed, how great an aversion there is to the completion of the work. How many things will a man lose of the old life, how near will he voluntarily come to death, and yet at the last point refuse to " lose his life." The evil *doings* of the old or natural life may be put aside to a large extent, but the life itself, though nigh unto death, is retained by some apparently slender thread of existence. This, however, is sufficient to sustain the vitality, which anon, in a most unexpected moment, springs up again in fearful energy.

Death is a bitter thing to nature, whether it be the death of the body, or the yielding up of "the flesh" to death; the crucifixion of "the old man, that the body of sin might be destroyed;" the burial "by baptism into death;" the reckoning ourselves "dead indeed unto sin." And yet, until this is known, it is a weary and unequal struggle between the flesh and the spirit, with often most God-dishonoring results.

When the Christian, who is as yet not fully at rest in the Lord, is honest before God, and when he will come to his knees in sincerity with the heart-prayer, "Search me, O God, and see if there be any wicked way in me, and lead me in the way everlasting," there will then always be found some point of will reserved from God, some secret place of the heart not yielded, some method of acting condemned by conscience and yet allowed, or some act of faith from which the soul yet shrinks. It is most important to come into the full light of God, that this may be defined to the soul, so that instead of a general and indefinite sense of soul-weariness and separation from God, there may be the distinct consciousness of what God calls for at his hands. This is often God's first answer to the prayer for a clean heart, the light exposing the evil before the blood can cleanse. It is the purpose of our Lord's work, accepted in all its blessed provisions, that our souls should be filled with love and obedience, and that dwelling in the full sunshine of His love and favor, we should realize His love and His joy fulfilled in ourselves. It is most blessed to have a hope opened to the soul of walking thus, not sometimes in special seasons of command, but always. What the soul needs is the Way in which this can be accomplished, definitely set before it.

This result is not attained unless there be that distinct work in the heart by which the temple is emptied of *all* defiling things, and cleansed by the blood of Jesus. It can then be filled with the love of God, and consciously and definitely established in entire consecration and obedience. "Whoso keepeth His word, in him verily is the love of God

perfected : *hereby* know we that we are in Him."
To this agrees that word of our Lord, " He that
keepeth My commandments, he it is that loveth
Me."

" Oh that I *could* live thus ! " exclaims some soul,
weary of its wanderings and falls, footsore and despairing of ever having a heart that shall condemn
it not, and leave it confidence before God,—able to
enter into God's dwelling-place of love. Do you
indeed desire it ? And if some Way, clearly proven
by Scripture, were set before you,—a Way possible to you just *now*,—would you at any sacrifice
enter upon it ?

We take it for granted that you so far trusted
Jesus, as to realize that He did indeed bear your
sins in His own body on the tree,—even though
you do not yet find the declared result of being
" dead unto sins, and alive unto righteousness,"—
and that you are not now in condemnation of soul
by the remembrance on your part of past " sins and
iniquities," which God is pledged to " remember no
more." We assume that you are not living wilfully
in any known sin or open act of rebellion, and that
you are groaning for that full union of soul with
Christ which the Scripture sets before you.

Can I cease from sin, and dwell in love and in God?

God is our Father. He does not reap where He has not sown. He commands no impossibilities of us. He is not more unreasonable than earthly parents. No command is without the means of its fulfilment attached to it. Faith and love can meet any requirement of God, for the one brings His own power into the scene, and the other places us in God's own atmosphere of love as our dwelling-place. "For this is the love of God, that we keep His commandments, and *His commandments are not grievous.*" It would seem to be beyond question that God has provided a Way of obedience and holiness, and if you have not attained to it yet, He whose command is "Awake to righteousness, and *sin not,*" tenderly assures your heart by these words, "And this is the confidence that we have in *Him*, that if we ask anything *according to His will*, He heareth us. And if we know that he heareth us, whatsoever we ask, we know that we have the petitions we desired of Him." If it be, then, according to His declared will that we "abide in Him" and "sin not," do not

hesitate to ask in confidence for such a grace, nor
fail to use the means which He has provided.

It may be, however, that your theory of what is
included, in this dispensation, in "the fulfilling of
the law," and "in pleasing God," may be different
from the definitions of Scripture. We are not
called to the standard of a different dispensation
from that in which our lives are to be lived. We
are not called to walk by the rule of angels who
"excel in strength," while we exceed all other creatures in weakness, nor yet even by the rule of the
yet unfallen Adam. Neither is our standard that
which will be ours in glorified bodies. "Like as
a father pitieth his children, *so* the Lord pitieth
them that fear Him ; for He knoweth our frame,
He remembereth that we are dust." The obedience
to which Christ is wooing us is not the legal obedience, a stainless perfection of knowledge and act
impossible to these clouded faculties. That would
indeed be an impossible and therefore grievous
command. "If ye are led of the Spirit, ye are not
under law." We are called to a hearty and supreme love of God, and to love our neighbour as
ourselves. "Love is the fulfilling of the law." "A
new commandment I give unto you, That ye love

one another ; as I have loved you, that ye also love one another." "For in Christ Jesus neither circumcision availeth anything, nor uncircumcision ; but faith which worketh by love." "Love is of God : and every one that loveth is born of God, and knoweth God." "If we love one another, God dwelleth in us, and His love is perfected in us." "Jesus said unto him, Thou shalt love the Lord thy God with all thy heart, and with all thy soul, and with all thy mind. . . . Thou shalt love thy neigbour as thyself. *On these two commandments* hang all the Law and the Prophets."

Any commandment beyond the plain requirements of Christian morals is all "briefly comprehended in this saying, namely, Thou shalt love thy neighbour as thyself." It was on the occasion of our Lord's enjoining the duties of love upon His disciples that He said, "that ye may be the children of your Father which is in heaven . . . . . Be ye *therefore* perfect, even as your Father in heaven is perfect." That is, as I judge, Receive "the love of God shed abroad in our hearts by the Holy Ghost," and let that love be "made perfect" in you as children of a heavenly Father. The Holy Ghost is given to accomplish what were indeed impossible otherwise,

It would seem, then, that love is God's law and standard in this dispensation, and that whatever is not contrary to love does not now bring condemnation upon our conscience ; entire obedience to the recognized guidance of God's Spirit being, of course, included in our love to God. A child's service may be accepted and acceptable, although not yet perfect. There may be many mistakes of judgment, things done through involuntary not wilful ignorance, that are not contrary to love,—on the principle that to him that knoweth to do good, and doeth it not, *to him* it is sin. And yet it is true that all our ignorance, all our failures in the best of our service, all our lack of conformity to the perfect example of Christ, need the application of "the blood of Christ, who through the eternal Spirit offered Himself without spot to God," that he might purge our conscience from the dead works of a legal obedience, to serve the living God through a divinely-implanted love. We cannot claim any perfection beyond this, that up to the furthest line of to-day's consciousness, we have the witness that we do love God and our brethren, and keep a conscience (or knowledge) void of offence.

It must, however, not be overlooked, that this

soul-attitude of obedience involves a perpetually increasing light, as well as a perpetually growing conscious conformity to God. Increasing light is the essential condition of obedience. Each day of full obedience is a day of advancing knowledge. Yesterday's standard of walk will not answer for to-day. The past twilight did not discover some defiling bone in my tent, and it did not then bring an evil conscience; but, in the clearer light of to-day, the same contact would bring condemnation. The essential thing is not perfect light or perfect knowledge, but perfect obedience to the light and knowledge already bestowed.

A just consideration of this truth would remove many difficulties from those in doubt about the possibilities of a full sanctification. It is not perfect knowledge, perfect wisdom, or perfect attainment, but simply a perfect heart—that is, a heart yielded without any reserve to God—to walk in entire obedience and perfect trust. It is that yielding ourselves to God, "*as those that are alive from the dead,*" which can only be known after a practical experience of having been "buried with [Christ] by baptism into death." It is the power of resurrection life with Jesus. So far from this experience of grace being the completion of God's work, as is sometimes understood, it is but the condition of soul-health, in which a continuous, unchecked progress in the divine life is possible. It is the well-grafted and healthy tree which can grow rapidly and mature its fruit. After having presented our bodies a living sacrifice to God, then, transformed by the renewing of our mind, we are privileged to " prove what is that good, and acceptable, and perfect will of God " in all the details of daily life.

A few days since, my gentle little girl, two years old, attracted by an inkstand, innocently picked it up, poured its contents over her new white dress, and, pleased with the performance, she finished the contents over my own clothes, and then looked joyously into my face for approval. Had the child been older and wiser it would have been a transgression, and she would have needed correction ; but, as I saw what was done, I could only say, " You knew no better, my little one ; "—and, I thought of my Father in Heaven, and said, " Does He exact impossibilities of my ignorance, while I walk in communion with Himself and up to the light He gives me ? "

" Beloved, if our heart condemn us not, then have

we confidence toward God. And whatsoever we ask we receive of Him, because we keep His commandments, and do those things that are pleasing in His sight. And *this is His commandment*, That we should believe on the name of His Son Jesus Christ, and love one another, as He gave us commandment. And he that keepeth His commandments dwelleth in Him, and He in him. And *hereby we know that He abideth in us by the Spirit which He hath given us.*" The Holy Spirit is the *direct* Witness to our spirits as to whether Christ is abiding in us and we in Him. Having this, we are satisfied. To any cavils from those who tell us that it is impossible, we may have little to answer, but our inward consciousness responds, "My Beloved is mine, and I am His!"

How can I attain to this dwelling in love and in God?

"Such a life seems impossible for *me*." So did the knowledge of the free, full, perfect forgiveness of past sins once seem. But it became true to faith.

"The placing it as a perfect love bestowed on us, rather than as a legal obedience, instead of lessening my difficulty, seems rather to increase it." So

did setting forgiveness of sins as the free gift of
God, and shutting you out from the least ray of
hope through your own legal obedience, once seem
to place salvation further off. But in like manner
we are now bringing you nearer to the attainment
of your soul's desires, for we are setting before
you God's own way.

"But the withdrawal of all hope of accomplishing this result by dependence on my prayers, vows,
and efforts, seems to take away all props and helps."
Such has been our principal aim in leading sinners
to the cross for remission of sins. In like manner,
when your present hopes and efforts are all proved
and acknowledged to be ineffectual, you will be
ready to lose your own life,—the self that must be
denied,—that you may find the resurrection-life of
Christ in all its glorious power. You may heretofore have somewhat denied self's evil doings ; now
you have to deny *self* in its very centre. You may
have heretofore denied some of the actings of the
old life ; but now you must lose that *life* itself, in
order that you may experience that "whatsoever is
born of God overcometh the world." You must
know that the old man *is* crucified with Him, that
the body of sin might be destroyed, that henceforth

we should not serve sin,—an actual transaction of your soul with God,—before you can say, "I am crucified with Christ: nevertheless I live ; yet not I, but Christ liveth in me: and the life which I now live in the flesh, I live by the faith of the Son of God, who loved me, and gave Himself for me."

"God is love. He that dwelleth in love dwell. eth in God, and God in him . . . . As He is, so are we in this world. There is no fear in love ; but perfect love casteth out fear." If the memory of all past failure, the sense of present despair and helplessness as to dwelling in love and in God, should bring you to the point of exclaiming, " 'O wretched man that I am ! Who shall deliver me ' from this corrupting body of sin ? " you are in such a place before the cross for inward cleansing, as you once were for the forgiveness of sins. Never had you been so near mercy's door as when you despaired utterly of self-merit, and of your own efforts. And now again, in that despairing of self and all its actings, of the old life and all its doings, you feel your need of the further results of the cross, for inwardly cleansing from all sin, and dwelling in love and in God, and you are just prepared to "thank God *through Jesus Christ* our

Lord," and to realize that "the law of the Spirit of life *in Christ Jesus* hath made me free from the law of sin and death, ... that the righteousness of the law might be fulfilled in us who walk not after the flesh, but after the Spirit."

What may be, in your case, the last weight to be laid aside, what the last item of self-will to be surrendered, the last thread of the old life to be severed, is known only to your own conscience, enlightened by the Spirit of God. It may be that you know of nothing in your present or future that you withhold from an entire consecration ; that you feel as though no self-will or mental reservation interfered with the yielding of the whole being as a living sacrifice laid upon God's altar. If so, and yet your soul has not entered into the full rest of God, there is but one thing remaining,—that is, to yield up your unbelief as to God's acceptance of the offering. The gift is sanctified by the altar, and what we bring to it, by touching the altar, becomes holy and acceptable to God. Our faculties and emotions are not in themselves unholy ; but have become so only by being yielded to Satan, and the *same* faculties and emotions yielded to God are made holy "instruments of righteousness to God."

"For as ye have yielded your members servants to uncleanness and to iniquity, unto iniquity ; even so *now* yield your members servants to righteousness, *unto holiness* . . . . *Now* being made free from sin, and become servants to God, *ye have your fruit unto holiness,* and the end everlasting life."

Can you not, dear Christian, believe that God *now* accepts and sanctifies that which you bring, and that *through faith it is now* and *may be henceforth,* yours to dwell in love and in God?

Plainly, as once the results of faith for the remission of sins were received the very moment that faith was exercised ; so now the very moment you trust Christ for realized deadness to sins and life unto righteousness, you shall find it accomplished ; and the foundation having been thus laid, your faith may extend to dwelling in love and in God. The very name of "*believer*" which you take, forbids that you should defer the reception of any blessing, for grasping which you are called to believe the promises of God.

The difficulty of realizing that this perfected trust and its accompanying perfect love is now for us, is lessened by the remembrance that it is not our own natural love, the emotions proceeding from

our own souls, which constitute "the love of God."
"The peace of God" is not our peace of soul to-
ward God, but His own eternal peace, in which He
dwells without change, amid all the convulsions of
His universe, throughout eternity ; and which He
sends down into the hearts of His trusting children.
In like manner, "the love of God" is not born of
"the will of the flesh, nor of the will of man, but of
God." It is an actual divine gift, like the Holy
Ghost, by which it "is shed abroad in our hearts."
It is not a condition of soul into which we ourselves can gradually grow, but a divine grace bestowed on and established in the trusting heart.
Since it is of God, it is perfect in its character, free
and immediate in its bestowal, and through a continuing faith and obedience, permanent in its results ; and since it is the soul's deepest need, now
is God's time for its reception. I see not how any
believer need despair of its full power, since *it is a
gift, and it is from God*, and is to be received as a
gift, undeserved but freely bestowed.

Once received, then follows the responsibility of
keeping ourselves in the love of God. This injunc-
tion is found between the "building up yourselves on your most holy faith, praying in the Holy

Ghost," and the joy of "looking for the mercy of
our Lord Jesus Christ unto eternal Life." The
path of faith is always an advancing path, and yesterday's building seems to-day but as a foundation
laid, so that there is the perpetual further building
on the foundation once laid. "Praying in the
Holy Ghost" surely authorizes prayer that God's
love may be "made perfect" in us up to the utmost limit of the present capacity of these small
vessels.

Oh that this gift of God in all its fulness might
be received into hearts which have too long dwelt
in the changing atmosphere of failing natural
emotions! Listen to the tender tones of thy
Beloved who speaks, and NOW says, "Rise up, my
love, my fair one, and come away. For, lo, the
winter is past, the rain is over and gone ; the flowers appear on the earth ; the time of the singing
of birds is come, and the voice of the turtle is
heard in our land : the fig-tree putteth forth her
green figs, and the vines with the tender grape
give a good smell. Arise, my love, my fair one,
and come away." Oh, that thou wouldst *abandon*
thyself to this love of Jesus until thou canst say,
"He brought me to the banqueting-house, and his

banner over me was love. Stay me with flagons, comfort me with apples ; for I am sick of love." There are those whose very hearts do melt within them as they experience this divinely-begotten love of God. Such an one, a simple child-like heart, a few evenings ago, in the prayer-meeting, said, "I've had *just one drop* of the love of Jesus, and just that one drop would fill all your souls."

It is the full acceptance of this love of God, and the creation of its response by the Holy Ghost in the heart, which can alone satisfy the claims of the Heavenly Bridegroom, who tells us that his "love is strong as death : . . . . many waters cannot quench love, neither can the floods drown it ; if a man would give all the substance of his house for love, it would utterly be contemned." Jesus tenderly both offers and claims such a divinely, inwrought love for us when He says, "Love Me."

Thank God, if the feeling of the need of this overcoming divine love has been created in the heart of my reader, even though it be, for the moment, nigh unto despair as to experiencing it. The creation of the felt need of a grace promised to faith in the Word, is the first step, and a great one, toward the supply of that need. Lay that need before God,—not to go away and forget it amid the myriad voices that are in the world and in the heart ; but to keep it as the soul's cry continually before the throne.   Can there be any doubt as to the result ?

living in the busy whirl of large commercial operations, writes, " I have great joy in recalling the time when first those words were effectually illuminated to my soul by the Holy Spirit: *'God is love. He that dwelleth in love, dwelleth in God, and God in him.'*   I could not deny that a marvellous work had been already done in my soul, in a divinely inwrought faith, which placed Christ between me and temptation, just as a screen, placed before the fire, shuts out the fire, leaving only the grateful colors of the screen before the eye.   I had already known the faith which overcomes the world, inward or outward, and something, at least, of what it was to abide in Christ, with its blessed results.   Yet in the thought of *dwelling* in love, and in God, and God in me, there was a vista opened before me that seemed at first to overwhelm my faith with a sense of impossibility.   I dared not say, however, that any promise of God was 'not for me,' and I felt that God's hand was on me for this also. I do not remember any sudden baptism of love or of joy, but as I *continued* in prayer and faith for this gift of God, I became conscious of a marked change in my inward life. The stirrings of bitterness or contention seemed to die out. I shrunk from thinking or hearing evil of any one. There seemed an atmosphere of divine love graciously formed around and within me, so that it did not now seem so much effort or restraint to meet sudden injury or insult with love, as the simple and natural expression of the inward life of God in the soul. I remember the hour in which I became conscious that my prayer had been in a measure answered. Although I feel that all yet received from God is but a drop from the ocean of divine love,—yet it *is* that drop, and I *know* that 'God is love. And he that dwelleth in love, dwelleth in God, and God in him.' 'And hereby we know that He abideth in us, by the Spirit, which He hath given us.'"

We find, then, that—

I. Christ's command involves the truth that the believer CAN cease from conscious transgression, and dwell in love and in God.

II. It is in an unreserved abandonment of soul to Christ only, that the believer can learn HOW to dwell in love and in God.

III. Faith's NOW is the time WHEN the believer may dwell in love and in God.

We are called with Abraham, who left his *all* at God's command, to put our trust in "God, who quickeneth the dead, and calleth those things which be not as though they were ; " and follow "the Father of all them that believe," who "staggered not at the promise of God through unbelief, but was strong in faith, giving glory to God ; being fully persuaded that what He had promised He was able also to perform." This is the faith which brings God into the scene, negatives the verdict of experience, sight and sense,

"And cries, it shall be done."

"*Let us therefore as many as be perfect, be thus minded : and if in anything ye be otherwise minded, God shall reveal even this unto you. Nevertheless whereto we have already attained, let us walk by the same rule, let us mind the same thing.*"

CHAPTER VIII.

IT is manifest that every approach to God must humble him who draws near, and the nearer the place into which faith brings the believer, the more entire the withering of the flesh and self. The two evils which separate the soul from the Saviour are sin and self-righteousness; and of these two things, self-righteousness seemed to be the more effectual barrier during the days of our Lord's ministry on the earth. The self-righteous Pharisees, who wore Scripture texts up and down their garments, and who would not eat their soup till the tithe of their mint and anise had been paid, derided Him; but the publicans and sinners heard Him gladly, and were saved. We are all born Pharisees. Pharisaism is bred in our very natures; and, if we escape the upbraidings of conscience for gross sin, the natural resource of the evil of our hearts is this legal self-righteousness.

Although this evil of self-confidence is that with which the "Way of holiness through faith" is most frequently charged, and, although the confession of salvation in its full, practical, present sense might sometimes *seem* to give ground for it, yet in truth it is as effectual an antidote to pharisaical self-confidence as it is to sinning. It was precisely here, in the self-despairing confession of entire helplessness, the conviction burned into our very souls by the consciousness of inward failure, that we reached that point where a new view of the privilege of present redemption in Jesus, from all iniquity, made us burst into the exclamation, " I thank God through Jesus Christ our Lord ! " It then became *all* Christ ; and the soul, which could not stop to define the doctrine, joyously embraced the living Christ to receive from his hands a practical death to sins and life unto righteousness.

The *doctrine*, without the life-giving power of " Christ formed in you," is but the colorless shadow, the faint copy of the living, breathing reality. It is the possessors of this shadow who have brought reproach upon this " Way of holiness," by an imitation, which, while it presents some of the outlines, lacks the reality of the resurrection-life in Christ. We know that the devil always imitates, but never originates, and we ought not to be ignorant of his devices to throw at every point discredit on the truth of God. There seems to be a special and most marked effort by the evil one to destroy in every way the testimony of those who preach a redemption from all iniquity. We are not careful to reconcile the fleshly walk of those who evidently profess without possessing or practicing the truth of God, whether the "profession" be that of pardon of sins, or that of the faith which gives real victory over the world, the flesh, and the devil.

There is a wide difference between "professing" and "confessing." Peter professed what he would do, and he fell. Paul confessed Christ living in him, and he triumphed. In a more exact translation of the Epistles we should find the word "profess" applied in an evil sense to those who, "professing themselves to be wise, they became fools;" while we should read of Timothy that he "confessed a good confession before many witnesses." It is just here that the point now before us lies. We profess nothing of ourselves, but we *confess* that "Jesus, who delivered us from the wrath to come," now keeps us, by the power of God, practically within that kingdom which is righteousness, peace, and joy in the Holy Ghost.

So long as there is the least legal taint in our ideas as to how we were saved from just judgment for our sins, so long will the taint of self-confidence be found in the "professor of religion." But, as soon as the soul recognizes that " salvation is of the Lord," wholly of the Lord, without work or merit of our own, then at once the "profession" (implying something partly our own, which we will carry out), is changed to a " confession made unto salvation" of what Christ has freely done for us. Then, without any other trust, the soul rests on the sacrifice of Christ, and, for the first time, is thoroughly humbled before the Lord, finding it now *not* "presumption to be sure of heaven."

Those who have not the assurance of salvation, will not believe this ; but, judging such a confession by their own legal thoughts of salvation, they will insist that confidence in Christ is presuming on one's own merits. Only those who have found that holiness is no longer a desperate negative strife, but a blessed positive obtainment or gift, can know how exactly parallel to the above are the thoughts of brethren who charge with presumption and self-confidence those believers who *confess* Christ as a present Saviour from sinning.

It is because with us it is ALL Christ that we are so humbled, and that we have such confidence. We find, alas! that the moment anything else intrudes into the ground of our confidence, our strength is gone. This life is one of continuous self-despair, and of continuous trust. The instant that the soul pauses to rest in anything "already attained," in that moment our feet slide. Just so far as any element of unbelief qualifies the simple, absolute trust in Christ, just so far is there transgression. Faith is the measure of holiness. But, let us always remember, that uniformly victorious faith is not an impossible faith, but, that as Jesus is the author of faith, He is, also, the finisher or perfector of faith. Here again it is ALL Jesus ; and, while looking to him, we are not sent empty away. The vessel may be small, but it is filled to-day ; to-morrow it will be larger, and still its utmost capacity shall be filled. Truly, here all "boasting is excluded." By what law? Of works? Nay, but by the law of faith. And yet with David we say, "*In God we boast all the day long*, and praise thy name forever." Saved from Egyptian bondage by the outstretched arm of Jehovah alone, "neither did we get the land of Canaan in possession by our own sword, nor did our own arm save us, but Thy right hand and Thine arm, and the light of Thy countenance."

Contrast the holy and happy, yet humble confidence in Jehovah, which says of the Canaan of rest, "Let us go up at once and possess it, for we are well able to overcome it," with the faithless cry, "We be not able to go up against the people, for they are stronger than we ;" and we find the secret cause of the different positions of God's people. In a late church-meeting, an influential man arose and said that he loved the Lord Jesus in his weak way, but that he had sinned very much yesterday and to-day, and he expected that he should again to-morrow. The same was said by several others who had taken prominent positions among evangelical Christians.

It was not said of constitutional defects, nor of evil not yet discerned as such, but of known and conscious sins. And these frequently utter their belief that Christians necessarily commit known sins.

We could ask, How much sinning is of the nature of a necessity ? If a necessity, upon whom does it reflect ? Verily, such a doctrine is the very stronghold of Satan within our lines. The Lord have mercy on those who thus dishonor the work and power of Christ by saying that continuing in sin is inevitable ; and on those, too, who would not say it so broadly, but who cover up the essence of the doctrine by indefinite evasions of the issue. May we beware of this specious form of " humility," for, as the stream does not rise above its source, so their lives cannot rise above their faith, or rather faithlessness.

Such is the present experience of the church, her sins culminating in the charge against Israel, " They limited the Holy One of Israel." According to her faith she is cured, according to her unbelief the old sin-palsy returns. But we like not to hold up the unlovely picture. We would be found not so much testifying against error, as bearing a faithful witness to the truth as it is in Jesus. If we have to speak of error, it is sadly, and not for controversy. Nor does it befit one who looks back to so sad an experience of failure, and who stands from moment to moment by faith only, to judge his fellow-servants. We would rather say to them, We have found in Jesus treasures of present practical blessing, such as we had not, in our former dimness of sight, conceived of as for us in this life. "O taste and see that the Lord is good ; blessed is the man that trusteth in Him. .... They that seek the Lord shall not want any good thing."

We dare not withhold our testimony to the power of Christ to usward, when we are conscious before God that it is given in self humiliation and to his praise. We saw a part, but now in the light of God we see full salvation in its glorious proportions. We were unholy, but by his grace we are made holy,—saved from sin to the full measure of our trust in Jesus, and filled with the comforts of the Holy Ghost. Surely it is no pharisaism to proclaim, like Paul, what God is doing for us,— no vaunting to say that we find Jesus saving us from our sins. For it is never said by any walking in this sacred light, "I am holier than thou," or "I am holy of myself," or "I can be holy if I choose." The praise for these blessings, equally with deliverance from wrath, is all given to Jesus. We hear from such, "Jesus keeps me." "I find Him to be indeed the double cure." "The blood cleanses." "I am nothing, Christ is all." "I am kept by the power of God."

Dare you, my brother, reject such a present sal-

vation from sinning, every aspect of which is illustrated by the Word, by Christ, by the light of
Calvary, by the power of the Spirit, by victory
over sin, and by the genuine humility into which
it introduces the believer? I am not so careful
about our agreement in the doctrinal statement
of this glorious privilege, as for the reality in the
soul, which can only be rejected by any to their
most imminent peril. The substance of the life
may be held with some misapprehension of the doctrine. While I am divinely sure of the reality of
the experience that "Christ liveth in me," and
while, according to my small measure of capacity, I
know what it is to "be filled with the Spirit," I do
not feel perfect in knowledge, nor that I am able to
state the doctrine in the perfect harmony of its
several elements. Test all yourself by the Scriptures, *never bringing them down to the level of your
experience, but raising your experience by faith to
their full standard of holiness.*

If others can state these things, so as to reach
the hearts of their hearers, without illustrating
by personal experience, yet pardon me that in
these letters I have followed the best judgment
that I could gain in prayer. As the preacher's

9

confession of Christ as his own Saviour from wrath, is the best preface to his message, so I have judged that I must witness that I have myself partaken of the fruits, in order that I may not seem to hold out an impossible privilege to those for whom I write.

And now, for the future :—I feel it most important not to set before myself any *expectation* of ever again sinning against God.*   Although my past experience might seem against such a hope, and though I dare not either make vows or boast, I feel it to be most God-honoring to commit the keeping of my soul in well-doing unto God, as

---

* As long as David, without anxiety, trusted God without limit day by day, walking in full faith in that path appointed him, so long confidence toward God and holy communion were his. " Saul sought him every day ; but God delivered him not into his hand." But forgetting the miraculous preservation just experienced, and that he was God's appointed king, he looked at circumstances, instead of exercising that faith which is above circumstances. Then came in the evil heart of unbelief, and he " said *in his heart*, I shall now perish one day by the hand of Saul." This distrust of Him who had given him all his victories was the entrance on the shameful history of failure from which at length God restored him, a solemn warning, as once he had been an example. "Take heed, brethren, lest there be in any of you an evil heart of unbelief in departing from the living God." " For by faith ye stand "

unto a faithful Creator. *The very expectation of sinning would be its prelude,* and I must look not at sin, but at Him who saves from sinning. I can set no bounds to what God may do for the chief of sinners, now saved and kept by grace. When I have thought and asked my largest, I find that God does for me exceeding abundantly above and beyond it all. In fact, this seems to be my almost continual experience of surprise and wonder at the manifestation of God in *His* power, in *His* presence, in *His* imparted joy.

All this is accompanied by deeply increasing knowledge of self-weakness ; for the flesh does, indeed, wither at the presence of God in the soul, while yet the Spirit lives and reigns. And yet it is only by faith, and only a moment at a time, I am thus kept. The evil root is ready to spring up into bitter branches ; the flesh is near me, though I walk not in it ; and the " destroyed" body of sin is ready to " revive" at any moment. Oh, hourly miracle of grace ! Oh, blessed Saviour, to whom all thy children are privileged thus to cling !

CHAPTER IX.

I.—A REVIVAL.

THERE is a most important rule of the deal ing of God with his children embraced in the statement of the Psalmist, " He made known His ways unto Moses, His acts unto the children of Israel." Moses was on the mount, in communion with the *ways* and purposes of God, while the children of Israel trembled beneath acts which manifested the awful presence of God in their midst. Be it ours with Moses to commune with Jehovah in the knowledge of his *ways*, rather than to have our eyes so upon the world as to see his *acts* only. May we, like Abraham, the friend of God, dwell in heavenly separation, where God shall not hide from us what He is about to do !

A little church in the country had lost its pastor, and not being able to procure another, they desired a business man, who lived a few miles away, and who preached the Word, to minister among them. He found it in about the condition in which so many assemblies are found,—legal and uninstructed in some of the first principles of Scripture. Few, beside some young persons recently converted, could say with confidence that they had eternal life. One of the deacons, however, had a few months before entered with great power, into the experience of entire consecration to Christ and victory over sin. Full of faith and the Holy Ghost, his walk, and even his very appearance, were a testimony to the gospel. He was, however, comparatively untaught, and his power of expression was mostly limited to the simple, though convincing, statement of what the Lord had done for his soul. The arrangement of the meetings was of the usual kind—preaching on the Lord's day to a mixed company of saints and sinners, and on a week-day evening a prayer-meeting.

At first the gospel was preached, and strong appeals made to the unconverted, but without apparent fruit, save in two instances. Disheartened by the limited results, the preacher then, in anxiety, turned to do that which he should have done more fully at first—to ask the guidance of the Spirit, to wait for it, and to *act on it* alone.

The answer came with great distinctness in the words, " Oh, that salvation were come out of Zion ! *When God bringeth back the captivity of his people,* Jacob shall rejoice, and Israel shall be glad." It was seen that full salvation should be *in* the church, before salvation could flow forth to sinners. " He made known his ways," to his weak servant, and full faith was imparted, that when the believers were experimentally sanctified, *then* the power of God in His gospel would save sinners. Close and careful instruction from the Scriptures in much prayer was from that time addressed to the believers, leading them to look away from themselves to Jesus only as the ground of the forgiveness of their sins. One by one the members dismissed their Christ - dishonoring doubts, and rejoiced in the present possession of eternal life through faith in Christ only. But they were not suffered to rest here. The foundation having been laid in Christ, they were to be *built up* in their most holy faith. The confession made by two brethren in their midst of what God had done for their souls, made the church feel that they could not take up with any rest short of the true rest of receiving *all* from God, and giving

all to God. The aspect in which this practical
sanctification was presented was chiefly as the full
result of the atonement,—the privilege purchased
for us by Christ, the entrance upon which thus
became the most solemn obligation. The power
of God in this truth reached their souls one by
one, leading to full experimental union with
Christ, until nearly all shared the blessing. Then
it seemed as though the very windows of heaven
were opened upon them in the floods of spiritual
blessing and joy. The meetings were deeply quiet,
and more and more solemn. The power of the
Holy Ghost was seen wonderfully in the assemblies. As men are "drunk with wine," so were
they "filled with the Spirit, making melody in
"their hearts to the Lord ; giving thanks always."

Then with this fulness of joy came the willingness to "fill up that which is behind of the afflic-
tions of Christ in their flesh, for His body's sake,
which is the church." Then dawned in their souls
the glory of the humiliation. They saw that the
more they suffered with and for Christ, the more
their place was "without the camp ; " the less
that they kept to please the flesh and their natural
love of position, the more they would occupy the

real p_ace of spiritual blessing. Strong cries went
up to God to hide them, and to honor Christ.
They renounced all desire that, as a church, they
should have any honor in the community,—glad
themselves to be little and unknown, if only God
should be glorified in them. They asked one
thing alone,—to have Christ in their midst, ruling
effectually in their hearts and in their meetings,
and then that from them should sound out the
word of the Lord in all that region.

The answer came according to their prayer.
The worldly attenders left their meetings. Their
house of worship was taken from the church.
Some members removed, and others were estrang-
ed. They were stripped of numbers, their house
gone, and the places of loved ones were vacant.
Poverty, too, pressed upon them. They were
learning the lesson that God Himself was to be
their only hope and joy. The lessened meetings
were held in a private house, and limited to the
more faithful members only, But God was there.
He had now brought them to the place of need,
which is always the valley of blessing. He who
had "made known his ways" of first filling Zion
with blessing, in faith that thence salvation should

flow forth, now led their hearts to pray for sinners in prevailing power. It was not the restlessness of struggle and effort, so much as the calm confidence of faith, which, acting in the power of God, must command results,—the firm step of soul health rather than the struggle with spiritual paralysis. It was a solemn season of apparent failure of all things outwardly, and yet of the triumph of an anticipative faith. It was the Lord's way, his deep lesson in the school of God, the humiliation before the triumph.

After the more private meeting of the diminished though favored church, they were accustomed to join a much larger company on the Lord's-day evening near by, in a capacious building, erected for the joint use of all the religious denominations around. There were, however, but few meeting there who were walking even outwardly in Christian paths. Soon prayer was answered by a deepened interest in this meeting, and without any previous planning of revival services, continuous nightly meetings were called for. In these the attendance, though good, did not result in any conversions for near two weeks. The preacher who had labored in the smaller church proclaimed both God's judgments on sin, and a free, full salvation to contrite sinners. That there were no conversions closely tested the faith that seemed to be just grasping the promised results ; but the trial of faith was "precious" beyond gold in God's sight. God's ways, as foreseen some months, had all been realized up to this point ; praying for sinners had surely been "in the Spirit,"—and were the meetings to close without their seeing souls saved ? In the smaller and select meetings the cry went up, but "Jesus answered them not a word." The answer was delayed, however, but to bring out the deeper needs of their souls. At length it seemed as though prayer must be answered, or the preacher could hardly live. Night after night, as, after the hard work of the day, he rode alone through the darkness to the meetings, his cry went up to God, and the earnestness of the appeal was at length answered by the agonizing pleading becoming the effectual message of grace.

The answer came. Dead souls heard the voice of the Son of God and were quickened into life. Large numbers responded to the call to meet after the preaching those who could answer their question, "What shall I do to be saved?" As each one entered into peace, the loudest call was sounded by their confession of Christ, and the hearts of others were reached. Persons gathered from a distance; the word of the Lord was sounded all through that neighborhood; meetings were started in other places around, and thus the faith which had through all trusted in God was honored.

Before this time, often, in preaching the gospel, the joy of seeing souls come to Christ had been mingled with the deepest sadness in the anticipation that the saved ones would, alas! too probably, soon fall into the Christ-dishonoring, faithless ways of the professors around them; but now it was a wonderful and joyous privilege to set forth Christ to the young converts, not only as bearing their sins in his own body on the tree, but as proposing to make them by that very sacrifice " dead to sins," and alive to God; to show them *in Christ* a present and practical redemption from all iniquity; and to open out to them their privilege, having left Egypt, of entering at once into Canaan, or resurrection-life and victory over all enemies.

The type or character of the faith and life of converts is wonderfully affected by the character

of those who have been their spiritual parents.
Where these have been themselves groping in legal
twilight and spiritual paralysis, the same low type
is too often reproduced. But where the preachers
of the gospel have themselves had clear views of
divine grace, with corresponding entire consecration
to God and victory over sin, we generally see a
higher faith and walk in converts. Recent intercourse with some of those saved in the revival
here described, and reliable accounts from most of
the remainder, give us ground to believe that the
Holy Spirit who gave the victorious faith in their
spiritual parents, reproduced the "like-precious
faith," to a most satisfactory degree in those who
made a clear confession of Christ during these
services.

These special meetings presented many scenes
of deep interest. A praying father saw two of his
children, who were just arriving at maturity, confess Christ for the first time on the same evening.
The dividing line in families between faith and
unbelief was cancelled, and ties of blood were
eternally cemented by union in Christ. The numbering of converts is often an evil thing ; for we
may rejoice over those who may go out, "that

they might be made manifest that they were not all of us," and we may know as yet nothing of many whose repentance makes "joy in the presence of the angels of God." We leave all to be ascertained in "that 'day," when the wise, who turn many to righteousness, shall shine as the stars, and when all our crowns of rejoicing shall be laid at the Saviour's feet as the triumphs of his grace alone in us.

In a true revival, life is increased and developed by exercising its functions, instead of being merely stimulated and exhausted. Where there is excitement without development of life among Christians, the subsequent reaction places them in a condition as much below their ordinary level as the stimulus raised them above it. But in soul-health, scenes of protracted effort only develop the life within, so that increased power follows, and not reaction. It is therefore not only that sinners may be saved, that the privileges of a full soul-union with Christ are to be urged upon believers, but that, when special times of refreshing come, there may be spiritual capacity to retain the grace poured out.

The special work being ended, the little com-

pany of " faithful brethren," having done their
Lord's will, returned to their more private meetings,
their assembly being added to by the fellowship of
some of those lately saved.   Their meeting-house
was restored to them, and they are now worshipping on the Lord's day in great simplicity, and
holding frequent meetings through the week, in
the wonderful joy and power of the Holy Ghost.
He who had preached the word and taught among
them was suddenly removed to a distant field of
labor, but they realize the truth that " the anointing which ye have received of Him abideth in
you ; and ye need not that any man teach you ;
but as the same anointing teacheth you of all
things, and is truth, and is no lie, and even as it
hath taught you, ye shall abide in Him." Much as
they valued the gift of a teacher, they knew that
their assembly, with a public teacher or without
one, was " a house of God," " the church of the
living God."   Though they may wait on God for
another pastor, they do not for the want of one
cease to know the presence and power of the Divine
Teacher in their midst.

The lessons learned in this scene were,—first, the
guidance of the Spirit in the assembly, pointing

out the mind of God as to the present line of preaching; and, secondly, that to have a revival that can be fully owned of God, Zion must first herself be filled with salvation. We have more hope for the cause of God in seeing one intelligent soul led to this full practical sanctification in Christ, taking *all* from God, and giving *all* to Him, than in ten ordinary conversions, where the converts may probably, for want of knowledge and faith, fall into the usual ways of the correctly called "Christian *world*." For instead of a stumbling-block, the soul thus sanctified will be a power for God through a lifetime, leading many souls to like privileges.

"Oh, that the salvation of Israel were come out of Zion. When God bringeth back the captivity *of His people*, Jacob shall rejoice, and Israel shall be glad."

II.—KADESH BARNEA.

A young disciple under words of solemn warning to Christians not to be always asking God for a holiness that they could not exercise faith for, nor even hope to receive, was led to see what it was to be raised up with Christ in resurrection-life, to "sit in heavenly places in Jesus Christ," always walking in those "good works which God hath before-ordained that we should walk in them." An anxious inquiry after the meeting as to how he should attain practically to such a privilege, led to a conversation, of which the following is the substance :

"Do you desire to be *wholly* the Lord's? Are you willing to receive this full salvation at once, if God would give it to you ? "

"I do indeed desire it above everything in this world," he replied.

He was told, " You must yield to God your own will, as well as all its evil actings. Not that your sacrifice is the procuring cause of God's blessings, but it removes the obstacles to their reception. *We are neither saved nor sanctified by what we give up, but by what we receive.* It is no covenant of works that is set before you, but you must not frustrate the grace of God, which can only reign in the soul through righteousness. If in anything you were regarding iniquity in your heart, God could not answer your desires for holiness. Hence, you are wholly to yield yourself to God, as one alive from the dead, and your members as instru-

ments of righteousness. You are to realize yourself by faith as 'buried with Christ in baptism,
wherein also ye are risen with Him, through the
faith of the operation of God;' and this resurrection is to make you practically dead unto sins, and
alive unto righteousness. Can you die to all the
idols of your heart, that Christ may be formed
within, reigning in resurrection-life?"

"I do not know of anything that I have not
fully dedicated to God," was the reply, "but I
have not the victory you speak of yet."

"But there is one thing not yet given up, and
unless you part with it you can never hope for this
fulness of gospel blessing."

"What is that?" he eagerly inquired.

"*You have not yielded up your unbelief!*"

He saw this last step to be taken, and powerless
of himself to take it, we bowed before God for the
power of the Holy Spirit. The time of our interview was necessarily limited to about twenty
minutes, but God can bring a trusting soul into
the land of promise directly from Egypt as easily
as after forty years of faithlessness in the wilderness. Upon his knees before God, there stole over
his soul, as the dew from heaven, the God-given

10

faith by which he realized what it was to put off the old man, corrupt according to the deceitful lusts, and to put on the new man, which after God is created in righteousness and true holiness. The flesh was withered, but the spirit lived, and with a strange, humble joy, he learned the first great lesson in the way of holiness by faith in Jesus. By faith alone will he stand in this holy place. But, thank God, he *can* stand by faith in the power of the resurrection of Jesus Christ.

III.—A CITY PASTOR.

I parted with this rejoicing disciple to keep an engagement with another dear Christian, whose history may throw one more gleam of light on this highway of holiness cast up for the Lord's redeemed ones to walk in. Converted early in life, and well settled in the doctrine of justification by faith, his early joy had been chilled by some influences at a theological seminary, so that upon entering on the pastoral office, he had found a cold, professional feeling in all his work, that alarmed him. He had incurred a severe disease from laboring among the soldiers in the late Union war, which laid him by for a season, and gave him the opportunity of reviewing his past and present position before the Lord. God created in his soul deep longings for personal holiness, with a feeling of intense need for something far beyond his present life of inward failure and conscious lack of full communion with God. So deep were these convictions that after his recovery, and even during special services in the church under his care, he declined to preach, leaving the work to others.

At length, over-persuaded by those around him, he stood up to speak. In that moment, under a perfectly overwhelming sense of need, he cast himself unreservedly upon Christ, to live and act in Him ; and to his great surprise and joy, he found himself preaching the gospel with the Holy Ghost sent down from heaven, and witnessing to what God had done for his soul with a new and strange power never before known. For nearly a year he lived thus, carried above the world in the victory of faith. When he knelt for prayer, he knew not what he was about to pray for, but he felt conscious that what he should find himself asking should be done. It was the Spirit praying in him, according to the mind of God, and in the name and power of Jesus, for such things as God would bestow.

Difficulties, however, beset him. He found men
" professing sanctification," and evidently walking
in the flesh ; and instead of seeing that the counterfeit always presupposed a reality, he became
perplexed. The privilege of such a walk of faith
was not clearly set forth in the standards of the
denomination in which he preached. His brethren
told him it was a joy that could not last. Alas!
instead of going only to the oracles of God for
knowledge, and casting himself unreservedly upon
Him for power and guidance, he looked to man ;
he took his eye off Christ, was frightened by the
waves, and his feet sank. He limited the Holy One
of Israel, who had already gotten him so many
victories,—and fell from the resurrection walk of
victory over the world, the flesh, and the devil.
He ceased to be filled with the Spirit. Several
years had passed, and although considered an
earnest and a successful pastor, he was now under
so painful a sense of inward failure, and of want
of full communion and power with God, that he
was thinking of giving up his large metropolitan
charge for another profession.

On the evening preceding the prayer-meeting
above described, I had accepted his invitation to

call upon him. Although our first interview, he freely opened his history, as related above.

" I have for months been asking God for some one to be sent to lift me out of this condition. Can *you* tell me," said he, feelingly, " how I may regain the blessed experience of joy and power of service in which I once lived? "

We opened together on Romans vii., that chapter which holds up the mirror so effectually to the experience of the failing Christian. When at last we came to Paul's fresh vision of Christ doing all that Paul had failed in,—the law of the Spirit of life in Jesus Christ setting him free from the law of sin and death,—we felt that God's hand was upon us. On our knees we besought God to restore to him the joy of His salvation, and the power of resurrection-life. The prayer was answered. He thanked God, through Jesus Christ, and left behind him,—as we trusted for ever,— "the seventh of Romans," to live henceforth in the eighth, walking not after the flesh, but in the Spirit.

A striking feature of this interview was that to almost every difficulty suggested by the remaining legality of his soul, the only reply needed was,

" Answer as you would to the doubts of an awakened sinner." We found ourselves applying just such words as in his own mouth had been so often blessed to those inquiring the way of pardon— " Receive God's grace by faith alone,"—" Without or with emotion,"—" Now,"—" Step out in God's promises, and find them true,"—" It is no presumption to trust Christ for what He has promised." When delivered from his legal doubts, he confessed that while he had always preached immediate deliverance for sinners, he had indulged the subtle unbelief which argued that time, and sorrow, and certain methods of feeling, were needful to saints.

These instances of the entrance on a walk in the Spirit are selected among many as the freshest in my memory. The testimony of those who, beginning thus, have walked in God's highway of holiness for nearly half a century, could be added, were it needed. *The highway was cast up for the redeemed to walk in*, though some would seem to believe that it was only to be longingly gazed at.

A Presbyterian minister has very recently told me, that while he had not accepted either the doctrine or this " gift of righteousness," he must, in

candor, say that he had often wondered at, and
almost envied, the uniform elevation of piety, and
the practical resurrection power in which some
around him, and even in his own congregation,
walked,—a power to which he was, alas! himself a
stranger.

My brother, you believe in the resurrection of
Jesus Christ.   Have you not faith to realize practically your own resurrection?   Have you consciously given up ALL to God?   Is there no reserve,
no corner of your heart retained for yourself,—
the old hateful self, that must be denied, not in its
manifestations only, but in its centre.   If you
have, what hinders you from being practically
risen with Christ?   Give up your *unbelief* in the
fulness of God's present salvation!—but oh, do not
turn back to the old hopeless ways of self-effort, or
to a trusting in means while rejecting Christ's
power.

With your sins buried in the grave whence they
can have no resurrection, can you trust Christ for
a present resurrection-life that knows no eclipse?
Whether you sweep the streets, or ride in your
carriage, you can only fulfil God's purposes of love
by living and walking in Christ in heavenly places.

The believer dead with Christ should have done with the world, and find himself risen with Christ in a new life. Acceptance with God and separation from the flesh belong together. The same cross which connects me with God should be found to separate me from my old self, and not be taken as a reprieve to the flesh. Christ died that we might also die with Him, to self, to the world and to sin. The believer should not profess to enjoy the benefit of Christ's bearing his sins in His own body on the tree, and yet refuse to enter upon the experience of being "dead to sins," and of "living unto righteousness."

I do not feel at liberty to close without adding that there are many who *speak* of that which we do ourselves *know*. We are not exhorting to a path, the joy of which we are ignorant of. According to our small measure we are witnessing the results and power of our Lord's resurrection in the midst of lives of severe labor :

> "There are, in this loud and stunning tide
>   Of human care and crime,
>   With whom the melodies abide
>   Of the everlasting chime :
>   Who carry music in their heart.
>   Through crowded streets and wrangling mart ;
>   Plying their daily tasks with busier feet,
>   Because their hearts the sacred melodies repeat."

It is not a mere ideal, nor a translation, but an intensely child-like and simple life lived out in the duties and relationships in which God places us. We are conscious of no controversies in our souls with God; and, like breathing, it becomes the habit of the soul to trust God for everything. The cross-currents are controlled, the current of the whole being sets towards God, and the soul can take up the word, "How shall we that are dead to sin live any longer therein?" We boast not of yesterday, nor make vows for to-morrow. The blood of Christ *now* cleanseth, the bread come down from heaven *now* sustains, and the faith once delivered to the saints *now* gives the victory.

IV.

One or two incidents may be better than definitions. In the summer of 1868, I met, at a large conference, a young business man, with whose variable religious experience I had been familiar for some years. The company of some who were evidently walking in an atmosphere of Christian love, and of victory over the world, to which he was a stranger, led him to feel his need of a full salvation. One evening after an address on the soul's union with Christ, he was asked the question, "Do *you* need such a life?" "I do indeed," was the reply. "And are you ready to trust Christ for a full sanctification?" was asked. "I feel that I am," he responded. Then came the searching question, "WHEN?" to which he replied, "Now!" The conversation was so simple and brief, that often as I had witnessed the far-reaching results of an immediate and full surrender of soul to Christ, I could myself hardly believe all that seemed included in those few brief responses would be realized; but soon I heard in all directions of his gospel labors, and the wondrous results. He was like a flame lighting every circle it touched; and I could name few in private life who, in the two years that have passed since that brief interview, have done more for the cause of God than this young man, although up to that time he had rather needed to be himself helped than to be called on to help others. A few days since he told me that he was living in a cloudless rest in Christ.

I recently met in a railway car, a young lady, of whose remarkable success in gospel labors among the young and educated I had known. On asking her the secret of her power, she said, that after her large Bible-class one evening, under a deep sense of need of more power in the Spirit, she asked this same young man the secret of his power, and how to obtain it. "*Just abandon your soul to Christ,*" was the brief reply. Accompanied by the Holy Ghost, it was blessed to her heart, so that before she entered her father's door she felt that she had indeed "*abandoned*" her soul and her *all*, without reserve, to trust Christ for victory over every sin, and for every blessing promised in the Scriptures to faith. Her life since seems to have been a continuous act of trust, which like breathing has become the habit of her soul. Many stars are already in her crown of rejoicing, and I doubt not many more will be found "in that day."

I like that word "*abandon.*" It expresses the soul's attitude towards Christ. This attitude may be taken up at any moment, and continued without break through a lifetime — the perfect abandonment to Christ in all his offices of mercy, cleansing, power, and guidance. It places the soul in Christ's hands, and makes Him alone responsible, if we may so speak, for all results. Our responsibility ends with the abiding: for then He Himself works in us both *to will* and to do of his good pleasure. A life of abiding is a life in which we sin not (1 John iii. 6) ; we bear much fruit (John xv. 5) ; we ask what we will, and it shall be done unto us (John xv. 7) ; and then when He shall appear, we shall have confidence before Him at his coming. (1 John ii. 28.)

Oh, blessed abiding in his love! Oh, blessed keeping of his commandments! How can we ever enough praise God that, in the midst of all the evil of man and of Satan, God's power can be so exercised toward his saints as to keep them abiding in the Vine, as living fruit-bearing branches!

Let none stagger at the promises of God, or fail of recognizing his grace for making them to dwell in love, and dwell in God. Oh that the simple way of faith, rendered possible by an entire abandonment of soul to Him, might become plain to all of God's children!

May our reader see by the Spirit's illumination that God's now is the time for availing himself by faith of the provisions made for us in our King, our Sacrifice, our Life, our Conqueror, Sanctifier, our ALL IN ALL.

THE

CHRISTIAN'S SECRET

OF

A HAPPY LIFE.

BY

H. W. S.,

AUTHOR OF

"FRANK, OR THE RECORD OF A HAPPY LIFE";

"BIBLE READINGS," ETC.

New Edition, Revised and Enlarged.

THIRTY-FIFTH THOUSAND.

THE CHRISTIAN WITNESS CO.,

36 Bromfield Street,   57 Washington Street,
Boston.   Chicago.

PREFACE.

THIS is not a theological book. I frankly confess
I have not been trained in theological schools,
and do not understand their methods nor their terms.
But the Lord has taught me experimentally and
practically certain lessons out of his Word, which
have greatly helped me in my christian life, and
have made it a very happy one. And I want to tell
my secret, in the best way I can, in order that some
others may be helped into a happy life also.

I do not seek to change the theological views of
a single individual. I dare say most of my readers
know far more about theology than I do myself,
and perhaps may discover abundance of what will
seem to be theological mistakes. But let me ask
that these may be overlooked, and that my readers
will try, instead, to get at the experimental point of
that which I have tried to say, and if that is prac-

tical and helpful, forgive the blundering way in which
it is expressed. I have tried to reach the absolute
truth which lies at the foundation of all " creeds "
and " views," and to bring the soul into those personal relations with God which must exist alike in
every form of religion, let the expression of them
differ as they may.

I have committed my book to the Lord, and have
asked Him to counteract all in it that is wrong, and
to let only that which is true find entrance into any
heart. It is sent out in tender sympathy and yearning love for all the struggling, weary ones in the
Church of Christ, and its message goes right from
my heart to theirs. I have given the best I have,
and could do no more. May the blessed Holy
Spirit use it to teach some of my readers the true
secret of a happy life !

HANNAH WHITALL SMITH.

GERMANTOWN, PENNSYLVANIA.

CONTENTS.

THE

CHRISTIAN'S SECRET OF A HAPPY LIFE.

CHAPTER I.

INTRODUCTORY.

GOD'S SIDE AND MAN'S SIDE.

IN introducing this subject of the life and walk of faith, I desire, at the very outset, to clear away one misunderstanding which very commonly arises in reference to the teaching of it, and which effectually hinders a clear apprehension of such teaching. This misunderstanding comes from the fact that the *two* sides of the subject are rarely kept in view at the same time. People see distinctly the way in which one side is presented, and, dwelling exclusively upon this, without even a thought of any other, it is no wonder that distorted views of the whole matter are the legitimate consequence.

Now there are two very decided and distinct sides to this subject, and, like all other subjects, it cannot

be fully understood unless both of these sides are
kept constantly in view.   I refer, of course, to God's
side and man's side; or, in other words, to God's part
in the work of sanctification, and man's part.   These
are very distinct and even contrastive, but are not
contradictory; though, to a cursory observer, they
sometimes look so.

This was very strikingly illustrated to me not long
ago.   There were two teachers of this higher christian life holding meetings in the same place, at alternate hours.   One spoke only of God's part in the
work, and the other dwelt exclusively upon man's
part.   They were both in perfect sympathy with one
another, and realized fully that they were each teaching different sides of the same great truth; and this
also was understood by a large proportion of their
hearers.   But with some of the hearers it was different, and one lady said to me, in the greatest perplexity, "I cannot understand it at all.   Here are two
preachers undertaking to teach just the same truth,
and yet to me they seem flatly to contradict one
another."   And I felt at the time that she expressed
a puzzle which really causes a great deal of difficulty in the minds of many honest inquirers after
this truth.

Suppose two friends go to see some celebrated
building, and return home to describe it.   One has
seen only the north side, and the other only the
south.   The first says, "The building was built in
such a manner, and has such and such stories and
ornaments."   "Oh, no!" says the other, interrupting

him, "you are altogether mistaken; I saw the build
ing, and it was built in quite a different manner, and
its ornaments and stories were so and so." A lively
dispute would probably follow upon the truth of the
respective descriptions, until the two friends discover
that they have been describing different *sides* of the
building, and then all is reconciled at once.

I would like to state as clearly as I can what I
judge to be the two distinct sides in this matter; and
to show how the looking at one without seeing the
other, will be sure to create wrong impressions and
views of the truth.

To state it in brief, I would just say that man's
part is to trust, and God's part is to work; and it can
be seen at a glance how contrastive these two parts
are, and yet not necessarily contradictory. I mean
this. There is a certain *work* to be accomplished.
We are to be delivered from the power of sin, and
are to be made perfect in every good work to do the
will of God. "Beholding as in a glass the glory of
the Lord," we are to be actually "changed into the
same image from glory to glory, even as by the Spirit
of the Lord." We are to be transformed by the renewing of our minds, that we may prove what is that
good and acceptable and perfect will of God. A real
work is to be wrought in us and upon us. Besetting
sins are to be conquered. Evil habits are to be
overcome. Wrong dispositions and feelings are to
be rooted out, and holy tempers and emotions are to
be begotten. A positive transformation is to take
place. So at least the Bible teaches. Now some

body must do this. Either we must do it for oui
selves, or another must do it for us. We have most
of us tried to do it for ourselves at first, and have
grievously failed ; then we discover from the Scriptures and from our own experience that it is a work
we are utterly unable to do for ourselves, but that the
Lord Jesus Christ has come on purpose to do it, and
that He will do it for all who put themselves wholly
into His hand, and trust Him to do it. Now under
these circumstances, what is the part of the believer,
and what is the part of the Lord? Plainly the
believer can do nothing but trust; while the Lord,
in whom he trusts, actually does the work intrusted
to Him. *Trusting* and *doing* are certainly contrastive
things, and often contradictory ; but are they contradictory in this case? Manifestly not, because it is two
different parties that are concerned. If we should
say of one party in a transaction that he trusted his
case to another, and yet attended to it himself, we
should state a contradiction and an impossibility.
But when we say of two parties in a transaction that
one trusts the other to do something, and that that
other goes to work and does it, we are making a statement that is perfectly simple and harmonious. When
we say, therefore, that in this higher life, man's part
is to trust, and that God does the thing intrusted to
Him, we do not surely present any very difficult or
puzzling problem.

The preacher who is speaking on man's part in this
matter cannot speak of anything but surrender and
trust, because this is positively all the man can do.

We all agree about this. And yet such preachers are constantly criticised as though, in saying this, they had meant to imply there *was* no other part, and that therefore nothing but trusting is done. And the cry goes out that this doctrine of faith does away with all realities, that souls are just told to trust, and that is the end of it, and they sit down thenceforward in a sort of religious easy-chair, dreaming away a life fruitless of any actual results. All this misapprehension arises, of course, from the fact that either the preacher has neglected to state, or the hearer has failed to hear, the other side of the matter; which is, that when we trust, the Lord works, and that a great deal is done, not by us, but by Him. Actual results are reached by our trusting, because our Lord undertakes the thing trusted to Him, and accomplishes it. *We* do not do anything, but *He* does it; and it is all the more effectually done because of this. The puzzle as to the preaching of faith disappears entirely as soon as this is clearly seen.

On the other hand, the preacher who dwells on God's side of the question is criticised on a totally different ground. He does not speak of trust, for the Lord's part is not to trust, but to work. The Lord does the thing intrusted to Him. He disciplines and trains the soul by inward exercises and outward providences. He brings to bear all the resources of His wisdom and love upon the refining and purifying of that soul. He makes everything in the life and circumstances of such a one subservient to the one great purpose of making him grow in grace, and of conforming him, day by day and hour by hour, to the image of Christ. He carries him through a process of transformation, longer or shorter, as his peculiar case may require, making actual and experimental the results for which the soul has trusted. We have dared, for instance, according to the command in Rom. vi. 11, by faith to reckon ourselves "dead unto sin." The Lord makes this a reality, and leads us to victory over self, by the daily and hourly discipline of His providences. Our reckoning is available only because God thus makes it real. And yet the preacher who dwells upon this practical side of the matter, and tells of God's processes for making faith's reckonings experimenta. realities, is accused of contradicting the preaching of faith altogether, and of declaring only a process of gradual sanctification by works, and of setting before the soul an impossible and hopeless task.

Now, sanctification is both a sudden step of faith, and also a gradual process of works. It is a step as far as we are concerned; it is a process as to God's part. By a step of faith we get into Christ; by a process we are made to grow up unto Him in all things. By a step of faith we put ourselves into the hands of the Divine Potter; by a gradual process He makes us into a vessel unto His own honor, meet for His use, and prepared to every good work.

To illustrate all this: suppose I were to be describing to a person, who was entirely ignorant of the subject, the way in which a lump of clay is made into a beautiful vessel. I tell him first the part of the clay in the matter, and all I can say about this is, that the clay is put into the potter's hands, and then lies passive there, submitting itself to all the turnings and overturnings of the potter's hands upon it. There is really nothing else to be said about the clay's part. But could my hearer argue from this that nothing else is done, because I say that this is all the clay can do? If he is an intelligent hearer, he will not dream of doing so, but will say, " I understand. This is what the clay must do; but what must the potter do?" "Ah," I answer, "now we come to the important part. The potter takes the clay thus abandoned to his working, and begins to mould and fashion it according to his own will. He kneads and works it, he tears it apart and presses it together again, he wets it and then suffers it to dry. Sometimes he works at it for hours together, sometimes he lays it aside for days and does not touch it. And then, when by all these processes he has made it perfectly pliable in his hands, he proceeds to make it up into the vessel he has purposed. He turns it upon the wheel, planes it and smooths it, and dries it in the sun, bakes it in the oven, and finally turns it out of his workshop, a vessel to his honor and fit for his use."

Will my hearer be likely now to say that I am contradicting myself; that a little while ago I had said the clay had nothing to do but lie passive in the potter's hands, and that now I am putting upon it a great work which it is not able to perform : and that to make itself into such a vessel is an impossible and hopeless undertaking? Surely not. For he will see that, while before I was speaking of the clay's part in the matter, I am now speaking of the potter's part, and that these two are necessarily con- trastive, but not in the least contradictory, and that the clay is not expected to do the potter's work, but only to yield itself up to his working.

Nothing, it seems to me, could be clearer than the perfect harmony between these two *apparently* con- tradictory sorts of teaching on this subject. What *can* be said about man's part in this great work, but that he must continually surrender himself and con- tinually trust?

But when we come to God's side of the question, what is there that may not be said as to the manifold and wonderful ways in which He accomplishes the work intrusted to Him? It is here that the *growing* comes in. The lump of clay would never grow into a beautiful vessel if it stayed in the clay-pit for thousands of years. But once put into the hands of a skilful potter, and, under his fashioning, it grows rapidly into a vessel to his honor. And so the soul, abandoned to the working of the Heavenly Potter, is changed rapidly from glory to glory into the image of the Lord by His Spirit.

Having, therefore, taken the step of faith by which you have put yourself wholly and absolutely into His hands, you must now expect Him to begin to work. His way of accomplishing that which you have intrusted to Him may be different from your way. But He knows, and you must be satisfied.

I knew a lady who had entered into this life of faith with a great outpouring of the Spirit, and a wonderful flood of light and joy. She supposed, of course, this was a preparation for some great service, and expected to be put forth immediately into the Lord's harvest field. Instead of this, almost at once her husband lost all his money, and she was shut up in her own house, to attend to all sorts of domestic duties, with no time or strength left for any Gospel work at all. She accepted the discipline, and yielded herself up as heartily to sweep, and dust, and bake, and sew, as she would have done to preach, or pray or write for the Lord. And the result was that through this very training He made her into a vessel "meet for the Master's use, and prepared unto every good work."

Another lady, who had entered this life of faith under similar circumstances of wondrous blessing, and who also expected to be sent out to do some great work, was shut up with two peevish invalid nieces, to nurse, and humor, and amuse them all day long. Unlike the first lady, this one did not accept the training, but chafed and fretted, and finally rebelled, lost all her blessing, and went back into a state of sad coldness and misery. She had understood her part of trusting to begin with, but not understanding the divine process of accomplishing that for which she had trusted, she took herself out of the hands of the Heavenly Potter, and the vessel was marred on the wheel.

I believe many a vessel has been similarly marred

by a want of understanding these things. The maturity of christian experience cannot be reached in a moment, but is the result of the work of God's Holy Spirit, who, by His energizing and transforming power, causes us to grow up into Christ in all things. And we cannot hope to reach this maturity in any other way than by yielding ourselves up utterly and willingly to His mighty working. But the sanctification the Scriptures urge as a present experience upon all believers does not consist in maturity of growth, but in purity of heart, and this may be as complete in the babe in Christ as in the veteran believer.

The lump of clay, from the moment it comes under the transforming hand of the potter, is, during each day and each hour of the process, just what the potter wants it to be at that hour or on that day, and therefore pleases him. But it is very far from being matured into the vessel he intends in the future to make it.

The little babe may be all that a babe could be, or ought to be, and may therefore perfectly please its mother, and yet it is very far from being what that mother would wish it to be when the years of maturity shall come.

The apple in June is a perfect apple for June. It is the best apple that June can produce. But it is very different from the apple in October, which is a perfected apple.

God's works are perfect in every stage of their growth. Man's works are never perfect until they are in every respect complete.

All that we claim then in this life of sanctification is, that by a step of faith we put ourselves into the hands of the Lord, for Him to work in us all the good pleasure of His will; and that by a continuous exercise of faith we keep ourselves there. This is our part in the matter. And when we do it, and while we do it, we are, in the Scripture sense, truly pleasing to God, although it may require years of training and discipline to mature us into a vessel that shall be in all respects to His honor, and fitted to every good work.

Our part is the trusting, it is His to accomplish the results. And when we do our part, He never fails to do His, for no one ever trusted in the Lord and was confounded. Do not be afraid, then, that if you trust, or tell others to trust, the matter will end there. Trust is only the beginning and the continual foundation; when we trust, the Lord works, and His work is the important part of the whole matter. And this explains that apparent paradox which puzzles so many. They say, "In one breath you tell us to do nothing but trust, and in the next you tell us to do impossible things. How can you reconcile such contradictory statements?" They are to be reconciled just as we reconcile the statements concerning a saw in a carpenter's shop, when we say at one moment that the saw has sawn asunder a log, and the next moment declare that the carpenter has done it. The saw is the instrument used, the power that uses it is the carpenter's. And so we, yielding ourselves unto God, and our members as instruments of

2

righteousness unto Him, find that He works in us to will and to do of His good pleasure; and we can say with Paul, " I labored ; yet not I, but the grace of God which was with me." For we are to be His workmanship, not our own. (Eph. ii. 10.) And in fact, when we come to look at it, only God, who created us at first, can re-create us, for He alone understands the " work of His own hands." All efforts after self-creating, result in the marring of the vessel, and no soul can ever reach its highest fiulfilment except through the working of Him who " worketh all things after the counsel of His own will."

In this book I shall of course dwell mostly upon man's side in the matter, as I am writing for man, and in the hope of teaching believers how to fulfil their part of the great work. But I wish it to be distinctly understood all through, that unless I believed with all my heart in God's effectual working on His side, not one word of this book would ever have been written.

CHAPTER II.

WHEN I approach this subject of the true christian life, that life which is hid with Christ in
God, so many thoughts struggle for utterance that
I am almost speechless. Where shall I begin? What
is the most important thing to say? How shall I
make people read and believe? The subject is so
glorious, and human words seem so powerless!

But something I am impelled to say. The secret
must be told. For it is one concerning that victory
which overcometh the world, that promised deliverance from all our enemies, for which every child of
God longs and prays, but which seems so often and
so generally to elude their grasp. May God grant
me so to tell it, that every believer to whom this book
shall come, may have his eyes opened to see the
truth as it is in Jesus, and may be enabled to enter
into possession of this glorious life for himself!

For sure I am that every converted soul longs for
victory and rest, and nearly every one feels instinctively, at times, that they are his birthright. Can you

not remember, some of you, the shout of triumph your
souls gave when you first became acquainted with the
Lord Jesus, and had a glimpse of His mighty saving
power? How sure you were of victory then! How
easy it seemed, to be more than conquerors, through
Him that loved you! Under the leadership of a
Captain who had never been foiled in battle, how
could you dream of defeat? And yet, to many of
you, how different has been your real experience!
The victories have been but few and fleeting, the
defeats many and disastrous. You have not lived as
you feel children of God ought to live. There has
been a resting in a clear understanding of doctrinal
truth, without pressing after the power and life
thereof. There has been a rejoicing in the knowledge of things testified of in the Scriptures, without
a living realization of the things themselves, consciously felt in the soul. Christ is believed in, talked
about, and served, but He is not known as the soul's
actual and very life, abiding there forever, and
revealing Himself there continually in His beauty.
You have found Jesus as your Saviour and your
Master, and you have tried to serve Him and advance
the cause of His kingdom. You have carefully studied the Holy Scriptures and have gathered much
precious truth therefrom, which you have endeavored faithfully to practise. But notwithstanding all
your knowledge and all your activities in the service
of the Lord, your souls are secretly starving, and
you cry out again and again for that bread and water
of life which you see promised in the Scriptures to

all believers. In the very depths of your hearts you know that your experience is not a Scriptural experience; that, as an old writer says, your religion is "but a *talk* to what the early Christians enjoyed, possessed, and lived in." And your souls have sunk within you, as day after day, and year after year, your early visions of triumph have seemed to grow more and more dim, and you have been forced to settle down to the conviction that the best you can expect from your religion is a life of alternate failure and victory; one hour sinning, and the next repenting; and beginning again, only to fail again, and again to repent.

But *is* this all? Had the Lord Jesus only this in His mind when He laid down His precious life to deliver you from your sore and cruel bondage to sin? Did He propose to Himself only this partial deliverance? Did He intend to leave you thus struggling along under a weary consciousness of defeat and discouragement? Did He fear that a continuous victory would dishonor Him, and bring reproach on His name? When all those declarations were made concerning His coming, and the work He was to accomplish, did they mean only this that you have experienced? Was there a hidden reserve in each promise that was meant to deprive it of its complete fulfilment? Did "delivering us out of the hands of our enemies" mean only a few of them? Did "enabling us always to triumph" mean only sometimes; or being "more than conquerors through Him that loved us" mean constant defeat and failure? No,

no, a thousand times no! God is able to save us
to the uttermost, and He means to do it. His promise, confirmed by His oath, was that " He would grant
unto us, that we, being delivered out of the hand of
our enemies, might serve Him without fear, in holiness and righteousness before Him, all the days of
our life." It is a mighty work to do, but our Deliverer is able to do it. He came to destroy the works
of the devil, and dare we dream for a moment that
He is not able or not willing to accomplish His own
purposes?

In the very outset, then, settle down on this one
thing, that the Lord is able to save you fully, now,
in this life, from the power and dominion of sin, and
to deliver you altogether out of the hands of your
enemies. If you do not think He is, search your
Bible, and collect together every announcement or
declaration concerning the purposes and object of
His death on the cross. You will be astonished to
find how full they are. Everywhere and always His
work is said to be, to deliver us from our sins, from
our bondage, from our defilement; and not a hint is
given anywhere, that this deliverance was to be only
the limited and partial one with which the Church so
continually tries to be satisfied.

Let me give you a few texts on this subject. When
the angel of the Lord appeared unto Joseph in a
dream, and announced the coming birth of the
Saviour, he said, "And thou shalt call His name
Jesus, for He shall save His people from their sins."
When Zacharias was "filled with the Holy Ghost"

at the birth of his son, and "prophesied," he declared that God had visited His people in order to fulfil the promise and the oath He had made them, which promise was, "That He would grant unto us, that we, being delivered out of the hands of our enemies, might serve Him without fear, in holiness and right-eousness before Him, all the days of our life."

When Peter was preaching in the porch of the Temple to the wondering Jews, he said, "Unto you first, God, having raised up His Son Jesus, sent Him to bless you in turning away every one of you from his iniquities."

When Paul was telling out to the Ephesian church the wondrous truth that Christ had loved them so much as to give Himself for them, he went on to declare, that His purpose in thus doing was, "that He might sanctify and cleanse it by the washing of water by the word, that He might present it to Him-self a glorious church, not having spot or wrinkle, or any such thing; but that it should be holy and with-out blemish."

When Paul was seeking to instruct Titus, his own son after the common faith, concerning the grace of God, he declared that the object of that grace was to teach us "that denying ungodliness and worldly lusts, we should live soberly, righteously, and godly in this present world"; and adds, as the reason of this, that Christ "gave Himself for us that He might redeem us from all iniquity, and purify us unto Himself a peculiar people, zealous of good works."

When Peter was urging upon the christians, to

whom he was writing, a holy and Christ-like walk, he tells them that "even hereunto were ye called because Christ also suffered for us, leaving us an example that ye should follow His steps: who did no sin, neither was guile found in His mouth"; and adds, "who His own self bare our sins in His own body on the tree, that we, being dead to sins, should live unto right-eousness; by whose stripes ye were healed."

When Paul was contrasting in the Ephesians the walk suitable for a christian, with the walk of an unbeliever, he sets before them the truth in Jesus as being this, "that ye put off concerning the former conversation the old man, which is corrupt according to the deceitful lusts; and be renewed in the spirit of your mind; and that ye put on the new man, which after God is created in righteousness and true holiness."

And when, in Romans vi., he was answering for-ever the question as to continuing in sin, and showing how utterly foreign it was to the whole spirit and aim of the salvation of Jesus, he brings up the fact of our judicial death and resurrection with Christ as an un-answerable argument for our practical deliverance from it, and says, "God forbid. How shall we, that are dead to sin, live any longer therein? Know ye not that so many of us as were baptized into Jesus Christ were baptized into His death? Therefore we are buried with Him by baptism into death; that like as Christ was raised up from the dead by the glory of the Father, even so we also should walk in newness of life." And adds, "Knowing this, that

THE SCRIPTURALNESS OF THIS LIFE.   25

our old man is crucified with Him, that the body of
sin might be destroyed, that henceforth we should
not serve sin."

Dear christians, will you receive the testimony of
Scripture on this matter? The same questions that
troubled the Church in Paul's day are troubling it
now: first, "Shall we continue in sin that grace may
abound?" And second, "Do we then make void
the law through faith?" Shall not our answer to
these be Paul's emphatic "God forbid"; and his
triumphant assertions that instead of making it void
"we establish the law"; and that "what the law
could not do, in that it was weak through the flesh,
God sending His own Son in the likeness of sinful
flesh, and for sin, condemned sin in the flesh: that
the righteousness of the law might be fulfilled in us
who walk not after the flesh, but after the Spirit"?

Can we suppose for a moment that the holy God
who hates sin in the sinner, is willing to tolerate it
in the christian, and that He has even arranged the
plan of salvation in such a way as to make it impossible for those who are saved from the guilt of sin,
to find deliverance from its power?

As Dr. Chalmers well says, "Sin is that scandal
which must be rooted out from the great spiritual
household over which the Divinity rejoices. . . .
Strange administration, indeed, for sin to be so hateful to God as to lay all who had incurred it under
death, and yet when readmitted into life that sin
should be permitted; and that what was before the
object of destroying vengeance, should now become

the object of an upheld and protected toleration.
Now that the penalty is taken off, think you that
it is possible the unchangeable God has so given
up His antipathy to sin, as that man, ruined and redeemed man, may now perseveringly indulge under
the new arrangement in that which under the o.d
destroyed him? Does not the God who loved
righteousness and hated iniquity six thousand years
ago, bear the same love to righteousness and hatred
to iniquity still? . . . I now breathe the air of lov-
ing-kindness from Heaven, and can walk before
God in peace and graciousness; shall I again attempt the incompatible alliance of two principles
so adverse as that of an approving God and a per-
severing sinner? How shall we, recovered from
so awful a catastrophe, continue that which first involved us in it? The cross of Christ, by the same
mighty and decisive stroke wherewith it moved the
curse of sin away from us, also surely moves away
the power and the love of it from over us."

And not Dr. Chalmers only, but many other holy
men of his generation and of our own, as well as of
generations long past, have united in declaring that
the redemption accomplished for us by our Lord
Jesus Christ on the cross at Calvary is a redemption from the power of sin as well as from its guilt,
and that He *is* able to save to the uttermost all who
come unto God by Him.

A quaint old divine of the seventeenth century
says: " There is nothing so contrary to God as s'n,
and God will not suffer sin always to rule his master

piece, man. When we consider the infiniteness of God's power for destroying that which is contrary to Him, who can believe that the devil must always stand and prevail? I believe it is inconsistent and disagreeable with true faith for people to be christians, and yet to believe that Christ, the eternal Son of God, to whom all power in heaven and earth is given, will suffer sin and the devil to have dominion over them.

"But you will say no man by all the power he hath can redeem himself, and no man can live without sin. We will say, Amen, to it. But if men tell us, that when God's power comes to help us and to redeem us out of sin, that it cannot be effected, then this doctrine we cannot away with; nor I hope you neither.

"Would you approve of it, if I should tell you that God puts forth His power to do such a thing, but the devil hinders Him? That it is impossible for God to do it because the devil does not like it? That it is impossible that any one should be free from sin because the devil hath got such a power in them that God cannot cast him out? This is lamentable doctrine, yet hath not this been preached? It doth in plain terms say, though God doth interpose His power, it is impossible, because the devil hath so rooted sin in the nature of man. Is not man God's creature, and cannot He new make him, and cast sin out of him? If you say sin is deeply rooted in man, I say so, too; yet not so deeply rooted but Christ Jesus hath entered so deeply into the root of the nature of man that He hath received power to destroy

the devil and his works, and to recover and redeem
man into righteousness and holiness. Or else it is
false that ' He is able to save to the uttermost all
that come unto God by Him.' We must throw away
the Bible, if we say that it is impossible for God to
deliver man out of sin.

"We know," he continues, "when our friends are
in captivity, as in Turkey, or elsewhere, we pay our
money for their redemption; but we will not pay our
money if they be kept in their fetters still. Would
not any one think himself cheated to pay so much
money for their redemption, and the bargain be made
so that he shall be *said* to be redeemed, and be *called*
a redeemed captive, but he must wear his fetters
still ? How long? As long as he hath a day to live.

"This is for bodies, but now I am speaking of
souls. Christ must be made to me redemption, and
rescue me from captivity. Am I a prisoner anywhere? Yes, verily, verily, he that committeth sin,
saith Christ, he is a servant of sin, he is a slave of
sin. If thou hast sinned, thou art a slave, a captive
that must be redeemed out of captivity. Who will
pay a price for me? I am poor; I have nothing; I
cannot redeem myself; who will pay a price for me?
There is One come who hath paid a price for me.
That is well; that is good news, then I hope I shall
come out of my captivity. What is His name, is He
called a Redeemer? So, then, I do expect the benefit of my redemption, and that I shall go out of my
captivity. No, say they, you must abide in sin as
long as you live. What! must we never be delivered ?

Must this crooked heart and perverse will always remain?   Must I be a believer, and yet have no faith
that reacheth to sanctification and holy living?   Is
there no mastery to be had, no getting victory over
sin?   Must it prevail over me as long as I live?
What sort of a Redeemer, then, is this, or what benefit have I in this life, of my redemption?"

Similar extracts might be quoted from Marshall,
Romaine, and many others, to show that this doctrine
is no new one in the Church, however much it may
have been lost sight of by the present generation of
believers.   It is the same old story that has filled with
songs of triumph the daily lives of many saints of God
throughout all ages; and is now afresh being sounded
forth to the unspeakable joy of weary and burdened
souls.

Do not reject it, then, dear reader, until you have
prayerfully searched the Scriptures to see whether
these things be indeed so.   Ask God to open the
eyes of your understanding by His Spirit, that you
may "know what is the exceeding greatness of His
power to us-ward who believe, according to the working of His mighty power, which He wrought in
Christ, when He raised Him from the dead, and set
Him at His own right hand in the heavenly places."
And when you have begun to have some faint
glimpses of this power, learn to look away utterly
from your own weakness, and, putting your case into
His hands, trust Him to deliver you.

In Psalms viii. 6, we are told that God made man
to "have dominion over the works of His hands."

The fulfilment of this is declared in 2 Cor. ii. 4, where the apostle cries, "Thanks be unto God which always causeth us to triumph in Christ." If the maker of a machine should declare that he had made it to accomplish a certain purpose, and if upon trial it should be found incapable of accomplishing that purpose, we would all say of that maker that he was a fraud.

Surely then we will not dare to think that it is impossible for the creature whom God has made, to accomplish the declared object for which he was created. Especially when the Scriptures are so full of the assertions that Christ has made it possible.

The only thing that can hinder is the creature's own failure to work in harmony with the plans of his Creator, and if this want of harmony can be removed, then God can work. Christ came to bring about an at-onement between God and man, which should make it possible for God thus to work in man to will and to do of His good pleasure. Therefore we may be of good courage; for the work Christ has undertaken He is surely able and willing to perform. Let us then "walk in the steps of that faith of our father Abraham," who "staggered not at the promise of God through unbelief; but was strong in faith, giving glory to God; being fully persuaded that what He had promised, He was able also to perform."

CHAPTER III.

THE LIFE DEFINED.

IN my last chapter I tried to settle the question as to the scripturalness of the experience sometimes called the Higher Christian Life, but which to my own mind is best described in the words, the "life hid with Christ in God." I shall now, therefore, consider it as a settled point that the Scriptures do set before the believer in the Lord Jesus a life of abiding rest and of continual victory, which is very far beyond the ordinary line of christian experience; and that in the Bible we have presented to us a Saviour able to save us from the power of our sins, as really as He saves us from their guilt.

The point to be next considered is, as to what this hidden life consists in, and how it differs from every other sort of christian experience.

And as to this, it is simply letting the Lord carry our burdens and manage our affairs for us, instead of trying to do it ourselves.

Most christians are like a man who was toiling along the road, bending under a heavy burden, when a wagon overtook him, and the driver kindly offered to help him on his journey. He joyfully accepted the offer, but when seated, continued to bend beneath his burden, which he still kept on his shoulders. "Why do you not lay down your burden?" asked the kind-hearted driver. "Oh!" replied the man, " I feel that it is almost too much to ask you to carry me, and I could not think of letting you carry my burden too." And so christians, who have given themselves into the care and keeping of the Lord Jesus, still continue to bend beneath the weight of their burden, and often go weary and heavy-laden throughout the whole length of their journey.

When I speak of burdens, I mean everything that troubles us, whether spiritual or temporal.

I mean, first of all, ourselves. The greatest burden we have to carry in life is self. The most difficult thing we have to manage is self. Our own daily living, our frames and feelings, our especial weaknesses and temptations, and our peculiar temperaments, our inward affairs of every kind, these are the things that perplex and worry us more than anything else, and that bring us oftenest into bondage and darkness. In laying off your burdens, therefore, the first one you must get rid of is yourself. You must hand yourself and all your inward experiences, your temptations, your temperament, your frames and feelings, all over into the care and keeping of your God, and leave them there. He made you, and therefore He understands you and knows how to manage you, and you must trust Him to do it. Say to Him, "Here, Lord, I abandon myself to thee. I have tried in every way I could think of to manage myself, and to make myself what I know I ought to be, but have always failed. Now I give it up to thee Do thou take entire possession of me. Work in me all the good pleasure of thy will. Mould and fashion me into such a vessel as seemeth good to thee. I leave myself in thy hands, and I believe thou wilt, according to thy promise, make me into a vessel unto thine honor, 'sanctified, and meet for the Master's use, and prepared unto every good work.'" And here you must rest, trusting yourself thus to Him continually and absolutely.

Next, you must lay off every other burden, — your health, your reputation, your christian work, your houses, your children, your business, your servants; everything, in short, that concerns you, whether inward or outward.

Christians always commit the keeping of their souls for eternity to the Lord, because they know, without a shadow of a doubt, that they cannot keep these themselves. But the things of this present life they take into their own keeping, and try to carry on their own shoulders, with the perhaps unconfessed feeling that it is a great deal to ask of the Lord to carry them, and that they cannot think of asking Him to carry their burdens too.

I knew a christian lady who had a very heavy temporal burden. It took away her sleep and her appetite, and there was danger of her health breaking down under it. One day, when it seemed espe

3

cially heavy, she noticed lying on the table near her
a little tract called " Hannah's Faith." Attracted
by the title, she picked it up and began to read it,
little knowing, however, that it was to create a revo-
lution in her whole experience. The story was of
a poor woman who had been carried triumphantly
through a life of unusual sorrow. She was giving
the history of her life to a kind visitor on one occasion, and at the close the visitor said, feelingly, " O
Hannah, I do not see how you could bear so much
sorrow ! "   " I did not bear it," was the quick reply;
" the Lord bore it for me."   " Yes," said the visitor
" that is the right way. You must take your troubles
to the Lord." " Yes," replied Hannah, " but we
must do more than that ; we must *leave* them there.
Most people," she continued, " take their burdens to
Him, but they bring them away with them again, and
are just as worried and unhappy as ever. But I take
mine, and I leave them with Him, and come away
and forget them. And if the worry comes back, I
take it to Him again ; I do this over and over, until
at last I just forget that I have any worries, and am
at perfect rest."

My friend was very much struck with this plan
and resolved to try it. The circumstances of her
life she could not alter, but she took them to the
Lord, and handed them over into His management;
and tnen she believed that He took it, and she left
all the responsibility and the worry and anxiety with
Him. As often as the anxieties returned she took
them back ; and the result was that, although the

circumstances remained unchanged, her soul was kept in perfect peace in the midst of them. She felt that she had found out a blessed secret, and from that time she tried never again to carry her own burdens, nor to manage anything for herself.

And the secret she found so effectual in her outward affairs, she found to be still more effectual in her inward ones, which were in truth even more utterly unmanageable. She abandoned her whole self to the Lord, with all that she was and all that she had, and, believing that He took that which she had committed to Him, she ceased to fret and worry, and her life became all sunshine in the gladness of belonging to Him. And this was the Higher Christian Life! It was a very simple secret she found out. Only this, that it was possible to obey God's commandment contained in those words, "Be careful for nothing, but in everything by prayer and supplication, with thanksgiving, let your requests be made known unto God"; and that, in obeying it, the result would inevitably be, according to the promise, that the "peace of God which passeth all understanding shall keep your hearts and minds through Christ Jesus."

There are many other things to be said about this life hid with Christ in God, many details as to what the Lord Jesus does for those who thus abandon themselves to Him. But the gist of the whole matter is here stated, and the soul that has got hold of this secret has found the key that will unlock the whole treasure-house of God.

And now I do trust that I have made you hungry for this blessed life. Would you not like to get rid of your burdens? Do you not long to hand over the management of your unmanageable self into the hands of One who is able to manage you? Are you not tired and weary, and does not the rest I speak of look sweet to you?

Do you recollect the delicious sense of rest with which you have sometimes gone to bed at night, after a day of great exertion and weariness? How delightful was the sensation of relaxing every muscle, and letting your body go in a perfect abandonment of ease and comfort. The strain of the day had ceased for a few hours at least, and the work of the day had been thrown off. You no longer had to hold up an aching head or a weary back. You trusted yourself to the bed in an absolute confidence, and it held you up, without effort, or strain, or even thought on your part. You rested.

But suppose you had doubted the strength or the stability of your bed, and had dreaded each moment to find it giving away beneath you and landing you on the floor; could you have rested then? Would not every muscle have been strained in a fruitless effort to hold yourself up, and would not the weariness have been greater than not to have gone to bed at all?

Let this analogy teach you what it means to rest in the Lord. Let your souls lie down upon His sweet will, as your bodies lie down in your beds at night. Relax every strain and lay off every burden.

Let yourselves go in a perfect abandonment of ease
and comfort, sure that when He holds you up you
are perfectly safe.

Your part is simply to rest. His part is to sustain you, and He cannot fail.

Or take another analogy, which our Lord Himself
has abundantly sanctioned, that of the child-life.
For "Jesus called a little child unto Him, and set
him in the midst of them, and said, Verily I say unto
you, Except ye be converted and become as little
children, ye shall not enter the kingdom of Heaven."

Now, what are the characteristics of a little child
and how does he live? He lives by faith, and his
chiefest characteristic is thoughtlessness. His life is
one long trust from year's end to year's end. He
trusts his parents, he trusts his care-takers, he trusts
his teachers, he even trusts people often who are
utterly unworthy of trust, because of the confiding-
ness of his nature. And his trust is abundantly
answered. He provides nothing for himself, and yet
everything is provided. He takes no thought for the
morrow, and forms no plans, and yet all his life is
planned out for him, and he finds his paths made
ready, opening out to him as he comes to them day
by day, and hour by hour. He goes in and out of
his father's house with an unspeakable ease and
abandonment, enjoying all the good things it contains, without having spent a penny in procuring
them. Pestilence may walk through the streets of
his city, but he regards it not. Famine and fire and
war may rage around him, but under his father's

ɪender care he abides in utter unconcern and perfect
rest.   He lives in the present moment, and receives
his life without question as it comes to him day by
day from his father's hands.

I was visiting once in a wealthy house, where there
was one only adopted child, upon whom was lavished all the love and tenderness and care that
human hearts could bestow or human means procure.   And as I watched that child running in and
out day by day, free and light-hearted, with the
happy carelessness of childhood, I thought what a
picture it was of our wonderful position as children
in the house of our Heavenly Father.   And I said to
myself, " If nothing could so grieve and wound the
loving hearts around her, as to see this little child
beginning to be worried or anxious about herself in
any way, about whether her food and clothes would
be provided for her, or how she was to get her edu-
cation or her future support, how much more must
the great, loving heart of our God and Father be
grieved and wounded at seeing His children taking
so much anxious care and thought ! "   And I understood why it was that our Lord had said to us so
emphatically, " Take no thought for yourselves."

Who is the best cared for in every household ?   Is
it not the little children ?   And does not the least of
all, the helpless baby, receive the largest share ?   As
a late writer has said, the baby " toils not, neither
does he spin ; and yet he is fed, and clothed, and
loved, and rejoiced in," and none so much as he.

This life of faith, then, about which I am writing,

consists in just this; being a child in the Father's
house. And when this is said, enough is said to
transform every weary, burdened life into one of
blessedness and rest.

Let the ways of childish confidence and freedom
from care, which so please you and win your hearts in
your own little ones, teach you what should be your
ways with God; and leaving yourselves in His hands,
learn to be literally "careful for nothing"; and you
shall find it to be a fact that "the peace of God which
passeth all understanding shall keep (as in a garri-
son) your hearts and minds through Christ Jesus."
Notice the word "nothing" in the above passage, as
covering all possible grounds for anxiety, both inward and outward. We are continually tempted to
think it is our duty to be anxious about some things.
Perhaps our thought will be, "Oh, yes, it is quite
right to give up all anxiety in a general way; and in
spiritual matters of course anxiety is wrong; but
there *are* things about which it would be a sin not
to be anxious; about our children, for instance,
or those we love, or about our church affairs and the
cause of truth, or about our business matters. It
would show a great want of right feeling not to be
anxious about such things as these." Or else our
thoughts take the other tack, and we say to ourselves, "Yes, it is quite right to commit our loved
ones and all our outward affairs to the Lord, but
when it comes to our inward lives, our religious experiences, our temptations, our besetting sins, our
growth in grace, and all such things, these we *ought*

to be anxious about ; for if we are not, they will be
sure to be neglected."

To such suggestions, and to all similar ones, the
answer is found in our text, —

"In NOTHING be anxious."

In Matt. vi. 25-34, our Lord illustrates this being
without anxiety, by telling us to behold the fowls of
the air and the lilies of the field, as examples of the
sort of life He would have us live. As the birds
rejoice in the care of their God and are fed, and as
the lilies grow in His sunlight, so must we, without
anxiety, and without fear. Let the sparrows speak
to us : —

" I am only a tiny sparrow,
    A bird of low degree ;
  My life is of little value,
      But the dear Lord cares for me.

" I have no barn nor storehouse,
    I neither sow nor reap ;
  God gives me a sparrow's portion,
      But never a seed to keep.

" I know there are many sparrows ;
    All over the world they are found ;
  But our heavenly Father knoweth
      When one of us falls to the ground.

" Though small, we are never forgotten.
    Though weak, we are never afraid ;
  For we know the dear Lord keepeth
      The life of the creatures he made.

THE LIFE DEFINED.

" I fly through the thickest forest,
  I light on many a spray;
I have no chart nor compass,
  But I never lose my way.

" And I fold my wings at twilight
  Wherever I happen to be;
For the Father is always watching
  And no harm will come to me.

" I am only a little sparrow,
  A bird of low degree,
But I know the Father loves me:
  Have *you* less faith than *I* ?"

CHAPTER IV.

HOW TO ENTER IN.

HAVING tried to settle the question as to the scripturalness of the experience of this life of full trust, and having also shown a little of what it is; the next point is as to how it is to be reached and realized.

And first, I would say that this blessed life must not be looked upon in any sense as an attainment but as an obtainment. We cannot earn it, we cannot climb up to it, we cannot win it; we can do nothing but ask for it and receive it. It is the gift of God in Christ Jesus. And where a thing is a gift, the only course left for the receiver is to take it and thank the giver. We never say of a gift, " See to what I have attained," and boast of our skill and wisdom in having attained it ; but we say, " See what has been given me," and boast of the love and wealth and generosity of the giver. And everything in our salvation is a gift. From beginning to end, God is the giver and we are the receivers ; and it is

not to those who do great things, but to those who
receive abundance of grace, and of the gift of
righteousness," that the richest promises are made.

In order, therefore, to enter into a realized experience of this interior life, the soul must be in a recep-
tive attitude, fully recognizing the fact that it is to
be God's gift in Christ Jesus, and that it cannot be
gained by any efforts or works of our own. This
will simplify the matter exceedingly; and the only
thing left to be considered then will be to discover
upon whom God bestows this gift, and how they are
to receive it. And to this I would answer in short,
that He bestows it only upon the fully consecrated
soul, and that it is to be received by faith.

Consecration is the first thing. Not in any legal
sense, not in order to purchase or deserve the blessing, but to remove the difficulties out of the way and
make it possible for God to bestow it. In order for
a lump of clay to be made into a beautiful vessel, it
must be entirely abandoned to the potter, and must
lie passive in his hands. And in order for a soul to
be made into a vessel unto God's honor, " sanctified
and meet for the Master's use, and prepared unto
every good work," it must be entirely abandoned to
Him, and must lie passive in His hands. This is
manifest at the first glance.

I was once trying to explain to a physician, who
had charge of a large hospital, what consecration
meant, and its necessity, but he seemed unable to
understand. At last I said to him, "Suppose, in
going your rounds among your patients, you should

meet with one man who entreated you earnestly to
take his case under your especial care in order to
cure him, but who should at the same time refuse to
tell you all the symptoms, or to take all your pre-
scribed remedies; and should say to you, 'I am quite
willing to follow your directions as to certain things,
because they commend themselves to my mind as
good, but in other matters I prefer judging for myself and following my own directions.' What would
you do in such a case?" I asked. "Do!" he replied
with indignation, — "do! I would soon leave such a
man as that to his own care. For of course," he
added, "I could do nothing for him, unless he would
put his whole case into my hands without any reserves, and would obey my directions implicitly."
"It is necessary then," I said, "for doctors to be
obeyed, if they are to have any chance to cure their
patients?" "*Implicitly obeyed!*" was his emphatic
reply. "And that is consecration," I continued.
"God must have the whole case put into His hands
without any reserves, and His directions must be implicitly followed." "I see it," he exclaimed, — "I
see it! And I will do it. God shall have His own
way with me from henceforth."

Perhaps to some minds the word "abandonment"
might express this idea better. But whatever word
we use, we mean an entire surrender of the whole
being to God; spirit, soul, and body placed under
His absolute control, for Him to do with us just what
He pleases. We mean that the language of our
souls under all circumstances, and in view of every

act, is to be, "Thy will be done." We mean the giving up of all liberty of choice. We mean a life of
inevitable obedience.

To a soul ignorant of God, this may look hard.
But to those who know Him, it is the happiest and
most restful of lives. He is our Father, and He
loves us, and He knows just what is best, and therefore, of course, His will is the very most blessed
thing that can come to us under all circumstances.
I do not understand how it is that Satan has suc-
ceeded in blinding the eyes of the Church to this
fact. But it really would seem as if God's own
children were more afraid of His will than of anything
else in life; His lovely, lovable will, which only
means loving-kindnesses and tender mercies, and
blessings unspeakable to their souls. I wish I
could only show to every one the unfathomable
sweetness of the will of God. Heaven is a place of
infinite bliss because His will is perfectly done there,
and our lives share in this bliss just in proportion as
His will is perfectly done in them. He loves us,
loves us, and the will of love is always blessing for its
loved one. Some of us know what it is to love, and
we know that could we only have our way, our beloved ones would be overwhelmed with blessings.
All that is good, and sweet, and lovely in life would
be poured out upon them from our lavish hands, had
we but the power to carry out our will for them.
And if this is the way of love with us, how much
more must it be so with our God, who is love itself.
Could we but for one moment get a glimpse into the

mighty depths of His love, our hearts would spring out to meet His will, and embrace it as our richest treasure; and we would abandon ourselves to it with an enthusiasm of gratitude and joy, that such a wondrous privilege could be ours.

A great many christians actually seem to think that all their Father in heaven wants is a chance to make them miserable, and to take away all their blessings, and they imagine, poor souls, that if they hold on to things in their own will, they can hinder Him from doing this. I am ashamed to write the words, and yet we must face a fact which is making wretched hundreds of lives.

A Christian lady who had this feeling, was once expressing to a friend how impossible she found it to say, "Thy will be done," and how afraid she should be to do it. She was the mother of one only little boy, who was the heir to a great fortune, and the idol of her heart. After she had stated her difficulties fully, her friend said, "Suppose your little Charley should come running to you to-morrow and say, 'Mother, I have made up my mind to let you have your own way with me from this time forward. I am always going to obey you, and I want you to do just whatever you think best with me. I know you love me, and I am going to trust myself to your love.' How would you feel towards him? Would you say to yourself, 'Ah, now I shall have a chance to make Charley miserable. I will take away all his pleasures, and fill his life with every hard and disagreeable thing I can find. I will compel him to do just the things that are the most difficult for him to do, and will give him all sorts of impossible commands"? "Oh, no, no, no!" exclaimed the indignant mother. "You know I would not. You know I would hug him to my heart and cover him with kisses, and would hasten to fill his life with all that was sweetest and best." "And are you more tender and more loving than God?" asked her friend. "Ah, no," was the reply, "I see my mistake, and I will not be afraid of saying, 'Thy will be done,' to my Heavenly Father, any more than I would want my Charley to be afraid of saying it to me."

Better and sweeter than health, or friends, or money, or fame, or ease, or prosperity, is the adorable will of our God. It gilds the darkest hours with a divine halo, and sheds brightest sunshine on the gloomiest paths. He always reigns who has made it his kingdom; and nothing can go amiss to him. Surely, then, it is nothing but a glorious privilege that is opening before you when I tell you that the first step you must take, in order to enter into the life hid with Christ in God, is that of entire consecration. I cannot have you look at it as a hard and stern demand. You must do it gladly, thankfully, enthusiastically. You must go in on what I call the *privilege* side of consecration; and I can assure you, from a blessed experience, that you will find it the happiest place you have ever entered yet.

Faith is the next thing. Faith is an absolutely necessary element in the reception of any gift; for let our friends give a thing to us ever so fully, it is

not really ours until we believe it has been given
and claim it as our own.   Above all, this is true in
gifts which are purely mental or spiritual.   Love
may be lavished upon us by another without stint
or measure, but until we believe that we are loved,
it never really becomes ours.

I suppose most Christians understand this principle
in reference to the matter of their forgiveness.   They
know that the forgiveness of sins through Jesus might
have been preached to them forever, but it would
never have become theirs consciously until they believed this preaching, and claimed the forgiveness as
their own.   But when it comes to living the christian
life, they lose sight of this principle, and think that,
having been saved by faith, they are now to live by
works and efforts; and instead of continuing to *receive*,
they are now to begin to *do*.   This makes our declaration that the life hid with Christ in God is to be entered by faith, seem perfectly unintelligible to them.
And yet it is plainly declared, that "*as* we have received Christ Jesus the Lord, *so* we are to walk in
Him."   We received Him by faith, and by faith
alone ; therefore we are to walk in Him by faith, ar d
by faith alone.   And the faith by which we enter into
this hidden life is just the same as the faith by which
we were translated out of the kingdom of darkness
into the kingdom of God's dear Son, only it lays hold
of a different thing.   Then we believed that Jesus was
our Saviour from the guilt of sin, and according to
our faith it was unto us.   Now we must believe that
He is our Saviour from the power of sin, and accord

ing to our faith it shall be unto us. Then we trusted Him for our justification, and it became ours; now we must trust Him for our sanctification, and it shall become ours also. Then we took Him as a Saviour in the future from the penalties of our ʾins; now we must take Him as a Saviour in the present from the bondage of our sins. Then He was our Redeemer, now He is to be our Life. Then He lifted us out of the pit, now He is to seat us in heavenly places with Himself.

I mean all this of course experimentally and practically. Theologically and judicially I know that every believer has everything the minute he is converted. But experimentally nothing is his until by faith he claims it. " Every place that the sole of your foot shall tread upon, that have I given unto you." God " hath blessed us with all spiritual blessings in heavenly places in Christ," but until we set the foot of faith upon them they do not practically become ours. " According to our faith," is always the limit and the rule.

But this faith of which I am speaking must be a present faith. No faith that is exercised in the future tense amounts to anything. A man may believe forever that his sins will be forgiven at some future time, and he will never find peace. He has to come to the *now* belief, and say by faith, " My sins are now forgiven," before he can live the new life. And, similarly, no faith which looks for a future deliverance from the power of sin, will ever lead a soul into the life we are describing. The enemy delights in this

4

f.iture faith, for he knows it is powerless to accom
plish any practical results. But he trembles and
flees when the soul of the believer dares to claim a
present deliverance, and to reckon .itself now to be
free from his power.

To sum up, then: in order to enter into. this
blessed interior life of rest and triumph, you have
two steps to take: first, entire abandonment; and
second, absolute faith. No matter what may be the
complications of your peculiar experience, no matter
what your difficulties or your surroundings or your
associations, these two steps, definitely taken and
unwaveringly persevered in, will certainly bring you
out sooner or later into the green pastures and still
waters of this higher christian life. You may be
sure of this. And if you will let every other consid
eration go, and simply devote your attention to these
two points, and be very clear and definite about
them, your progress will be rapid, and your soul
will reach its desired haven far sooner than now
you can think possible.

Shall I repeat the steps, that there may be no mistake? You are a child of God, and long to please
Him. You love your precious Saviour, and are sick
and weary of the sin that grieves Him. You long to
be delivered from its power. Everything you have
hitherto tried has failed to deliver you; and now in
your despair you are asking if it can indeed be, as
these happy people say, that the Lord is able and
willing to deliver you. Surely you know in your very
soul that He is ; that to save you out of the hand of al.

your enemies is in fact just the very thing He came to do. Then trust Him. Commit your case to Him in an absolute abandonment, and believe that He undertakes it; and at once, knowing what He is and what He has said, claim that He does even now fully save. Just as you believed at first that He delivered you from the guilt of sin because He said so, believe now that He delivers you from the power of sin because He says so. Let your faith now lay hold of a new power in Christ. You have trusted Him as your dying Saviour, now trust Him as your living Saviour. Just as much as He came to deliver you from future punishment, did He also come to deliver you from present bondage. Just as truly as He came to bear your sins for you, has He come to live His life in you. You are as utterly powerless in the one case as in the other. You could as easily have got yourself rid of your own sins, as you could now accomplish for yourself practical righteousness. Christ, and Christ only, must do both for you, and your part in both cases is simply to give the thing to Him to do, and then believe that He does it.

A lady, now very eminent in this life of trust, when she was seeking in great darkness and perplexity to enter in, said to the friend who was trying to help her, " You all say, ' Abandon yourself, and trust, abandon yourself, and trust,' but I do not know how. I wish you would just do it out loud, so that I may see how you do it."

Shall I do it out loud for you ?

" Lord Jesus, I believe that Thou art able and

willing to deliver me from all the care, and unrest, and bondage of my christian life. I believe thou didst die to set me free, not only in the future, but now and here. I believe thou art stronger than Satan, and that thou canst keep me, even me, in my extreme of weakness, from falling into his snares or yielding obedience to his commands. And, Lord, I am going to trust thee to keep me. I have tried keeping myself, and have failed, and failed most grievously. I am absolutely helpless; so now I will trust thee. I will give myself to thee; I keep back no reserves. Body, soul, and spirit, I present myself to thee, a worthless lump of clay, to be made into anything thy love and thy wisdom shall choose. And now, I *am* thine. I believe thou dost accept that which I present to thee; I believe that this poor, weak, foolish heart has been taken possession of by thee, and thou hast even at this very moment begun to work in me to will and to do of thy good pleasure. I trust thee utterly, and I trust thee now!"

Are you afraid to take this step? Does it seem too sudden, too much like a leap in the dark? Do you not know that the steps of faith always "fall on the seeming void, but find the rock beneath"? A man, having to descend a well by a rope, found, to his horror, when he was a great way down, that it was too short. He had reached the end, and yet was, he estimated, about thirty feet from the bottom of the well. He knew not what to do. He had not the strength or skill to climb up the rope, and to let go was to be dashed to pieces. His arms began to fail, and at last he decided that as he could not hold on much longer, he might as well let go and meet his fate at once. He resigned himself to destruction, and loosened his grasp. He fell! To the bottom of the well it was — just three inches!

If ever your feet are to touch the "rock beneath," you must let go of every holding-place and drop into God; for there is no other way. And to do it now may save you months and even years of strain and weariness.

In all the old castles of England there used to be a place called the keep. It was always the strongest and best protected place in the castle, and in it were hidden all who were weak and helpless and unable to defend themselves in times of danger. Had you been a timid, helpless woman in such a castle during a time of siege, would it have seemed to you a leap in the dark to have hidden yourself there? Would you have been *afraid* to do it? And shall we be afraid to hide ourselves in the keeping power of our Divine Keeper, who neither slumbers nor sleeps, and who has promised to preserve our going out and our coming in, from this time forth and even forever more?

CHAPTER V.

DIFFICULTIES CONCERNING CONSECRATION.

IT is very important that christians should not be ignorant of the devices of the enemy; for he stands ready to oppose every onward step of the soul's progress. And especially is he busy when he sees a believer awakened to a hunger and thirst after righteousness, and seeking to reach out to apprehend all the fulness that is in the Lord Jesus' Christ for him.

One of the first difficulties he throws in the way of such a one is concerning consecration. The seeker after holiness is told that he must consecrate himself; and he endeavors to do so. But at once he meets with a difficulty. He has done it, as he thinks, and yet does not feel differently from before; nothing seems changed, as he has been led to expect it would be, and he is completely baffled, and asks the question almost despairingly, " How am I to know when I am consecrated?"

The one grand temptation which has met such a

soul at this juncture is the temptation which never fails to assert itself on every possible occasion, and generally with marked success, and that is in reference to feeling. The soul cannot believe it is consecrated until it *feels* that it is; and because it does not *feel* that God has taken it in hand, it cannot believe that He has. As usual, it puts feeling first and faith second. Now, God's invariable rule is faith first and feeling second, in everything; and it is striving against the inevitable when we seek to make it different.

The way to meet this temptation, then, in reference to consecration, is simply to take God's side in the matter, and to put faith before feeling. Give yourself to the Lord definitely and fully, according to your present light, asking the Holy Spirit to show you all that is contrary to God, either in your heart or life. If He shows you anything, give it to the Lord immediately, and say in reference to it, "Thy will be done." If He shows you nothing, then you must believe that there is nothing, and must conclude that you have given Him all. Then you must believe that He takes you. You positively must not wait to *feel* either that you have given yourself or that He has taken you. You must simply believe it, and reckon it to be the case.

If you were to give an estate to a friend, you would have to give it, and he would have to receive it by faith. An estate is not a thing that can be picked up and handed over to another; the gift of it and its reception are altogether a mental transaction,

and therefore one of faith.   Now, if you should give
an estate one day to a friend, and then should go
away and wonder whether you really had given it,
and whether he had actually taken it and considered
it his own, and should feel it necessary to go the
next day and renew the gift; and if on the third day
you should still feel a similar uncertainty about it,
and should again go and renew the gift, and on the
fourth day go through a like process, and so on, day
after day for months and years, what would your
friend think, and what at last would be the condition
of your own mind in reference to it?   Your friend
certainly would begin to doubt whether you ever had
intended to give it to him at all; and you yourself
would be in such hopeless perplexity about it, that
you would not know whether the estate was yours,
or his, or whose it was.

Now, is not this very much the way in which you
have been acting towards God in this matter of con
secration?   You have given yourself to Him over
and over daily, perhaps for months, but you have invariably come away from your seasons of consecration wondering whether you really have given yourself after all, and whether He has taken you; and
because you have not *felt* any differently, you have
concluded at last, after many painful tossings, that
the thing has not been done.   Do you know, dear
believer, that this sort of perplexity will last forever,
unless you cut it short by faith?   You must come to
the point of reckoning the matter to be an accomplished and settled thing, and leaving it there, before

you can possibly expect any change of feeling whatever.

The very law of offerings to the Lord settles this
as a primary fact,.that everything which is given to
Him becomes by that very act something holy, set
apart from all other things, and cannot without sac-
rilege be put to any other uses.   " Notwithstanding,
no devoted thing that a man shall devote unto the
Lord of all that he hath, both of man and beast, and
of the field of his possession, shall be sold or redeemed : every devoted thing is most holy unto the
Lord."   Having once given it to the Lord, the devoted thing henceforth was reckoned by all Israel as
being the Lord's, and no one dared to stretch forth
a hand to retake it.   The giver might have made his
offering very grudgingly and half-heartedly, but having made it, the matter was taken out of his hands
altogether, and the devoted thing by God's own law
became "most holy unto the Lord."   It was not the
intention of the giver that made it holy, but the holiness of the receiver. " The altar sanctifies the gift."
And an offering once laid upon the altar, from that
moment belonged to the Lord.   I can imagine an
offerer who had deposited a gift, beginning to search
his heart as to his sincerity and honesty in doing it,
and coming back to the priest to say that he was
afraid after all he had not given it right, or had not
been perfectly sincere in giving it.   I feel sure that
the priest would have silenced him at once with saying, " As to how you gave your offering, or what were
your motives in giving it, I do not know.   The facts

are that you did give it, and that it is the Lord's, for every devoted thing is most holy unto Him. It is too late to recall the transaction now." And not only the priest but all Israel would have been aghast at the man who, having once given his offering, should have reached out his hand to take it back. And yet, day after day, earnest-hearted christians, who would have shuddered at such an act of sacri- lege on the part of a Jew, are guilty in their own experience of a similar act, by giving themselves to the Lord in solemn consecration, and then through unbelief taking back that which they have given.

Because God is not visibly present to the eye, it is difficult to feel that a transaction with Him is real. I suppose if, when we made our acts of consecration, we could actually see Him present with us, we should feel it to be a very real thing, and would realize that we had given our word to Him and could not dare to take it back, no matter how much we might wish to do so. Such a transaction would have to us the binding power that a spoken promise to an earthly friend always has to a man of honor. And what we need is to see that God's presence is a certain fact always, and that every act of our soul is done right before Him, and that a word spoken in prayer is as really spoken to Him, as if our eyes could see Him and our hands could touch Him. Then we shall cease to have such vague conceptions of our rela- tions with Him, and shall feel the binding force of every word we say in His presence.

I know some will say here, " Ah, yes; but if He

would only speak to me, and say that He took me
when I gave myself to Him, I would have no trouble
then in believing it." No, of course you would not;
but He does not generally say this until the soul has
first proved its loyalty by believing what He has
already said. It is he that *believeth* who has the witness, not he that *doubteth*. And by His very command to us to present ourselves to Him a living
sacrifice, He has pledged Himself to receive us. I
cannot conceive of an honorable man asking another
to give him a thing which, after all, he was doubtful
about taking; still less can I conceive of a loving
parent acting so towards a darling child. " My son,
give me thy heart," is a sure warrant for knowing
that the moment the heart is given, it will be taken
by the One who has commanded the gift. We may,
nay we must, feel the utmost confidence then that
when we surrender ourselves to the Lord, according
to His own command, He does then and there receive
us, and from that moment we are His. A real transaction has taken place, which cannot be violated
without dishonor on our part, and which we know
will not be violated by Him.

In Deut. xxvi. 17, 18, 19, we see God's way of working under these circumstances : —

"Thou hast avouched the Lord this day to be thy
God, and to walk in His ways and to keep His statutes, and His commandments, and His judgments,
and to hearken unto His voice; and the Lord hath
avouched thee this day to be His peculiar people, as
He hath promised thee, and that thou shouldst keep

all His commandments; . . . and that thou mayst
be an holy people unto the Lord, as He hath spoken."

When we avouch the Lord to be our God, and
that we *will* walk in His ways and keep His commandments, He avouches us to be His, and that we
shall keep all His commandments. And from that
moment He takes possession of us. This has always
been His principle of working, and it continues to
be so. "Every devoted thing is most holy to the
Lord." This seems to me so plain as scarcely to
admit of a question.

But if the soul still feels in doubt or difficulty, let
me refer you to a New Testament declaration which
approaches the subject from a different side, but
which settles it, I think, quite as definitely. It is in
1 John v. 14, 15, and reads: "And this is the confidence that we have in Him, that if we ask anything
according to His will, He heareth us; and if we
know that He hear us, whatsoever we ask, we know
that we *have* the petitions that we desired of Him."
Is it according to His will that you should be entirely
consecrated to Him? There can be, of course, but
one answer to this, for He has *commanded* it. Is it
not also according to His will that He should work
in you to will and to do of His good pleasure? This
question also can have but one answer, for He has
declared it to be His purpose. You know, then, that
these things are according to His will, therefore on
God's own word you are obliged to know that He
hears you; and knowing this much, you are compelled to go further and know that you have the

petitions that you have desired of Him. That you *have*, I say, not will have, or may have, but have now in actual possession. It is thus that we "obtain promises" by faith. It is thus that we have "access by faith" into the grace that is given us in our Lord Jesus Christ. It is thus, and thus only, that we come to know our hearts "purified by faith," and are enabled to live by faith, to stand by faith, to walk by faith.

I desire to make this subject so plain and practical that no one need have any further difficulty about it, and therefore I will repeat again just what must be the acts of your soul in order to bring you out of this difficulty about consecration.

I suppose that you have trusted the Lord Jesus for the forgiveness of your sins, and know something of what it is to belong to the family of God, and to be made an heir of God through faith in Christ. And now you feel springing up in your soul the longing to be conformed to the image of your Lord. In order for this, you know there must be an entire surrender of yourself to Him, that He may work in you all the good pleasure of His will; and you have tried over and over to do it, but hitherto without any apparent success. At this point it is that I desire to help you. What you must do now is to come once more to Him in a surrender of your whole self to His will, as complete as you know how to make it. You must ask Him to reveal to you by His Spirit any hidden rebellion; and if He reveals nothing, then you must believe that there is nothing, and that the surrender is

complete. This must, then, be considered a settled
matter. You have abandoned yourself to the Lord,
and from henceforth you do not in any sense belong
to yourself ; you must never even so much as listen
to a suggestion to the contrary. If the temptation
comes to wonder whether you really have completely
surrendered yourself, meet it with an assertion that
you have. Do not even argue the matter. Repel
any such idea instantly and with decision. You
meant it then, you mean it now, you have really done
it. Your emotions may clamor against the surrender,
but your will must hold firm. It is your purpose
God looks at, not your feelings about that purpose
and your purpose, or will, is therefore the only thin
you need attend to.

The surrender, then, having been made, never to
be questioned or recalled, the next point is to believe
that God takes that which you have surrendered, and
to reckon that it is His. Not that it will be at some
future time, but is now ; and that He has begun to
work in you to will, and to do, of His good pleasure.
And here you must rest. There is nothing more for
you to do, for you are the Lord's now, absolutely and
entirely in His hands, and He has undertaken the
whole care and management and forming of you; and
will, according to His word, " work in you that which
is well-pleasing in His sight through Jesus Christ."
But you must hold steadily here. If you begin to
question your surrender, or God's acceptance of it,
then your wavering faith will produce a wavering experience, and He cannot work. But while you trust,

He works, and the result of His working always is to change you into the image of Christ, from glory to glory, by His mighty Spirit.

Do you, then, now at this moment surrender yourself wholly to Him? You answer, Yes. Then, my dear friend, begin at once to reckon that you are His; that He has taken you, and that He is working in you to will and to do of His good pleasure. And keep on reckoning this. You will find it a great help to put your reckoning into words, and to say over and over to yourself and to your God, " Lord, I am thine ; I do yield myself up to thee entirely, and I believe that thou dost take me. I leave myself with thee. Work in me all the good pleasure of thy will, and I will only lie still in thy hands, and trust thee."

Make this a daily definite act of your will, and many times a day recur to it, as being your continual attitude before Him. Confess it to yourself. Confess it to your God. Confess it to your friends. Avouch the Lord to be your God continually and unwaveringly, and declare your purpose of walking in His ways and keeping His statutes ; and you will find in practical experience that He has avouched you to be His peculiar people and that you shall keep all His commandments, and that you will be "an holy people unto the Lord, as He hath spoken."

A few simple rules may be found helpful here. I would advise the use of them in daily times of devotion, making them the definite test and attitude of the soul, until the light shines clearly on this matter.

I. Express in definite words your faith in Christ
as your Saviour; and acknowledge definitely that you
believe He *has* reconciled you to God; according to
2 Cor. v. 18, 19.

II. Definitely acknowledge God as your Father,
and yourself as His redeemed and forgiven child;
according to Gal. `v : 6.

III. Definitely surrender yourself to be all the
Lord's, body, soul, and spirit; and to obey Him in
everything where His will is made known; according to Rom. xii. 1, 2.

IV. Believe and continue to believe, against all
seemings, that God takes possession of that which
you thus abandon to Him, and that He will henceforth work in you to will and to do of His good pleasure, unless you consciously frustrate His grace;
according to 2 Cor. vi. 17, 18, and Phil. ii. 13.

V. Pay no attention to your *feelings* as a test of
your relations with God, but simply attend to the
state of your *will* and of your *faith.* And count all
these steps you are now taking as settled, though the
enemy may make it *seem* otherwise.   Heb. x. 22, 23.

VI. Never, under any circumstances, give way for
one single moment to doubt or discouragement.
Remember, that all discouragement is from the devil,
and refuse to admit it; according to John xiv. 1, 27.

VII. Cultivate the habit of expressing your faith
in definite words, and repeat often, " I *am* all the
Lord's and He *is* working in me now to will and to
do of His good pleasure; according to Heb. xiii. 21.

CHAPTER VI.

DIFFICULTIES CONCERNING FAITH.

THE next step after consecration, in the soul's progress out of the wilderness of christian experience, into the land that floweth with milk and honey, is that of faith. And here, as in the first step, the enemy is very skilful in making difficulties and interposing obstacles.

The child of God, having had his eyes opened to see the fulness there is in Jesus for him, and having been made to long to appropriate that fulness to himself, is met with the assertion on the part of every teacher to whom he applies, that this fulness is only to be received by faith. But the subject of faith is involved in such a hopeless mystery in his mind, that this assertion, instead of throwing light upon the way of entrance, only seems to make it more difficult and involved than ever.

"Of course it is to be by faith," he says, "for I know that everything in the christian life is by faith. But then, that is just what makes it so hard, for I have no faith, and I do not even know what it is, nor how to get it." And, baffled at the very outset by this insuperable difficulty, he is plunged into darkness, and almost despair.

This trouble all arises from the fact that the subject of faith is very generally misunderstood; for in reality faith is the plainest and most simple thing in the world, and the most easy of attainment.

Your idea of faith, I suppose, has been something like this. You have looked upon it as in some way a sort of *thing*, either a religious exercise of soul, or an inward gracious disposition of heart; something tangible, in fact, which, when you have got, you can look at and rejoice over, and use as a passport to God's favor, or a coin with which to purchase His gifts. And you have been praying for faith, expecting all the while to get something like this, and never having received any such thing, you are insisting upon it that you have no faith. Now faith, in fact, is not in the least this sort of thing. It is nothing at all tangible. It is simply believing God, and, like sight, it is nothing apart from its object. You might as well shut your eyes and look inside to see whether you have sight, as to look inside to discover whether you have faith. You see something, and thus know that you have sight; you believe something, and thus know that you have faith. For, as sight is only seeing, so faith is only believing. And as the only necessary thing about seeing is, that you see the thing as it is, so the only necessary thing about believing is, that you believe the thing as it is. The virtue does not lie in your believing, but in the thing you believe. If you believe the truth you are saved; if you believe a lie you are lost. The believing in both cases is the same; the things believed in are exactly opposite, and it is this which makes the mighty difference. Your salvation comes, not because your faith saves you, but because it links you on to the Saviour who saves; and your believing is really nothing but the link.

I do beg of you to recognize, then, the extreme simplicity of faith; that it is nothing more nor less than just believing God when He says He either has done something for us, or will do it; and then trusting Him to do it. It is so simple that it is hard to explain. If any one asks me what it means to trust another to do a piece of work for me, I can only answer that it means letting that other one do it, and feeling it perfectly unnecessary for me to do it myself. Every one of us has trusted very important pieces of work to others in this way, and has felt perfect rest n thus trusting, because of the confidence we have had in those who have undertaken to do it. How constantly do mothers trust their most precious infants to the care of nurses, and feel no shadow of anxiety? How continually we are all of us trusting our health and our lives, without a thought of fear, to cooks and coachmen, engine-drivers, railway conductors, and all sorts of paid servants, who have us completely at their mercy, and could plunge us into misery or death in a moment, if they chose to do so, or even if they failed .n the necessary carefulness ? All this we do, and make no fuss about it. Upon the slightest acquaint ance, often, we thus put our trust in people, requiring only the general knowledge of human nature, and the common rules of human intercourse ; and we never feel as if we were doing anything in the least remarkable.

You have done all this yourself, dear reader, and are doing it continually. You would not be able to live in this world and go through the customary routine of life a single day, if you could not trust your fellow-men. And it never enters into your head to say you cannot.

But yet you do not hesitate to say, continually, that you cannot trust your God !

I wish you would just now try to imagine yourself acting in your human relations as you do in your spiritual relations. Suppose you should begin to-morrow with the notion in your head that you could not trust anybody, because you had no faith. When you sat down to breakfast you would say, " I cannot eat anything on this table, for I have no faith, and I cannot believe the cook has not put poison in the coffee, or that the butcher has not sent home diseased meat." So you would go starving away. Then when you went out to your daily avocations, you would say, "I cannot ride in the railway train, for I have no faith, and therefore I cannot trust the engineer, nor the conductor, nor the builders of the carriages, nor the managers of the road." So you would be compelled to walk everywhere, and grow unutterably weary in the effort, besides being actually unable to reach many of the places you could have reached in the train. Then, when your friends met you with any statements, or your business agent with any accounts, you would say, "I am very sorry that I cannot believe you, but I have no faith, and never can believe anybody." If you opened a newspaper you would be forced to lay it down again, saying, "I really cannot believe a word this paper says, for I have no faith; I do not believe there is any such person as the queen, for I never saw her; nor any such country as Ireland, for I was never there. And I have no faith, so of course I cannot believe anything that I have not actually felt and touched myself. It is a great trial, but I cannot help it, for I have no faith."

Just picture such a day as this, and see how disastrous it would be to yourself, and what utter folly it would appear to any one who should watch you through the whole of it. Realize how your friends would feel insulted, and how your servants would refuse to serve you another day. And then ask yourself the question, if this want of faith in your fellow-men would be so dreadful, and such utter folly, what must it be when you tell God that you have no power to trust Him nor to believe His word; that "it is a great trial, but you cannot help it, for you have no faith"?

Is it possible that you can trust your fellow-men and cannot trust your God? That you can receive the "witness of men," and cannot receive the "witness of God"? That you can believe man's records, and cannot believe God's record? That you can commit your dearest earthly interests to your weak, failing fellow-creatures without a fear, and are afraid to commit your spiritual interests to the blessed Saviour who shed His blood for the very purpose of saving you, and who is declared to be "able to save you to the uttermost"?

Surely, surely, dear believer, you, whose very name of believer implies that you can believe, will never again dare to excuse yourself on the plea of having no faith. For when you say this, you mean of course that you have no faith in God, since you are not asked to have faith in yourself, and you would be in a very wrong condition of soul if you had. Let me beg of you then, when you think or say these things, always to complete the sentence and say, "I have no faith in God, I cannot believe God"; and this I am sure will soon become so dreadful to you, that you will not dare to continue it.

But you say, I cannot believe without the Holy Spirit. Very well; will you conclude that your want of faith is because of the failure of the blessed Spirit to do His work? For if it is, then surely *you* are not to blame, and need feel no condemnation; and all exhortations to you to believe are useless.

But, no! Do you not see that, in taking up this position, that you have no faith and cannot believe, you are not only "making God a liar," but you are also manifesting an utter want of confidence in the Holy Spirit? For He is always ready to help our infirmities. We never have to wait for Him, He is always waiting for us. And I for my part have such absolute confidence in the blessed Holy Ghost, and in His being always ready to do his work, that I dare to say to every one of you, that you *can* believe now, at this very moment, and that if you do not, it is not the Spirit's fault, but your own.

Put your will then over on to the believing side. Say, " Lord I will believe, I do believe," and continue to say it.   Insist upon believing, in the face of every suggestion of doubt with which you may be tempted. Out of your very unbelief, throw yourself headlong on to the word and promises of God, and dare to abandon yourself to the keeping and saving power of the Lord Jesus.   If you have ever trusted a precious interest in the hands of any earthly friend, I conjure you, trust yourself now and all your spiritual interests in the hands of your Heavenly Friend, and never, *never*, NEVER allow yourself to doubt again.

And remember, there are two things which are more utterly incompatible than even oil and water, and these two are trust and worry.   Would you call it trust, if you should give something into the hands of a friend to attend to for you, and then should spend your nights and days in anxious thought and worry as to whether it would be rightly and success-fully done?   And can you call it trust, when you have given the saving and keeping of your soul into the hands of the Lord, if day after day and night after night you are spending hours of anxious thought and questionings about the matter?   When a be-liever really trusts anything, he ceases to worry about that thing which he has trusted.   And when he worries, it is a plain proof that he does not trust. Tested by this rule, how little real trust there is in the Church of Christ! No wonder our Lord asked the pathetic question, " When the Son of Man cometh shall he find faith on the earth? " He will find plenty of activity, a great deal of earnestness, and doubtless many consecrated hearts ; but shall he find *faith*, the one thing He values more than all the rest? It is a solemn question, and I would that every christian heart would ponder it well. But may the time past of our lives suffice us to have shared in the unbelief of the world; and let us every one, who know our blessed Lord and His unspeakable trustworthiness, set to our seal that He is true, by our generous abandonment of trust in Him.

I remember, very early in my christian life, having every tender and loyal impulse within me stirred to its depths by an appeal I met with in a volume of old sermons to all who loved the Lord Jesus, that they should show to others how worthy He was of being trusted, by the steadfastness of their own faith in Him. And I remember my soul cried out with an eager longing that I might be called to walk in paths so dark, that an utter abandonment of trust might be my blessed and glorious privilege.

" Ye have not passed this way heretofore," it may be ; but to-day it is your happy privilege to prove, as never before, your loyal confidence in the Lord by starting out with Him on a life and walk of faith, lived moment by moment in absolute and childlike trust in Him.

You have trusted Him in a few things, and He has not failed you. Trust Him now for everything, and see if He does not do for you exceeding abundantly above all that you could ever have asked or thought; not according to your power or capacity, but according to His own mighty power, that will work in you all the good pleasure of His most blessed will.

You find no difficulty in trusting the Lord with the management of the universe and all the outward creation, and can your case be any more complex or difficult than these, that you need to be anxious or troubled about his management of it. Away with such unworthy doubtings! Take your stand on the power and trustworthiness of your God, and see how quickly all difficulties will vanish before a steadfast determination to believe. Trust in the dark, trust in the light, trust at night, and trust in the morning, and you will find that the faith, which may begin by a mighty effort, will end sooner or later by becoming the easy and natural habit of the soul.

All things are possible to God, and " all things are possible to him that believeth." Faith has, in times past, " subdued kingdoms, wrought righteousness, obtained promises, stopped the mouths of lions, quenched the violence of fire, escaped the edge of the sword, waxed valiant in fight, turned to flight the armies of the aliens"; and faith can do it again. For our Lord Himself says unto us, "If ye have faith as a grain of mustard seed, ye shall say unto this mountain, Remove hence to yonder place, and it shall remove; and nothing shall be impossible unto you."

If you are a child of God at all, you must have at least as much faith as a grain of mustard seed, and therefore you dare not say again that you cannot trust because you have no faith. Say rather, "I can trust my Lord, and I will trust Him, and not all the powers of earth or hell shall be able to make me doubt my wonderful, glorious, faithful Redeemer!"

In that greatest event of this century, the emancipation of our slaves, there is a wonderful illustration of the way of faith. The slaves received their freedom by faith, just as we must receive ours. The good news was carried to them that the government had proclaimed their freedom. As a matter of fact they were free the moment the Proclamation was issued, but as a matter of experience they did not come into actual possession of their freedom until they had heard the good news and had believed it. The fact had to come first, but the believing was necessary before the fact became available, and the feeling would follow last of all. This is the divine order always, and the order of common-sense as well. I. The fact. II. The faith. III. The feeling. But man reverses this order and says, I. The feeling. II. The faith. III. The fact. Had the slaves followed man's order in regard to their emancipation, and refused to believe in it until they had first felt it, they might have remained in slavery a long while. I have heard of one instance where this was the case. In a little out-of-the-way Southern town a Northern lady found, about two or three years after the war was over, some slaves who had not yet taken posses- sion of their freedom.   An assertion of hers, that the North had set them free, aroused the attention of an old colored auntie, who interrupted her with the eager question, —

"O missus, *is* we free ? "

"Of course you are," replied the lady.

"O missus, is you *sure?* " urged the woman, with intensest eagerness.

"Certainly, I am sure," answered the lady.   "Why, is it possible you did not know it ? "

"Well," said the woman, "we heered tell as how we was free, and we asked master, and he 'lowed we was n't, and so we was afraid to go.   And then we heered tell again, and we went to the cunnel, and he 'lowed we 'd better stay with ole massa.   And so we 's just been off and on.   Sometimes we 'd hope we was free, and then again we 'd think we was n't.   But now, missus, if you is *sure* we is free, won't you tell me all about it ? "

Seeing that this was a case of real need, the lady took the pains to explain the whole thing to the poor woman ; all about the war, and the Northern army, and Abraham Lincoln, and his Proclamation of Emancipation, and the present freedom.

The poor slave listened with the most intense eagerness.   She heard the good news.   She believed it.   And when the story was ended, she walked out of the room with an air of the utmost independence, saying as she went, —

"I's free! I's ain't a-going to stay with ole
massa any longer!"

She had at last received her freedom, and she had
received it by faith. The government had declared
her to be free long before, but this had not availed
her, because she had never yet believed in this
declaration. The good news had not profited her,
not being "mixed with faith" in the one who heard
it. But now she believed, an , believing, she dared
to reckon herself to be free. And this, not because
of any change in herself or her surroundings, not
because of any feelings or emotions of her own heart,
but because she had confidence in the word of
another, who had come to her proclaiming the good
news of her freedom.

Need I make the application? In a hundred different messages God has declared to us our freedom,
and over and over He urges us to reckon ourselves
'ree. Let your faith then lay hold of His proclamation, and assert it to be true. Declare to yourself,
to your friends, and in the secret of your soul to God,
that you *are* free. Refuse to listen for a moment to
the lying assertions of your old master, that you are
still his slave. Let nothing discourage you, no inward feelings nor outward signs. Hold on to your
reckoning in the face of all opposition, and I can
promise you, on the authority of our Lord, that according to your faith it shall be unto you.

Of all the worships we can bring our God, none
is so sweet to Him as this utter self-abandoning
trust, and none brings Him so much glory. There

fore in every dark hour remember that "though now for a season, if need be, ye are in heaviness through manifold temptations," it is in order that "the trial of your faith, being much more precious than of gold that perisheth, though it be tried with fire, might be found unto praise, and honor, and glory, at the appearing of Jesus Christ.'

CHAPTER VII.

DIFFICULTIES CONCERNING THE WILL.

WHEN the child of God has, by the way of entire abandonment and absolute trust, stepped out of himself into Christ, and has begun to know something of the blessedness of the life hid with Christ in God, there is one form of difficulty which is very likely to start up in his path. After the first emotions of peace and rest have somewhat subsided, or if, as is sometimes the case, they have never seemed to come at all, he begins to feel such an utter unreality in the things he has been passing through, that he seems to himself like a hypocrite, when he says or even thinks they are real. It seems to him that his belief does not go below the surface, that it is a mere lip-belief, and therefore of no account, and that his surrender is not a surrender of the heart, and therefore cannot be acceptable to God. He is afraid to say he is altogether the Lord's, for fear he will be telling an untruth, and yet he cannot bring himself to say he is not, because he longs for

it so intensely. The difficulty is real and very disheartening.

But there is nothing here which will not be very
easily overcome, when the christian once thoroughly
understands the principles of the new life, and has
learned *how* to live in it. The common thought is,
that this life hid with Christ in God is to be lived in
the emotions, and consequently all the attention of
the soul is directed towards them, and as they are
satisfactory or otherwise, the soul rests or is troubled.
Now the truth is that this life is not to be lived in
the emotions at all, but in the will, and therefore the
varying states of emotion do not in the least disturb or affect the reality of the life, if only the will
is kept steadfastly abiding in its centre, God's will.

To make this plain, I must enlarge a little. Fene-
lon says somewhere, that " pure religion resides in
the will alone." By this he means that as the will is
the governing power in the man's nature, if the will
is set straight, all the rest of the nature must come
into harmony. By the will I do not mean the wish
of the man, nor even his purpose, but the choice, the
deciding power, the king, to which all that is in the
man must yield obedience. It is the man, in short,
the " *Ego*," that which we feel to be ourselves.

It is sometimes thought that the emotions are the
governing power in our nature. But, as a matter of
practical experience, I think we all of us know that
there is something within us, behind our emotions,
and behind our wishes, — an independent self, — that
after all decides everything and controls everything.

Our emotions belong to us, and are suffered and en joyed by us, but they are not ourselves; and if God is to take possession of us, it must be into this cen tral will or personality that He shall enter.   If, then, He is reigning there by the power of His Spirit, all the rest of our nature must come under His sway; and as the will is, so is the man.

The practical bearing of this truth upon the diffi- culty I am considering is very great.   For the decis- ions of our will are often so directly opposed to the decisions of our emotions, that, if we are in the habit of considering our emotions as the test, we shall be very apt to feel like hypocrites in declaring those things to be real which our will alone has decided. But the moment we see that the will is king, we shall utterly disregard anything that clamors against it, and shall claim as real its decisions, let the emotions rebel as they may.

I am aware that this is a difficult subject to deal with, but it is so exceedingly practical in its bearing upon the life of faith, that I beg of you, dear reader, not to turn from it until you have mastered it.

Perhaps an illustration will help you.   A young man of great intelligence, seeking to enter into this new life, was utterly discouraged at finding himself the slave to an inveterate habit of doubting.   To his emotions nothing seemed true, nothing seemed real; and the more he struggled the more unreal did it all become.   He was told this secret concern- ing the will, that if he would only put his will over on to the believing side; if he would choose to be

lieve; if, in short, he would, in the Ego of his nature,
say, " I will believe ! I do believe !" he need not
trouble about his emotions, for they would find themselves compelled, sooner or later, to come into harmony. " What ! " he said, " do you mean to tell me
that I can *choose* to believe in that way, when nothing
seems true to me; and will that kind of believing be
real?" " Yes," was the answer, "your part is only
this, — to put your will over on God's side in this
matter of believing; and when you do this, God immediately takes possession of it, and works in you
to will of His good pleasure, and you will soon find
that He has brought all the rest of your nature into
subjection to Himself." " Well," was the answer, " I
can do this. I cannot control my emotions, but I
can control my will, and the new life begins to look
possible to me, if it is only my will that needs to be
set straight in the matter. I *can* give my will to God,
and I do ! " From that moment, disregarding all the
pitiful clamoring of his emotions, which continually
accused him of being a wretched hypocrite, this
young man held on steadily to the decision of his
will, answering every accusation with the continued
assertion that he chose to believe, he meant to be
lieve, he did believe; until at the end of a few days he
found himself triumphant, with every emotion and
every thought brought into captivity to the mighty
power of the blessed Spirit of God, who had taken
possession of the will thus put into His hands. He
had held fast the *profession* of his faith without wavering, although it had seemed to him that, as to real

6

faith itself, he had none to hold fast.   At times it
had drained all the will power he possessed to his
lips, to say that he believed, so contrary was it to all
the evidence of his senses or of his emotions.   But he
had caught the idea that his will was, after all, himself, and that if he kept that on God's side, he was
doing all *he* could do, and that God alone could
change his emotions or control his being.   The result has been one of the grandest christian lives I
know of, in its marvellous simplicity, directness, and
power over sin.

The secret lies just here.   That our will, which is
the spring of all our actions, is in our natural state
under the control of self, and self has been working
it in us to our utter ruin and misery.   Now God
says, "Yield yourselves up unto Me, as those that are
alive from the dead, and I will work in you to will
and to do of my good pleasure."   And the moment
we yield ourselves, He of course takes possession of
us, and does work in us "that which is well pleasing
in His sight through Jesus Christ," giving us the
mind that was in Christ, and transforming us into
His image.   (See Rom. xii. 1, 2.)

Let us take another illustration.   A lady, who had
entered into this life hid with Christ, was confronted
by a great prospective trial.   Every emotion she
had within her rose up in rebellion against it, and
had she considered her emotions to be her king, she
would have been in utter despair.   But she had
learned this secret of the will, and knowing that, at
the bottom, she herself did really choose the will of

God for her portion, she did not pay the slightest attention to her emotions, but persisted in meeting every
thought concerning the trial, with the words, repeated
over and over, " Thy will be done ! Thy will be done ! "
asserting in the face of all her rebelling feelings, that
she did submit her will to God's, that she chose to
submit, and that His will should be and was her delight ! The result was, that in an incredibly short
space of time every thought was brought into captivity;
and she began to find even her very emotions rejoicing in the will of God.

Again, there was a lady who had a besetting sin,
which in her emotions she dearly loved, but which in
her will she hated. Having believed herself to be
necessarily under the control of her emotions, she
had therefore thought she was unable to conquer it,
unless her emotions should first be changed. But she
learned this secret concerning the will, and going to
her knees she said, " Lord, Thou seest that with one
part of my nature I love this sin, but in my real
central self I hate it. And now I put my will over
on thy side in the matter. I will not do it any
more. Do thou deliver me." Immediately God took
possession of the will thus surrendered to Himself,
and began to work in her, so that His will in the
matter gained the mastery over her emotions, and
she found herself delivered, not by the power of an
outward commandment, but by the inward power of
the Spirit of God working in her that which was well
pleasing in His sight.

And now, dear christian, let me show you how to

apply this principle to your difficulties. Cease to consider your emotions, for they are only the servants; and regard simply your will, which is the real king in your being. Is that given up to God? Is that put into His hands? Does your will decide to believe? Does your will choose to obey? If this is the case, then *you* are in the Lord's hands, and you decide to believe, and you choose to obey; for your will is yourself. And the thing is done. The transaction with God is as real, where only your will acts, as when every emotion coincides. It does not seem as real to you; but in God's sight it is as real. And when you have got hold of this secret, and have discovered that you need not attend to your emotions, but simply to the state of your will, all the Scripture commands, to yield yourself to God, to present yourself a living sacrifice to Him, to abide in Christ, to walk in the light, to die to self, become possible to you ; for you are conscious that, in all these, your will can act, and can take God's side : whereas, if it had been your emotions that must do it, you would sink down in despair, knowing them to be utterly uncontrollable.

When, then, this feeling of unreality or hypocrisy comes, do not be troubled by it. It is only in your emotions, and is not worth a moment's thought. Only see to it that your will is in God's hands; that your inward self is abandoned to His working; that your choice, your decision, is on His side; and there leave it. Your surging emotions, like a tossing vessel, which, by degrees, yields to the steady pull of the cable, finding themselves attached to the mighty power of God by the choice of your will, must inevitably come into captivity, and give in their allegiance to Him; and you will verify the truth of the saying that, "If any man will do His will, he shall know of the doctrine."

The will is like a wise mother in a nursery; the feelings are like a set of clamoring, crying children. The mother decides upon a certain course of action, which she believes to be right and best. The children clamor against it, and declare it shall not be. But the mother, knowing that she is mistress and not they, pursues her course calmly, unmoved by their clamors, and takes no notice of them except in trying to soothe and quiet them. The result is that the children are sooner or later compelled to yield, and fall in with the decision of the mother. Thus order and harmony are preserved. But if that mother should for a moment let in the thought that the children were the mistresses instead of herself, confusion would reign unchecked. Such instances have been known in family life! And in how many souls at this very moment is there nothing but confusion, simply because the feelings are allowed to govern, instead of the will!

Remember, then, that the real thing in your experience is what your will decides, and not the verdict of your emotions; and that you are far more in danger of hypocrisy and untruth in yielding to the assertions of your feelings, than in holding fast to the decision of your will. So that, if your will is on

God's side, you are no hypocrite at this moment in claiming as your own the blessed reality of belonging altogether to Him, even though your emotions may all declare the contrary.

I am convinced that, throughout the Bible, the expressions concerning the "heart" do not mean the emotions, that which we now understand by the word "heart"; but they mean the will, the personality of the man, the man's own central self; and that the object of God's dealings with man is, that this "I" may be yielded up to Him, and this central life abandoned to His entire control. It is not the feelings of the man God wants, but the man himself.

Have you given Him yourself, dear reader? Have you abandoned your will to His working? Do you consent to surrender the very centre of your being into His hands? Then, let the outposts of your nature clamor as they may, it is your right to say, even now, with the apostle, "I am crucified with Christ; nevertheless, I live; yet not I, but Christ liveth in me: and the life which I now live in the flesh, I live by the faith of the Son of God, who loved me, and gave Himself for me."

———

After this chapter had been enclosed to the printer, the following remarkable practical illustration of its teaching was presented by Pasteur T. Monod, of Paris. It is the experience of a Presbyterian minister, which this *pasteur* had carefully kept for many years.

NEWBURGH, Sept. 26, 1842.

Dear Brother, — I take a few moments of that time which I have devoted to the Lord, in writing a short epistle to you, His servant. It is sweet to feel we are wholly the Lord's, that He has received us and called us His. This is religion, — a relinquishment of the principle of self-ownership, and the adoption in full of the abiding sentiment, "I am not my own, I am bought with a price." Since I last saw you, I have been pressing forward, and yet there has been nothing remarkable in my experience of which I can speak; indeed I do not know that it is best to look for remarkable things; but *strive to be holy,* as God is holy, pressing right on toward the mark of the prize.

I do not feel myself qualified to instruct you; I can only tell you the way in which I was led. The Lord deals differently with different souls, and we ought not to attempt to copy the experience of others, yet there are certain things which must be attended to by every one who is seeking after a clean heart.

There must be a personal consecration of all to God, a covenant made with God, that we will be wholly and forever His. This I made intellectually without any change in my feelings with a heart full of hardness and darkness, unbelief and sin and insensibility.

I covenanted to be the Lord's, and laid all upon the altar, a living sacrifice, to the best of my ability. And after I rose from my knees, I was conscious of no change in my feelings. I was painfully conscious that there was no change. But yet I was sure that I did, with all the sincerity and honesty of purpose of which I was capable, make an entire and eternal consecration of myself to God. I did not then consider the work as done by any means, but I engaged to abide in a state of entire devotion to God, a living perpetual sacrifice. And now came the effort to do this.

I knew that I must believe that God did accept me, and did come in to dwell in my heart. I was conscious I did not believe this, and yet I desired to do so. I read with much prayer John's

First Epistle, and endeavored to assure my heart of God's love to me as an individual. I was sensible that my heart was full of evil. I seemed to have no power to overcome pride, or to repel evil thoughts, which I abhorred. But Christ was manifested to destroy the works of the devil, and it was clear that the sin in my heart was the work of the devil. I was enabled, therefore, to believe that God was working in me, to will and to do, while I was working out my own salvation with fear and trembling.

I was convinced of unbelief, that it was *voluntary and criminal.* I clearly saw that unbelief was an awful sin, it made the faithful God a liar. The Lord brought before me my besetting sins which had dominion over me, especially preaching myself instead of Christ, and indulging self-complacent thoughts after preaching. I was enabled to make myself of no reputation, and to seek the honor which cometh from God only Satan struggled hard to beat me back from the Rock of Ages, but thanks to God I finally hit upon the method of living by the moment, and then I found rest.

I trusted in the blood of Jesus already shed, as a sufficient atonement for all my past sins, and the future I committed wholly to the Lord, agreeing to do His will under all circumstances as He should make it known, and I saw that all I had to do was to look to Jesus for a present supply of grace, and to trust Him to cleanse my heart and keep me from sin at the present moment.

I felt shut up to a momentary dependence upon the grace of Christ. I would not permit the adversary to trouble me about the past or future, for I each moment looked for the supply for that moment. I agreed that I would be a child of Abraham, and walk by naked faith in the Word of God, and not by inward feelings and emotions : I would seek to be a Bible Christian. Since that time the Lord has given me a steady victory over sins which before enslaved me. I delight in the Lord, and in His Word. I delight in my work as a minister: my fellowship is with the Father and with His Son Jesus Christ. I am a babe in Christ; I know my progress has been small compared with that made by many. My feelings vary, but when I have feelings, I praise God, and I trust in His word; and when I am empty and my feelings are gone, I do the same. I have covenanted to walk by faith and not by feelings.

The Lord, I think, is beginning to revive His work among my people. " Praise the Lord." May the Lord fill you with all His fulness and give you all the mind of Christ. Oh, be faithful! Walk before God and be perfect. Preach the Word. Be instant in season and out of season. The Lord loves you. He works with you. Rest your soul fully upon that promise, " Lo, I am with you alway, even unto the end of the world."

Your fellow-soldier,

WILLIAM HILL.

There may be some who will object to this teaching, that it ignores the work of the blessed Holy Spirit. But I must refer such to the introductory chapter of this book, in which I have fully explained myself. I am not writing upon that side of the subject; I am considering man's part in the matter, and not the part of the Spirit. I realize intensely that all a man can do or try to do would be utterly useless, if the Holy Spirit did not work in that man continually. And it is only because I believe in the Spirit as a mighty power, ever present and always ready to do his work, that I can write as I do. But, like the wind that bloweth where it listeth, and thou hearest the sound thereof, but canst not tell whence it cometh, and whither it goeth, the operations of the Spirit are beyond our control, and also beyond our comprehension. The results we know, and the steps on our part which lead to those results, but we know nothing more. And yet, like a workman in a great

manufactory, who does not question the commands
of his employer, and is not afraid to undertake
apparent impossibilities, because he knows there is
a mighty unseen power, called steam, behind his
machinery, which can accomplish it all, so we dare
to urge upon men that they shall simply and coura-
geously set themselves to do that which they are commanded to do, because we know that the mighty
Spirit will never fail to supply at each moment the
necessary power for that moment's act.   And we
boldly claim that we who thus write can say from
our very hearts, as earnestly and as solemnly as any
other christians, We believe in the Holy Ghost.

CHAPTER VIII.

IS GOD IN EVERYTHING?

ONE of the greatest obstacles to living unwaveringly this life of entire surrender is the difficulty of seeing God in everything. People say, " I can easily submit to things which come from God ; but I cannot submit to man, and most of my trials and crosses come through human instrumentality." Or they say, " It is all well enough to talk of trusting ; but when I commit a matter to God, man is sure to come in and disarrange it all ; and while I have no difficulty in trusting God, I do see serious difficulties in the way of trusting men."

This is no imaginary trouble, but it is of vital importance, and if it cannot be met, does really make the life of faith an impossible and visionary theory. For nearly everything in life comes to us through human instrumentalities, and most of our trials are the result of somebody's failure, or ignorance, or carelessness, or sin. We know God cannot be the author of these things, and yet unless He is the agent in the matter, how can we say to Him about it, " Thy will be done " ?

Besides, what good is there in trusting our affairs to God, if, after all, man is to be allowed to come in and disarrange them ; and how is it possible to live by faith, if human agencies, in whom it would be wrong and foolish to trust, are to have a predominant influence in moulding our lives ?

Moreover, things in which we can see God's hand always have a sweetness in them which consoles while it wounds. But the trials inflicted by man are full of bitterness.

What is needed, then, is to see *God in everything*, and to receive everything directly from His hands, with no intervention of second causes. And it is just to this that we must be brought, before we can know an abiding experience of entire abandonment and perfect trust. Our abandonment must be *to God*, not to man, and our trust must be in Him, not in any arm of flesh, or we shall fail at the first trial.

The question here confronts us at once, " But *is* God in everything, and have we any warrant from the Scripture for receiving everything from His hands, without regarding the second causes which may have been instrumental in bringing it about ? " I answer to this, unhesitatingly, YES. To the children of God everything comes directly from their Father's hand, no matter who or what may have been the apparent agents. There are no " second causes " for them.

The whole teaching of the Bible asserts and implies this. "Not a sparrow falls to the ground without our Father." The very hairs of our head are all numbered. We are not to be careful about anything, because our Father cares for us. We are not to avenge ourselves, because our Father has charged Himself with our defence. We are not to fear, for the Lord is on our side. No one can be against us, because He is for us. We shall not want, for He is our Shepherd. When we pass through the rivers they shall not overflow us, and when we walk through the fire we shall not be burned, because He will be with us. He shuts the mouths of lions, that they cannot hurt us. "He delivereth and rescueth." "He changeth the times and the seasons; He removeth kings and setteth up kings." A man's heart is in His hand, and, "as the river of water, He turneth it whithersoever He will." He ruleth over all the kingdoms of the heathen; and in His hand there is power and might, "so that none is able to withstand" Him. "He ruleth the raging of the sea; when the waves thereof arise, He stilleth them." He "bringeth the counsel of the heathen to nought; He maketh the devices of the people of none effect." "Whatsoever the Lord pleaseth, that does He in heaven, and in earth, in the seas, and all deep places."

"If thou seest the oppression of the poor, and violent perverting of judgment and justice in a province, marvel not at the matter; for He that is higher than the highest regardeth; and there be higher than they."

"Lo, these are a part of His ways; but how little
a portion is heard of Him? But the thunder of His
power who can understand?" "Hast thou not
known, hast thou not heard, that the everlasting
God, the Lord, the Creator of the ends of the earth,
fainteth not, neither is weary? There is no searching of His understanding."

And this "God is our refuge and strength, a very
present help in trouble. Therefore will not we fear,
though the earth be removed, and though the mountains be carried into the midst of the sea; though the
waters thereof roar and be troubled; though the
mountains shake with the swelling thereof." "I will
say of the Lord, He is my refuge and my fortress,
my God, in Him will I trust. Surely He shall deliver thee from the snare of the fowler, and from the
noisesome pestilence. He shall cover thee with His
feathers, and under His wings shalt thou trust. His
truth shall be thy shield and buckler. Thou shalt
not be afraid for the terror by night, nor for the
arrow that flieth by day, nor for the pestilence that
walketh in darkness, nor for the destruction that
wasteth at noonday. A thousand shall fall at thy
side, and ten thousand at thy right hand; but it
shall not come nigh thee." "Because thou hast
made the Lord, which is my refuge, even the Most
High, thy habitation, there shall no evil befall thee,
neither shall any plague come nigh thy dwelling.
For He shall give His angels charge over thee, to
keep thee in all thy ways."

To my own mind, these Scriptures, and many

others like them, settle forever the question as to
the power of second causes in the life of the children
of God. They are all under the control of our
Father, and nothing can touch us except with His
knowledge and by His permission. It may be the
sin of man that originates the action, and therefore
the thing itself cannot be said to be the will of God
but by the time it reaches us, it has become God'
will for us, and must be accepted as directly from
His hands. No man or company of men, no power
in earth or heaven, can touch that soul which is abiding in Christ, without first passing through Him, and
receiving the seal of His permission. If God be
for us, it matters not who may be against us; nothing can disturb or harm us, except He shall see that
it is best for us, and shall stand aside to let it pass.

An earthly parent's care for his helpless child is a
feeble illustration of this. If the child is in its father's
arms, nothing can touch it without that father's consent, unless he is too weak to prevent it. And even
if this should be the case, he suffers the harm first in
his own person, before he allows it to reach his child.
And if an earthly parent would thus care for his little
helpless one, how much more will our Heavenly
Father, whose love is infinitely greater, and whose
strength and wisdom can never be baffled! I am
afraid there are some, even of God's own children,
who scarcely think that He is equal to themselves in
tenderness, and love, and thoughtful care ; and who
in their secret thoughts, charge Him with a neglect
and indifference of which they would feel themselves

incapable. The truth really is, that His care is infinitely superior to any possibilities of human care;
and that He who counts the very hairs of oui heads,
and suffers not a sparrow to fall without Him, takes
note of the minutest matters that can affect the lives
of His children, and regulates them all according to
His own sweet will, let their origin be what they may.

The instances of this are numberless. Take
Joseph. What could have seemed more apparently
on the face of it to be the result of sin, and utterly
contrary to the will of God, than his being sold into
slavery? And yet Joseph, in speaking of it, said,
"As for you, ye thought evil against me: but
God meant it unto good." "Now, therefore, be not
grieved nor angry with yourselves, that ye sold me
hither, for God did send me before you to preserve
life." To the eye of sense it was surely Joseph's
wicked brethren who had sent him into Egypt; and
yet Joseph, looking at it with the eye of faith, could
say, "God sent me." It had been undoubtedly a
grievous sin in his brethren, but, by the time it had
reached Joseph, it had become God's will for him,
and was in truth, though at first it did not look so,
the greatest blessing of his whole life. And thus
we see how the Lord can make even the wrath of
man to praise Him, and how all things, even the sins
of others, shall work together for good to them that
love Him.

I learned this lesson practically and experimentally
long years before I knew the scriptural truth concerning it. I was attending a prayer-meeting held for

the promotion of scriptural holiness, when a strange lady rose to speak, and I looked at her, wondering who she could be, little thinking she was to bring a message to my soul which would teach me such a grand lesson. She said she had had great difficulty in living the life of faith, on account of the second causes that seemed to her to control nearly everything that concerned her. Her perplexity became so great, that at last she began to ask God to teach her the truth about it, whether He really was in everything or not. After praying this for a few days, she had what she described as a vision. She thought she was in a perfectly dark place, and that there advanced towards her from a distance a body of light, which gradually surrounded and enveloped her and everything around her. As it approached, a voice seemed to say, " This is the presence of God; this is the presence of God." While surrounded with this presence, all the great and awful things in life seemed to pass before her, — fighting armies, wicked men, raging beasts, storms and pestilences, sin and suffering of every kind. She shrank back at first in terror, but she soon saw that the presence of God so surrounded and enveloped each one of these, that not a lion could reach out its paw, nor a bullet fly through the air, except as His presence moved out of the way to permit it. And she saw that, let there be ever so thin a sheet, as it were, of this glorious presence between herself and the most terrible violence, not a hair of her head could be ruffled, nor anything touch her, unless the presence divided to let the evil

through. Then all the small and annoying things
of life passed before her, and equally she saw that
these all were so enveloped in this presence of God,
that not a cross look, not a harsh word, nor petty
trial of any kind, could reach her unless His presence moved out of the way to let them through.

Her difficulty vanished. Her question was answered forever. God was in everything; and to her
henceforth there were no second causes. She saw
that her life came to her day by day and hour by
hour directly from His hand, let the agencies which
should seem to control it be what they might. And
never again had she found any difficulty in an abid
ing consent to His will and an unwavering trust in
His care.

If we look at the seen things, we shall not be able
to understand the secret of this. But the children
of God are called to look, " not at the things which
are seen : for the things which are seen are temporal,
but the things which are not seen are eternal."
Could we but see with our bodily eyes His unseen
forces surrounding us on every side, we would walk
through this world in an impregnable fortress, which
nothing could ever overthrow or penetrate, for " the
angel of the Lord encampeth round about them that
fear Him, and delivereth them."

We have a striking illustration of this in the history
of Elisha. The king of Syria was warring against
Israel, but his evil designs were continually frustrated
by the prophet ; and at last he sent his army to the
prophet's own city for the express purpose of taking

him captive. We read, " He sent thither horses and chariots and a great host; and they came by night and compassed the city about." This was the seen thing. And the servant of the prophet, whose eyes had not yet been opened to see the unseen things, was alarmed. And we read, " And when the servant of the man of God was risen early and gone forth, behold an host compassed the city, both with horses and chariots. And his servant said unto him, Alas, my master, how shall we do?" But his master could see the unseen things, and he replied, ' Fear not; for they that be with us are more than they that be with them." And then he prayed, saying, " Lord, I pray thee, open his eyes that he may see. And the Lord opened the eyes of the young man, and he saw; and behold, the mountain was full of horses and chariots of fire round about Elisha."

The presence of God is the fortress of His people. Nothing can withstand it. At His presence the wicked perish; the earth trembles; the hills melt like wax; the cities are broken down; " the heavens also dropped, and Sinai itself was moved at the presence of God." And in the secret of this presence He has promised to hide His people from the pride of man, and from the strife of tongues. " My presence shall go with thee," He says, "and I will give thee rest."

I wish it were only possible to make every christian see this truth as plainly as I see it; for I am convinced it is the only clew to a completely restful life. Nothing else will enable a soul to live only in the present moment, as we are commanded to do, and to take no thought for the morrow. Nothing else will take all the risks and "supposes" out of a christian's heart, and enable him to say, "Surely goodness and mercy shall follow me all the days of my life." Abiding in God's presence, we run no risks; and such a soul can triumphantly say, —

> "I know not what it is to doubt,
> My heart is always gay;
> I run no risks, for, come what will,
> God always has His way."

I once heard of a colored woman who earned a precarious living by daily labor, but who was a joyous, triumphant christian. "Ah! Nancy," said a gloomy christian lady to her one day, who almost disapproved of her constant cheerfulness, and yet envied it, — "ah! Nancy, it is all well enough to be happy now; but I should think the thoughts of your future would sober you. Only suppose, for instance, that you should have a spell of sickness and be unable to work; or suppose your present employers should move away, and no one else should give you anything to do; or suppose — " "Stop!" cried Nancy, "I never supposes. De Lord is my shepherd, and I knows I shall not want. And, honey," she added to her gloomy friend, "it's all dem *supposes* as is makin' you so mis'able. You'd better give dem all up, and just trust de Lord."

There is one text that will take all the "supposes" out of a believer's life, if only it is received and acted out in a childlike faith; it is in Heb. xiii. 5, 6 :

"Be content, therefore, with such things as ye have; for He hath said I will never leave thee, nor forsake thee"; so that we may boldly say, "THE LORD IS MY HELPER, AND I WILL NOT FEAR WHAT MAN SHALL DO UNTO ME." What if dangers of all sorts shall threaten you from every side, and the malice or foolishness or ignorance of men shall combine to do you harm? You may face every possible contingency with these triumphant words, "The Lord is my helper, and I will not fear what man shall do unto me." If the Lord is your helper, how *can* you fear what man may do unto you? There is no man in this world, nor company of men, that can touch you, unless your God, in whom you trust, shall please to let them. "He will not suffer thy foot to be moved: He that keepeth thee will not slumber. Behold, He that keepeth Israel shall neither slumber nor sleep. The Lord is thy keeper; the Lord is thy shade upon thy right hand. The sun shall not smite thee by day nor the moon by night. The Lord shall preserve thee from all evil: He shall preserve thy soul. The Lord shall preserve thy going out, and thy coming in, from this time forth, and even forevermore."

Nothing else but this seeing God in everything will make us loving and patient with those who annoy and trouble us. They will be to us then only the instruments for accomplishing His tender and wise purposes towards us, and we shall even find ourselves at last inwardly thanking them for the blessings they bring us.

Nothing else will completely put an end to all mur
muring or rebelling thoughts.   Christians often feel a
liberty to murmur against man, when they would not
dare to murmur against God.   But this way of receiving things would make it impossible ever to
murmur.   If our Father permits a trial to come, it
must be because that trial is the sweetest and best
thing that could happen to us, and we must accept it
with thanks from His dear hand.   The trial itself
may be hard to flesh and blood, and I do not mean
that we can like or enjoy the suffering of it.   But
we can and must love the will of God *in* the trial,
for His will is always sweet, whether it be in joy or
'n sorrow.

Our trials may be our chariots.   We long for some
rictory over sin and self, and we ask God to grant it
to us.   His answer comes in the form of a trial
which He means shall be the chariot to bear us to
the longed-for triumph.   We may either let it roll
over us and crush us as a Juggernaut car, or we may
mount into it and ride triumphantly onward.   Joseph's
chariots, which bore him on to the place of his exaltation, were the trials of being sold into slavery, and
being cast unjustly into prison.   Our chariots may
be much more insignificant things than these; they
may be nothing but irritating people or uncomfortable circumstances.   But whatever they are, God
means them to be our cars of triumph, which shall
bear us onward to the victories we have prayed for
If we are impatient in our dispositions and long to
be made patient, our chariot will probably be a try-

ing person to live in the house with us, whose ways or words will rasp our very souls. If we accept the trial as from God, and bow our necks to the yoke, we shall find it just the discipline that will most effectually produce in us the very grace of patience for which we have asked.

God does not *order* the wrong thing, but He *uses* it for our blessing; just as He used the cruelty of Joseph's wicked brethren, and the false accusations of Pharaoh's wife.

In short, this way of seeing our Father in everything makes life one long thanksgiving, and gives a rest of heart, and more than that, a gayety of spirit, that is unspeakable. Some one says, "God's will on earth is always joy, always tranquility." And since He must have His own way concerning His children, into what wonderful green pastures of inward rest, and beside what blessedly still waters of inward refreshment, is the soul led that learns this secret.

If the will of God is our will, and if He always has His way, then we always have our way also, and we reign in a perpetual kingdom. He who sides with God cannot fail to win in every encounter; and whether the result shall be joy or sorrow, failure or success, death or life, we may, under all circumstances, join in the apostle's shout of victory, "Thanks be unto God, which always causeth us to triumph in Christ!"

CHAPTER IX.

GROWTH.

WHEN the believer has been brought to the point of entire surrender and perfect trust, and finds himself dwelling and walking in a life of happy communion and perfect peace, the question naturally arises, "Is this the end?" I answer emphatically, "No, it is only the beginning."

And yet this is so little understood, that one of the greatest objections made against the advocates of this life of faith, is, that they do not believe in growth in grace. They are supposed to teach that the soul arrives at a state of perfection beyond which there is no advance, and that all the exhortations in the Scripture which point towards growth and development are rendered void by this teaching.

As exactly the opposite of this is true, I have thought it important next to consider this subject carefully, that I may, if possible, fully answer such objections, and may also show what is the scriptural place to grow in, and how the soul is to grow.

The text which is most frequently quoted is 2 Pet.
iii. 18, "But grow in grace, and in the knowledge
of our Lord and Saviour Jesus Christ." Now this
text exactly expresses what we believe to be God's
will for us, and what also we believe He has made it
possible for us to experience. We accept, in their
very fullest meaning, all the commands and promises
concerning our being no more children, and our
growing up into Christ in all things, until we come
unto a perfect man, unto the measure of the stature
of the fulness of Christ. We rejoice that we need
not continue always to be babes, needing milk; but
that we may, by reason of use and development
become such as have need of strong meat, skilful in
the word of righteousness, and able to discern both
good and evil. And none would grieve more than
we at the thought of any finality in the christian life
beyond which there could be no advance.

But then we believe in a growing that does really
produce maturity, and in a development that, as a
fact, does bring forth ripe fruit. We expect to reach
the aim set before us, and if we do not, we feel sure
there must be some fault in our growing. No parent
would be satisfied with the growth of his child, if,
day after day, and year after year, it remained the
same helpless babe it was in the first months of its
life; and no farmer would feel comfortable under
such growing of his grain as should stop short at
the blade, and never produce the ear, nor the full
corn in the ear. Growth, to be real, must be progressive, and the days and weeks and months must

see a development and increase of maturity in the thing growing. But is this the case with a large part of that which is called growth in grace? Does not the very christian who is the most strenuous in his longings and in his efforts after it, too often find that at the end of the year he is not as far on in his christian experience as at the beginning, and that his zeal, and his devotedness, and his separation from the world are not as whole-souled or complete as when his christian life first began?

I was once urging upon a company of christians the privileges and rest of an immediate and definite step into the land of promise, when a lady of great intelligence interrupted me, with what she evidently felt to be a complete rebuttal of all I had been saying, exclaiming, "Ah! but, my dear friend, I believe in *growing* in grace." "How long have you been growing?" I asked. "About twenty-five years," was her answer. "And how much more unworldly and devoted to the Lord are you now than when you began your christian life?" I continued. "Alas!" was the answer, "I fear I am not nearly so much so"; and with this answer her eyes were opened to see that at all events her way of growing had not been successful, but quite the reverse.

The trouble with her, and every other such case, is simply this, they are trying to grow *into* grace, instead of *in* it. They are like a rose-bush which the gardener should plant in the hard, stony path, with a view to its growing *into* the flower-bed, and which would of course dwindle and wither in consequence,

instead of flourishing and maturing. The children
of Israel wandering in the wilderness are a perfect
picture of this sort of growing. They were travel-
ling about for forty years, taking many weary steps,
and finding but little rest from their wanderings, and
yet, at the end of it all, were no nearer the promised land than they were at the beginning. When
they started on their wanderings at Kadesh Barnea,
they were at the borders of the land, and a few
steps would have taken them into it. When they
ended their wanderings in the plains of Moab, they
were also at its borders; only with this great difference, that now there was a river to cross, which
at first there would not have been. All their wanderings and fightings in the wilderness had not put
them in possession of one inch of the promised land.
In order to get possession of this land it was necessary first to be in it; and in order to grow in
grace, it is necessary first to be planted in grace.
But when once in the land, their conquest was very
rapid; and when once planted in grace, the growth
of the soul in one month will exceed that of years in
any other soil. For grace is a most fruitful soil, and
the plants that grow therein are plants of a marvellous growth. They are tended by a Divine Husbandman, and are warmed by the Sun of Righteousness, and watered by the dew from Heaven. Surely
it is no wonder that they bring forth fruit, "some
an hundred-fold, some sixty-fold, some thirty-
fold."

But, it will be asked, what is meant by growing

in grace? It is difficult to answer this question, because so few people have any conception of what the grace of God really is. To say that it is free, unmerited favor, only expresses a little of its meaning. It is the wondrous, boundless love of God, poured out upon us without stint or measure, not according to our deserving, but according to His infinite heart of love, which passeth knowledge, so unfathomable are its heights and depths. I sometimes think we give a totally different meaning to the word "love" when it is associated with God, from that we so well understand in its human application. But if ever human love was tender and self-sacrificing and devoted; if ever it could bear and forbear; if ever it could suffer gladly for its loved ones; if ever it was willing to pour itself out in a lavish abandonment for the comfort or pleasure of its objects, — then infinitely more is Divine love tender and self-sacrificing and devoted, and glad to bear and forbear, and to suffer, and to lavish its best of gifts and blessings upon the objects of its love. Put together all the tenderest love you know of, dear reader, the deepest you have ever felt, and the strongest that has ever been poured out upon you, and heap upon it all the love of all the loving human hearts in the world, and then multiply it by infinity, and you will begin perhaps to have some faint glimpses of what the love of God in Christ Jesus is. And this is grace. And to be planted in grace is to live in the very heart of this love, to be enveloped by it, to be steeped in it, to revel in it, to know nothing else but love only and love always, to grow day by day in the knowledge of it, and in faith in it, to intrust everything to its care, and to have no shadow of a doubt but that it will surely order all things well.

To grow in grace is opposed to all self-dependence, to all self-effort, to all legality of every kind. It is to put our growing, as well as everything else, into the hands of the Lord, and leave it with Him. It is to be so satisfied with our Husbandman, and with His skill and wisdom, that not a question will cross our minds as to His modes of treatment or His plan of cultivation. It is to grow as the lilies grow, or as the babes grow, without a care and without anxiety; to grow by the power of an inward life principle that cannot help but grow; to grow because we live and therefore must grow; to grow because He who has planted us has planted a growing thing, and has made us to grow.

Surely this is what our Lord meant when He said, "Consider the lilies, how they grow; they toil not, neither do they spin: and yet I say unto you, that even Solomon in all his glory was not arrayed like one of these." Or, when He says again, "Which of you by taking thought can add one cubit unto his stature?" There is no effort in the growing of a child or of a lily. They do not toil nor spin, they do not stretch nor strain, they do not make any effort of any kind to grow; they are not conscious even that they are growing; but by an inward life principle, and through the nurturing care of God's providence, and the fostering of care-taker or gardener, by the heat of the sun and the falling of the rain, they grow and grow.

And the result is sure. Even Solomon, our Lord says, in all his glory, was not arrayed like one of these. Solomon's array cost much toiling and spinning, and gold and silver in abundance, but the lily's array costs none of these. And though we may toil and spin to make for ourselves beautiful spiritual garments, and may strain and stretch in our efforts after spiritual growth, we shall accomplish nothing; for no man by taking thought *can* add one cubit to his stature; and no array of ours can ever equal the beautiful dress with which the great Husbandman clothes the plants that grow in His garden of grace and under His fostering care.

If I could but make each one of my readers realize how utterly helpless we are in this matter of growing, I am convinced a large part of the strain would be taken out of many lives at once. Imagine a child possessed of the monomania that he would not grow unless he made some personal effort after it, and who should insist upon a combination of rope and pulleys whereby to stretch himself up to the desired height. He might, it is true, spend his days and years in a weary strain, but after all there would be no change in the inexorable fiat, " No man by taking thought can add one cubit unto his stature "; and his years of labor would be only wasted, if they did not really hinder the longed-for end.

Imagine a lily trying to clothe itself in beautiful colors and graceful lines, stretching its leaves and

stems to make them grow, and seeking to manage
the clouds and the sunshine, that its needs might be
all judiciously supplied!

And yet in these two pictures we have, I conceive.
only too true a picture of what many christians are
trying to do; who, knowing they ought to grow, and
feeling within them an instinct that longs for growth,
yet think to accomplish it by toiling, and spinning,
and stretching, and straining, and pass their lives in
such a round of self-effort as is a weariness to con-
template.

Grow, dear friends, but grow, I beseech you, in
God's way, which is the only effectual way. See to
it that you are planted in grace, and then let the
Divine Husbandman cultivate you in His own way
and by His own means. Put yourselves out in the
sunshine of His presence, and let the dew of heaven
come down upon you, and see what will come of it.
Leaves and flowers and fruit must surely come in
their season, for your Husbandman is a skilful one,
and He never fails in His harvesting. Only see to
it that you oppose no hindrance to the shining of
the Sun of Righteousness or the falling of the dew
from Heaven. A very thin covering may serve to
keep off the heat or the moisture, and the plant may
wither even in their midst; and the slightest barrier
between your soul and Christ may cause you to
dwindle and fade as a plant in a cellar or under a
bushel. Keep the sky clear. Open wide every
avenue of your being to receive the blessed influences
your Divine Husbandman may bring to bear upon

you. Bask in the sunshine of His love. Drink in
of the waters of His goodness. Keep your face up-
turned to Him. Look, and your soul'shall live.

You need make no efforts to grow; but let your
efforts instead be all concentrated on this, that you
abide in the Vine. The Husbandman who has the
care of the vine, will care for its branches also, and
will so prune and purge and water and tend them
that they will grow and bring forth fruit, and their
fruit shall remain; and, like the lily, they shall find
themselves arrayed in apparel so glorious that that
of Solomon will be as nothing to it.

What if you seem to yourselves to be planted at this
moment in a desert soil where nothing can grow!
Put yourself absolutely into the hands of the great
Husbandman, and He will at once make that desert
blossom as the rose, and will cause springs and foun-
tains of water to start up out of its sandy wastes:
for the promise is sure, that the man who trusts in
the Lord "shall be as a tree planted by the waters,
and that spreadeth out her roots by the river, and
shall not see when heat cometh, but her leaf shall
be green; and shall not be careful in the year of
drought, neither shall cease from yielding fruit." It
is the great prerogative of our Divine Husbandman
that He is able to turn any soil, whatever it may be
like, into the soil of grace, the moment we put our
growing into His hands. He does not need to trans-
plant us into a different field, but right where we
are, with just the circumstances that surround us,
He makes His sun to shine and His dew to fall

upon us, and transforms the very things that were before our greatest hindrances into the chiefest and most blessed means of our growth. I care not what the circumstances may be, His wonder-working power can accomplish this. And we must trust Him with it all. Surely He is a Husbandman we *can* trust. And if He sends storms, or winds, or rains, or sunshine, all must be accepted at His hands with the most unwavering confidence that He who has undertaken to cultivate us, and to bring us to maturity, knows the very best way of accomplishing His end, and regulates the elements, which are all at His disposal, expressly with a view to our most rapid growth.

Let me entreat of you, then, to give up all your efforts after growing, and simply to *let* yourselves grow. Leave it all to the Husbandman, whose care it is, and who alone is able to manage it. No difficulties in your case can baffle Him. No dwarfing of your growth in years that are past, no apparent dryness of your inward springs of life, no crookedness or deformity in any of your past development, can in the least mar the perfect work that He will accomplish, if you will only put yourselves absolutely into His hands, and let Him have His own way with you. His own gracious promise to His backsliding children assures you of this. " I will heal their backslidings," He says: "I will love them freely, for mine anger is turned away from him. I will be as the dew unto Israel; he shall grow as the lily, and cast forth his roots as Lebanon. His branches shall spread, and his beauty shall be as the olive-tree, and his smell as Lebanon. They that dwell under His shadow shall return; they shall revive as the corn, and grow as the vine; the scent thereof shall be as the wine of Lebanon." And again He says, " Be not afraid, for the pastures of the wilderness do spring, for the tree beareth her fruit, the fig-tree and the vine do yield their strength. And the floors shall be full of wheat, and the fats shall overflow with wine and oil. And I will restore to you the years that the locust hath eaten; and ye shall eat in plenty and be satisfied, and praise the name of the Lord your God, who hath dealt wondrously with you; and my people shall never be ashamed."

Oh! that you could but know just what your Lord meant when He said, " Consider the lilies, *how they grow;* for they toil not, neither do they spin." Surely these words give us a picture of a life and of a growth far different from the ordinary life and growth of christians; a life of rest, and a growth without effort; and yet a life and a growth crowned with glorious results. And to every soul that will thus become a lily in the garden of the Lord, and will grow as the lilies grow, the same glorious array will be surely given as is given them; and they will know the fulfilment of that wonderful mystical passage concerning their Beloved, that "He feedeth among the lilies."

This is the sort of growth in grace in which we who have entered into the life of full trust believe a growth which brings the desired results, which blossoms out into flower and fruit, and becomes like a tree planted by the rivers of water, that bringeth forth his fruit in his season; whose leaf also does not wither, and who prospers in whatsoever he doeth. And we rejoice to know that there are growing up now in the Lord's heritage many such plants, who, as the lilies behold the face of the sun and grow thereby, are, by beholding as in a glass the glory of the Lord, being changed into the same image from glory to glory, even as by the spirit of the Lord.

Should you ask such, how it is that they grow so rapidly and with such success, their answer would be that they are not concerned about their growing, and are hardly conscious that they do grow; that their Lord has told them to abide in Him, and has promised that if they do thus abide, they shall certainly bring forth much fruit; and that they are concerned only about the abiding, which is their part, and leave the cultivating and the growing and the training and pruning to their good Husbandman, who alone is able to manage these things or bring them about. You will find that such souls are not engaged in watching self, but in looking unto Jesus. They do not toil nor spin for their spiritual garments, but leave themselves in the hands of the Lord to be arrayed as it may please Him. Self-effort and self-dependence are at an end with them. Their interest in self is gone, transferred over into the hands of another. Self has become really nothing, and Christ alone is all in all to such as these. And the blessed result is, that not even Solomon, in all his glory, was arrayed like these shall be.

Let us look at this subject practically. We all know that growing is not a thing of effort, but is the result of an inward life, a principle of growth. All the stretching and pulling in the world could not make a dead oak grow. But a live oak grows without stretching. It is plain, therefore, that the essential thing is to get within you the growing life, and then you cannot help but grow. And this life is the life hid with Christ in God, the wonderful divine life of an indwelling Holy Ghost. Be filled with this, dear believer, and, whether you are conscious of it or not, you must grow, you cannot help growing. Do not trouble about your growing, but see to it that you have the growing life. Abide in the Vine. Let the life from Him flow through all your spiritual veins. Interpose no barrier to His mighty life-giving power, working in you all the good pleasure of His will. Yield yourself up utterly to His sweet control. Put your growing into His hands, as completely as you have put all your other affairs. Suffer Him to manage it as He will. Do not concern yourself about it, nor even think of it. Trust Him absolutely, and always. Accept each moment's dispensation as it comes to you, from His dear hands, as being the needed sunshine or dew for that moment's growth. Say a continual "Yes" to your Father's will.

Heretofore you have perhaps tried, as so many do, to be both the lily and the gardener, both the vineyard and the husbandman. You have taken upon your shoulders the burdens and responsibilities that

belong only to the Divine Husbandman, and which
He alone is able to bear. Henceforth consent to take
your rightful place and to *be* only what you really *are*.
Say to yourself, If I am the garden only, and not the
gardener, if I am the vine only, and not the husbandman, it is surely essential to my right growth
and well being that I should keep the place and
act the part of the garden, and should not usurp
the gardener's place, nor try to act the gardener's
part.

Do not seek then to choose your own soil, nor the
laying out of your borders; do not plant your own
seeds, nor dig about, nor prune, nor watch over your
own vines. Be content with what the Divine Husbandman arranges for you, and with the care He
gives. Let Him choose the sort of plants and fruits
He sees best to cultivate, and grow a potato as
gladly as a rose, if such be His will, and homely
every-day virtues as willingly as exalted fervors.
Be satisfied with the seasons He sends, with the sunshine and rain He gives, with the rapidity or slowness of your growth, in short, with all His dealings
and processes, no matter how little we may comprehend them.

There is infinite repose in this. As the viole
rests in its little nook, receiving contentedly its daily
portion, satisfied to let rains fall, and suns rise, and
the earth to whirl, without one anxious pang, so must
we repose in the present as God gives it to us, ac-
cepting contentedly our daily portion, and with no
anxiety as to all that may be whirling around us, in
His great creative and redemptive plan.

The wind that blows can never kill
 The tree God plants;
It bloweth east, it bloweth west,
The tender leaves have little rest,
But any wind that blows is best.
 The tree God plants
Strikes deeper root, grows higher still,
Spreads wider boughs, for God's good-will
 Meets all its wants.

There is no frost hath power to blight
 The tree God shields;
The roots are warm beneath soft snows,
And when spring comes it surely knows,
And every bud to blossom grows.
 The tree God shields
Grows on apace by day and night,
Till, sweet to taste and fair to sight,
 Its fruit it yields.

There is no storm hath power to blast
 The tree God knows;
No thunder-bolt, nor beating rain,
Nor lightning flash, nor hurricane;
When they are spent it doth remain.
 The tree God knows
Through every tempest standeth fast,
And, from its first day to its last,
 Still fairer grows.

If in the soul's still garden-place
 A seed God sows —
A little seed — it soon will grow,
And far and near all men will know
For heavenly land He bids it blow.
 A seed God sows,
And up it springs by day and night;
Through life, through death, it groweth right,
 Forever grows.

CHAPTER X.

SERVICE.

THERE is, perhaps, no part of christian experience where a greater change is known upon entering into the life hid with Christ in God, than in the matter of service.

In all the lower forms of christian life, service is apt to have more or less of bondage in it; that is, it is done purely as a matter of duty, and often as a trial and a cross. Certain things, which at the first may have been a joy and delight, become weary tasks, performed faithfully, perhaps, but with much secret disinclination, and many confessed or unconfessed wishes that they need not be done at all, or at least that they need not be done so often. The soul finds itself saying, instead of the "May I" of love, the "Must I" of duty. The yoke, which was at first easy, begins to gall, and the burden feels heavy instead of light.

One dear christian expressed it once to me in this way. "When I was first converted," she said, "I

was so full of joy and love that I was only too glad
and thankful to be allowed to do anything for my
Lord, and I eagerly entered every open door.   But
after a while, as my early joy faded away, and my
love burned less fervently, I began to wish I had not
been quite so eager ; for I found myself involved in
lines of service which were gradually becoming very
distasteful and burdensome to me.   I could not very
well give them up, since I had begun them, without
exciting great remark, and yet I longed to do so increasingly.   I was expected to visit the sick, and
pray beside their beds.   I was expected to attend
prayer-meetings, and speak at them.   I was expected to be always ready for every effort in christian work, and the sense of these expectations bowed
me down continually.   At last it became so unspeakably burdensome to me to live the sort of
christian life I had entered upon, and was expected
by all around me to live, that I felt as if any kind of
manual labor would have been easier, and I would
have preferred, infinitely, scrubbing all day on my
hands and knees, to being compelled to go through
the treadmill of my daily christian work.   I envied," she said, "the servants in the kitchen, and the
women at the wash-tubs."

This may seem to some like a strong statement :
but does it not present a vivid picture of some of
your own experiences, dear christian ?   Have you
never gone to your work as a slave to his daily task,
knowing it to be your duty, and that therefore you
must do it, but rebounding like an india-rubber ball

back into your real interests and pleasures the moment your work was over?

Of course you have known this was the wrong way to feel, and have been ashamed of it from the bottom of your heart, but still you have seen no way to help it. You have not *loved* your work, and, could you have done so with an easy conscience, you would have been glad to have given it up altogether.

Or, if this does not describe your case, perhaps another picture will. You do love your work in the abstract; but, in the doing of it, you find so many cares and responsibilities connected with it, so many misgivings and doubts as to your own capacity or fitness, that it becomes a very heavy burden, and you go to it bowed down and weary, before the labor has even begun. Then also you are continually distressing yourself about the results of your work, and greatly troubled if they are not just what you would like, and this of itself is a constant burden.

Now from all these forms of bondage the soul is entirely delivered that enters fully into the blessed life of faith. In the first place, service of any sort becomes delightful to it, because, having surrendered its will into the keeping of the Lord, He works in it to will and to do of His good pleasure, and the soul finds itself really *wanting* to do the things God wants it to do. It is always very pleasant to do the things we *want* to do, let them be ever so difficult of accomplishment, or involve ever so much of bodily weariness. If a man's *will* is really set on a thing, he regards with a sublime indifference the obstacles that lie in the way of his reaching it, and laughs to himself at the idea of any opposition or difficulties hindering him. How many men have gone gladly and thankfully to the ends of the world in search of worldly fortunes, or to fulfil worldly ambitions, and have scorned the thoughts of any cross connected with it! How many mothers have congratulated themselves and rejoiced over the honor done their sons in being promoted to some place of power and usefulness in their country's service, although it has involved perhaps years of separation, and a life of hardship for their dear ones! And yet these same men and these very mothers would have felt and said that they were taking up crosses too heavy almost to be borne, had the service of Christ required the same sacrifice of home, and friends, and worldly ease. It is altogether the way we look at things, whether we think they are crosses or not. And I am ashamed to think that any christian should ever put on a long face and shed tears over doing a thing for Christ, which a worldly man would be only too glad to do for money.

What we need in the christian life is to get believers to *want* to do God's will, as much as other people want to do their own will. And this is the idea of the Gospel. It is what God intended for us; and it is what He has promised. In describing the new covenant in Heb. viii. 6–13, He says it shall no more be the old covenant made on Sinai, that is, a law given from the outside, controlling a man by force, but it shall be a law written *within*.

constraining a man by love. "I will put my laws,"
He says, "in their mind, and write them in their
hearts." This can mean nothing but that we shall
love His law, for anything written on our hearts we
must love. And putting it into our minds is surely
the same as God working in us to "will and to do of
His good pleasure," and means that we shall will
what God wills, and shall obey His sweet commands,
not because it is our duty to do so, but because we
ourselves want to do what He wants us to do.
Nothing could possibly be conceived more effectual
than this. How often have we thought when dealing with our children, "Oh, if I could only get inside
of them and make them *want* to do just what I want,
how easy it would be to manage them then !" And
how often practically in experience we have found
that, to deal with cross-grained people, we must carefully avoid suggesting our wishes to them, but must
in some way induce them to suggest them themselves,
sure that then there will be no opposition to contend
with. And we, who are by nature a stiff-necked people, always rebel more or less against a law from
outside of us, while we joyfully embrace the same
law springing up within.

God's plan for us therefore is to get possession of
the inside of a man, to take the control and management of his will, and to work it for him; and then
obedience is easy and a delight, and service becomes
perfect freedom, until the christian is forced to ex-
claim, "This happy service ! Who could dream
earth had such liberty ? "

What you need to do then, dear christian, if you are in bondage, is to put your will over completely into the hands of your Lord, surrendering to Him the entire control of it. Say, "Yes, Lord, YES!" to everything; and trust Him so to work in you to will, as to bring your whole wishes and affections into conformity with His own sweet and lovable and most lovely will. I have seen this done over and over, in cases where it looked beforehand an utterly impossible thing. In one case, where a lady had been for years rebelling fearfully against a thing which she knew was right, but which she hated, I saw her, out of the depths of despair and without any feeling, give her will in that matter up into the hands of her Lord, and begin to say to Him, "Thy will be done; *Thy will be done!*" And in one short hour that very thing began to look sweet and precious to her. It is wonderful what miracles God works in wills that are utterly surrendered to Him. He turns hard things into easy, and bitter things into sweet. It is not that He puts easy things in the place of the hard, but He actually changes the hard thing into an easy one. And this is salvation. It is grand. Do try it, you who are going about your daily christian living as to a hard and weary task, and see if your divine Master will not transform the very life you live now as a bondage, into the most delicious liberty!

Or again, if you do love His will in the abstract, but find the doing of it hard and burdensome, from this also there is deliverance in the wonderful life of faith. For in this life no burdens are carried, nor anxieties felt. The Lord is our burden-bearer, and upon Him we must lay off every care. He says, in effect, Be careful for nothing, but just make your requests known to Me, and I will attend to them all. Be careful for *nothing*, He says, not even your service. Above all, I should think, our service, because we know ourselves to be so utterly helpless in this, that even if we were careful, it would not amount to anything. What have we to do with thinking whether we are fit or not! The Master-workman surely has a right to use any tool He pleases for His own work, and it is plainly not the business of the tool to decide whether it is the right one to be used or not. He knows; and if He chooses to use us, of course we must be fit. And in truth, if we only knew it, our chiefest fitness is in our utter helplessness. His strength can only be made perfect in our weakness. I can give you a convincing illustration of this.

I was once visiting an idiot asylum and looking at the children going through dumb-bell exercises. Now we all know that it is a very difficult thing for idiots to manage their movements. They have strength enough, generally, but no skill to use this strength, and as a consequence cannot do much. And in these dumb-bell exercises this deficiency was very apparent. They made all sorts of awkward movements. Now and then, by a happy chance, they would make a movement in harmony with the music and the teacher's directions, but for the most part all was out of

harmony. One little girl, however, I noticed, who
made perfect movements. Not a jar nor a break
disturbed the harmony of her exercises. And the
reason was, not that she had more strength than the
others, but that she had no strength at all. She
could not so much as close her hands over the
dumb-bells, nor lift her arms, and the master had to
stand behind her and do it all. She yielded up her
members as instruments to him, and his strength
was made perfect in her weakness. He knew how
to go through those exercises, for he himself had
planned them, and therefore when he did it, it was
done right. She did nothing but yield herself up
utterly into his hands, and he did it all. The yielding
was her part, the responsibility was all his. It was
not her skill that was needed to make harmonious
movements, but only his. The question was not of
her capacity, but of his. Her utter weakness was her
greatest strength. And if this is a picture of our
christian life, it is no wonder that Paul could say,
" Most gladly therefore will I rather *glory* in my
infirmities, that the power of Christ may rest upon
me." Who would not glory in being so utterly weak
and helpless, that the Lord Jesus Christ should find
no hindrance to the perfect working of His mighty
power through us and in us?

Then, too, if the work is His, the responsibility is
His, and we have no room left for worrying about
it. Everything in reference to it is known to Him,
and He can manage it all. Why not leave it all with
Him then, and consent to be treated like a child

and guided where to go? It is a fact that the most effectual workers I know are those who do not feel the least care or anxiety about their work, but who commit it all to their dear Master, and, asking Him to guide them moment by moment in reference to it, trust Him implicitly for each moment's needed supplies of wisdom and of strength. To see such, you would almost think perhaps that they were too free from care, where such mighty interests are at stake. But when you have learned God's secret of trusting, and see the beauty and the power of that life which is yielded up to His working, you will cease to condemn, and will begin to wonder how any of God's workers can dare to carry burdens, or assume responsibilities which He alone is able to bear.

There are one or two other bonds of service from which this life of trust delivers us. We find out that we are not responsible for all the work in the world. The commands cease to be general, and become personal and individual. The Master does not map out a general course of action for us and leave us to get along through it by our own wisdom and skill as best we may, but He leads us step by step, giving us each hour the special guidance needed for that hour. His blessed Spirit dwelling in us, brings to our remembrance *at the time* the necessary command; so that we do not need to take any thought ahead, but simply to take each step as it is made known to us, following our Lord whithersoever He leads us. "The *steps* of a good man are ordered of the Lord" not his way only, but each separate step in that

way. Many christians make the mistake of expecting to receive God's commands all in a lump, as it
were. They think because He tells them to give a
tract to one person in a railway train, for instance,
that He means them always to give tracts to every-
body, and they burden themselves with an impossible
command.

There was a young christian once, who, because
the Lord had sent her to speak a message to one
soul whom she met in a walk, took it as a general
command for always, and thought she must speak to
every one she met about their souls. This was, of
course, impossible, and as a consequence she was
soon in hopeless bondage about it. She became
absolutely afraid to go outside of her own door, and
lived in perpetual condemnation. At last she dis-
closed her distress to a friend who was instructed in
the ways of God with His servants, and this friend
told her she was making a great mistake; that the
Lord had His own especial work for each especial
workman, and that the servants in a well-regulated
household might as well each one take it upon himself to try and do the work of all the rest, as for
the Lord's servants to think they were each one
under obligation to do everything. He told her just
to put herself under the Lord's personal guidance as
to her work, and trust Him to point out to her each
particular person to whom He would have her speak,
assuring her that He never puts forth His own sheep
without going before them, and making a way for
them Himself. She followed this advice, and laid

the burden of her work on the Lord, and the result was a happy pathway of daily guidance, in which she was led into much blessed work for her Master, but was able to do it all without a care or a burden, because He led her out and prepared the way before her.

Putting ourselves into God's hands in this way, seems to me just like making the junction between the machinery and the steam engine. The power is not in the machinery, but in the steam; disconnected from the engine, the machinery is perfectly useless; but let the connection be made, and the machinery goes easily and without effort, because of the mighty power there is behind it. Thus the christian life becomes an easy, natural life when it is the development of the divine working within. Most christians live on a strain, because their wills are not fully in harmony with the will of God, the connection is not perfectly made at every point, and it requires an effort to move the machinery. But when once the connection is fully made, and the law of the Spirit of life in Christ Jesus can work in us with all its mighty power, we are then indeed made free from the law of sin and death, and shall know the glorious liberty of the children of God. We shall lead *frictionless* lives.

Another form of bondage as to service, from which the life of faith delivers the soul, is in reference to the after-reflections which always follow any christian work. These self-reflections are of two sorts. Either the soul congratulates itself upon its success, and is lifted up; or it is distressed over its failure, and is utterly cast down. One of these is *sure* to come, and of the two I think the first is the more to be dreaded, although the last causes at the time the greater suffering. But in the life of trust, neither will trouble us; for, having committed ourselves and our work to the Lord, we will be satisfied to leave it to Him, and will not think about ourselves in the matter at all.

Years ago I came across this sentence in an old book: "Never indulge, at the close of an action, in any self-reflective acts of any kind. whether of self-congratulation or of self-despair. Forget the things that are behind, the moment they are past, leaving them with God." It has been of unspeakable value to me. When the temptation comes, as it always does, to indulge in these reflections, either of one sort or the other, I turn from them at once, and positively refuse to think about my work at all, leaving it with the Lord to overrule the mistakes, and to bless it as He chooses.

To sum it all up then, what is needed for happy and effectual service is simply to put your work into the Lord's hands, and leave it there. Do not take it to Him in prayer, saying, "Lord, guide me; Lord, give me wisdom; Lord, arrange for me," and then arise from your knees, and take the burden all back, and try to guide and arrange for yourself. *Leave* it with the Lord, and remember that what you trust to Him, you must not worry over nor feel anxious about. Trust and worry cannot go together. If your work is a burden, it is because you are not trusting it to Him. But if you do trust it to Him, you will surely find that the yoke He puts upon you is easy, and the burden He gives you to carry is light, and even in the midst of a life of ceaseless activity you shall find rest to your soul.

But some may say that this teaching would make us into mere puppets. I answer, No, it would simply make us into servants. It is required of a servant, not that he shall plan, or arrange, or decide, or supply the necessary material, but simply and only that he shall obey. It is for the Master to do all the rest. The servant is not responsible, either, for results. The Master alone knows what results he wished to have produced, and therefore he alone can judge of them. Intelligent service will, of course, include some degree of intelligent sympathy with the thoughts and plans of the Master, but after all there cannot be a full comprehension, and the responsibility cannot be transferred from the Master's shoulders to the servant's. And in our case, where our outlook is so limited and our ignorance so great, we can do very little more than be in harmony with the will of our Divine Master, without expecting to comprehend it very fully, and we *must* leave all the results with Him. What looks to us like failure on the seen side, is often, on the unseen side, the most glorious success; and if we allow ourselves to lament and worry, we shall often be doing the foolish and useless thing of weeping where we ought to be singing and rejoicing.

Far better is it to refuse utterly to indulge in any self-reflective acts at all; to refuse, in fact, to think about self in any way, whether for good or evil. We are not our own property, nor our own business. We belong to God, and are His instruments and His business; and since He always attends to His own business, He will of course attend to us.

I heard once of a slave who was on board a vessel in a violent storm, and who was whistling contentedly while every one else was in an agony of terror. At last some one asked him if he was not afraid he would be drowned. He replied with a broad grin, " Well, missus, s'pose I is. I don't b'long to myself, and it will only be massa's loss any how."

Something of this spirit would deliver us from many of our perplexities and sufferings in service. And with a band of servants thus abandoned to our Master's use and to His care, what might He not accomplish? Truly one such would " chase a thousand, and two would put ten thousand to flight"; and nothing would be impossible to them. For it is nothing with the Lord "to help, whether with many or with them that have no power."

May God raise up such an army speedily !

And may you, my dear reader, enroll your name in this army to-day, and, yielding yourself unto God as one who is alive from the dead, may every one of your members be also yielded unto Him as instruments of righteousness, to be used by Him as He pleases.

CHAPTER XI.

DIFFICULTIES CONCERNING GUIDANCE.

YOU have now begun, dear reader, the life of faith. You have given yourself to the Lord to be His wholly and altogether, and He has taken you and has begun to mould and fashion you into a vessel unto His honor. Your one most earnest desire is to be very pliable in His hands, and to follow Him whithersoever He may lead you, and you are trusting Him to work in you to will and to do of His good pleasure. But you find a great difficulty here. You have not learned yet to know the voice of the Good Shepherd, and are therefore in great doubt and perplexity as to what really is His will concerning you.

Perhaps there are certain paths into which God seems to be calling you, of which your friends utterly disapprove. And these friends, it may be, are older than yourself in the christian life, and seem to you also to be much further advanced. You can scarcely

bear to differ from them or distress them ; and you feel
also very diffident of yielding to any seeming impressions of duty of which they do not approve.   And yet
you cannot get rid of these impressions, and you are
plunged into great doubt and uneasiness.

There is a way out of all these difficulties, to the
fully surrendered soul.   I would repeat, *fully* surrendered, because if there is any reserve of will upon any
point, it becomes almost impossible to find out the
mind of God in reference to that point; and therefore
the first thing is to be sure that you really do *purpose*
to obey the Lord in every respect.   If however this is
the case, and your soul only needs to know the will of
God in order to consent to it, then you surely cannot
doubt His willingness to make His will known, and to
guide you in the right paths.   There are many very
clear promises in reference to this. Take, for instance,
John x. 3, 4 : "He calleth His own sheep by name,
and leadeth them out.   And when He putteth forth
His own sheep He goeth before them, and the sheep
follow Him, for they know His voice."   Or, John xiv.
26 : "But the Comforter, which is the Holy Ghost,
whom the Father will send in my name, He shall teach
you all things, and bring all things to your remembrance, whatsoever I have said unto you."   Or, James
i. 5, 6 : "If any of you lack wisdom, let Him ask of
God, that giveth to all men liberally, and upbraideth
not ; and it shall be given him."   With such passages
as these, and many more like them, we must believe
that Divine guidance is promised to us, and our faith
must confidently look for and expect it.   This is essen-

tial ; for in James i. 6, 7, we are told, " Let him ask in faith nothing wavering.   For he that wavereth is like a wave of the sea, driven with the wind and tossed. For let not such a man think that he shall receive anything of the Lord."

Settle this point then first of all, that Divine guidance has been promised, and that you are sure to have it, if you ask for it; and let no suggestion of doubt turn you from this.

Next, you must remember that our God has all knowledge and all wisdom, and that therefore it is very possible He may guide you into paths wherein *He* knows great blessings are awaiting you, but which to the short-sighted human eyes around you seem sure to result in confusion and loss.   You must recognize the fact that God's thoughts are not as man's thoughts, nor His ways as man's ways ; and that He who knows the end of things from the beginning, alone can judge of what the results of any course of action may be.   You must therefore realize that His very love for you may perhaps lead you to run counter to the loving wishes of even your dearest friends.   You must learn from Luke xiv. 26-33, and similar passages, that in order, not to be saved only, but to be a disciple or follower of your Lord, you may perhaps be called upon to forsake all that you have, and to turn your backs on even father or mother, or brother or sister, or husband or wife, or it may be your own life also.   Unless the possibility of this is clearly recognized, the soul would be very likely to get into difficulty, because it often happens that the

child of God who enters upon this life of obedience is
sooner or later led into paths which meet with the
disapproval of those he best loves ; and unless he is
prepared for this, and can trust the Lord through it
all, he will scarcely know what to do.

All this, it will of course be understood, is perfectly in harmony with those duties of honor and love
which we owe to one another in the various relations
of life.   The nearer we are to Christ, the more shall
we be enabled to exemplify the meekness and gentleness of our Lord, and the more tender will be our
consideration for those who are our natural guardians
and counsellors.   The Master's guidance will always
manifest itself by the Master's Spirit, and where, in
obedience to Him, we are led to act contrary to
the advice or wishes of our friends, we shall prove
that this is our motive, by the love and patience
which will mark our conduct.

But this point having been settled, we come now
to the question as to how God's guidance is to come
to us, and how we shall be able to know His voice.

There are four especial ways in which God speaks ·
by the voice of Scripture, the voice of the inward
impressions of the Holy Spirit, the voice of our own
higher judgment, and the voice of providential circumstances.

Where these four harmonize, it is safe to say that
God speaks.   For I lay it down as a foundation
principle, which no one can gainsay, that of course
His voice will always be in harmony with itself, no
matter in how many different ways He may speak.

The voices may be many, the message can be but one. If God tells me in one voice to do or to leave undone anything, He cannot possibly tell me the opposite in another voice. If there is a contradiction in the voices, the speaker cannot be the same. Therefore, my rule for distinguishing the voice of God would be to bring it to the test of this harmony.

If I have an impression, therefore, I must see if it is in accordance with Scripture, and whether it commends itself to my own higher judgment, and also whether, as we Quakers say, "way opens" for its carrying out. If either one of these tests fail, it is not safe to proceed; but I must wait in quiet trust until the Lord shows me the point of harmony, which He surely will, sooner or later, if it is His voice that has spoken.

For we must not overlook the fact that there are other voices that speak to the soul. There is the loud and clamoring voice of self, that is always seeking to be heard. And there are the voices, too, of evil and deceiving spirits, who lie in wait to entrap every traveller entering these higher regions of the spiritual life. In the same epistle which tells us that we are seated in "heavenly places in Christ" (Eph. ii. 6), we are also told that we shall have to fight there with spiritual enemies (Eph. vi. 12). These spiritual enemies, whoever or whatever they may be, must necessarily communicate with us by means of our spiritual faculties, and their voices, therefore, will be, as the voice of God is, an inward

impression made upon our spirits.   Therefore, just
as the Holy Spirit may tell us, by impressions, what
is the will of God concerning us, so also will these
spiritual enemies tell us, by impressions, what is their
will concerning us, though not of course giving it
their name.   It is very plain, therefore, that we must
have some test or standard by which to try these
inward impressions, in order that we may know
whose voice it is that is speaking.   And that test
will always be the harmony to which I have referred.
Sometimes, under a mistaken idea of exalting the
Divine Spirit, earnest and honest christians have
ignored and even violated the teachings of Scripture,
have disregarded the plain pointings of Providence,
and have outraged their own higher judgment.   God,
who sees the sincerity of their hearts, can and does
pity and forgive, but the consequences as to this life
are often very sad.

Our first test, therefore, of the Divine authority of
any voice which may seem to speak to us, must be its
harmony in moral character with the mind and will
of God, as revealed to us in the Gospel of Christ.
Whatever is contrary to this, cannot be Divine,
because God cannot contradict Himself.

Until we have found and obeyed God's will in
reference to any subject, as it is revealed in the
Bible, we cannot expect a separate direct personal
revelation.   A great many fatal mistakes are made
in this matter of guidance, by the overlooking of this
simple rule.   Where our Father has written out for
us plain directions about anything, He will not of

course, make an especial revelation to us concerning it. No man, for instance, needs or could expect any direct revelation to tell him not to steal, because God has already in the Scriptures plainly declared His will about it. This seems such an obvious thing that I would not speak of it, but that I have frequently met with christians who have altogether overlooked it, and have gone off into fanaticism as the result. For the Scriptures are far more explicit even about details than most people think. And there are not many important affairs in life for which a clear direction may not be found in God's book. Take the matter of dress, and we have 1 Pet. iii. 3, 4, and 1 Tim. ii. 9, 10. Take the matter of conversation, and we have Eph. iv. 29, and v. 4. Take the matter of avenging injuries and standing up for your rights, and we have Rom. xii. 19, 20, 21, and Matt. v. 38–48, and 1 Pet. ii. 19–21. Take the matter of forgiving one another, and we have Eph. iv. 32, and Mark xi. 25, 26. Take the matter of conformity to the world, and we have Rom. xii. 2, and 1 John ii. 15–17, and James iv. 4. Take the matter of anxieties of all kind, and we have Matt. vi. 25–34, and Phil. iv. 6, 7.

I only give these as examples to show how very full and practical the Bible guidance is. If, therefore, you find yourself in perplexity, first of all search and see whether the Bible speaks on the point in question, asking God to make plain to you by the power of His Spirit, through the Scriptures, what is His mind. And whatever shall seem to you to be plainly taught there, that you must obey.

When we read and meditate upon this record of God's mind and will, with our understandings thus illuminated by the inspiring Spirit, our obedience will be as truly an obedience to a present, living word, as though it were afresh spoken to us to-day by our Lord from Heaven.   The Bible is not only an ancient message from God sent to us many ages ago, but it is a present message sent to us now each time we read it. " The words that I speak unto you, they are spirit, and they are life," and obedience to these words now is a living obedience to a present and personal command.

But it is essential in this connection to remember that the Bible is a book of principles, and not a book of disjointed aphorisms.   Isolated texts may often be made to sanction things, to which the principles of Scripture are totally opposed.   I heard not long ago of a christian woman in a Western meeting, who, having had the text, " For we walk by faith, and not by sight," brought very vividly before her mind, felt a strong impression that it was a command to be literally obeyed in the outward ; and, blindfolding her eyes, insisted on walking up and down the aisle of the meeting-house, as an illustration of the walk of faith.   She very soon stumbled and fell against the stove, burning herself seriously, and then wondered at the mysterious dispensation. The *principles* of Scripture, and her own sanctified common-sense, if applied to this case, would have saved her from the delusion.

The second test, therefore, to which our impressions

must be brought, is that of our own higher judgment, or common-sense.

It is as true now as in the days when Solomon wrote, that a "man of *understanding* shall attain unto wise counsels"; and his exhortation still continues binding upon us: "Wisdom is the principal thing, therefore get wisdom; and with all thy getting, get *understanding.*"

As far as I can see, the Scriptures everywhere make it an essential thing for the children of God to use all the faculties which have been given them, in their journey through this world. They are to use their outward faculties for their outward walk, and their inward faculties for their inward walk. And they might as well expect to be "kept" from dashing their feet against a stone in the outward, if they walk blindfold, as to be "kept" from spiritual stumbling, if they put aside their judgment and common-sense in their interior life.

I asked a christian of "sound mind" lately how she distinguished between the voice of false spirits and the guidance of the Holy Spirit, and she replied promptly, "I rap them over the head, and see if they have any common-sense."

Some, however, may say here, "But I thought we were not to depend on our human understanding in Divine things." I answer to this, that we are not to depend on our unenlightened human understanding, but upon our human judgment and common-sense, enlightened by the Spirit of God. That is, God will speak to us through the faculties He has

Himself given us, and not independently of them. That is, just as we are to use our eyes when we walk, no matter how full of faith we may be, so also we are to use our mental faculties in our inward life.

The third and last test to which our impressions must be brought is that of providential circumstances. If a "leading" is of God, way will always open for it. Our Lord assures us of this when He says in John 10. 4, "And when He putteth forth His own sheep *He goeth before them*, and the sheep *follow* Him, for they know his voice." Notice here the expression "goeth before," and "follow." He goes before to open a way, and we are to follow in the way thus opened. It is never a sign of a Divine leading when the christian insists on opening his own way, and riding rough-shod over all opposing things. If the Lord "goes before" us, He will open all doors for us, and we shall not need ourselves to hammer them down.

The fourth point I would make is this: that, just as our impressions must be tested, as I have shown, by the other three voices, so must these other voices be tested by our inward impressions; and if we feel a "stop in our minds" about anything, we must wait until that is removed before acting. A christian who had advanced with unusual rapidity in the Divine life, gave me as her secret this simple receipt: "I always mind the checks." We must not ignore the voice of our inward impressions, nor ride rough-shod over them, any more than we must the other three voices of which I have spoken

These four voices, then, will always be found to agree in any truly Divine leading, *i. e.*, the voice of our impressions, the voice of Scripture, the voice of our own sanctified judgment, and the voice of providential circumstances; and where these four do not all agree at first, we must wait until they do.

A divine sense of "oughtness," derived from the harmony of all God's various voices, is the only safe foundation for any action.

And now I have guarded the points of danger, do permit me to let myself out for a little to the blessedness and joy of this direct communication of God's will to us. It seems to me to be the grandest of privileges. In the first place, that God should love me enough to *care* about the details of my life is perfectly wonderful. And then that He should be willing to tell me all about it, and to let me know just now to live and walk so as to perfectly please Him, seems almost too good to be true. We never care about the little details of people's lives unless we love them. It is a matter of indifference to us with the majority of people we meet, as to what they do or how they spend their time; but as soon as we begin to love any one, we begin at once to care. That God cares, therefore, is just a precious proof of His love; and it is most blessed to have Him speak to us about everything in our lives, about our duties, about our pleasures, about our friendships, about our occupations, about all that we do, or think, or say. You *must* know this in your own experience, dear reader, if you would come into the full joy and privilege of this life hid with Christ in God, for it is one of its most precious gifts !

God's promise is, that He will work in us to *will* as well as to do of His good pleasure.   This, of course, means that He will take possession of our will, and work it for us, and that His suggestions will come to us, not so much commands from the outside, as desires springing up within.   They will originate in our will ; we shall feel as though we *wanted* to do so and so, not as though we *must*.   And this makes it a service of perfect liberty ; for it is always easy to do what we desire to do, let the accompanying circumstances be as difficult as they may.   Every mother knows that she could secure perfect and easy obedience in her child, if she could only get into that child's will and work it for him, making him want himself to do the things she willed he should.   And this is what our Father does for His children in the new dispensation ; He writes His laws on our hearts and on our minds, and we love them, and are drawn to our obedience by our affections and judgment, not driven by our fears.

The way in which the Holy Spirit, therefore, usually works in His direct guidance is to impress upon the mind a wish or desire to do or leave undone certain things.

The soul when engaged, perhaps, in prayer, feels a sudden suggestion made to its inmost consciousness in reference to a certain point of duty.   "I would like to do this or the other," it thinks, "I wish I could."   Or perhaps the suggestion may come as

a question, " I wonder whether I had not better do so
and so?" Or it may be only at first in the way of
a conviction that such is the right and best thing to
be done.

At once the matter should be committed to the
Lord, with an instant consent of the will to obey
Him; and if the suggestion is in accordance with the
Scriptures, and a sanctified judgment, and with Providential circumstances, an immediate obedience is
the safest and easiest course. At the moment when
the Spirit speaks, it is always easy to obey; if the
soul hesitates and begins to reason, it becomes more
and more difficult continually. As a general rule,
the first convictions are the right ones in a fully surrendered heart; for God is faithful in His dealings
with us, and will cause His voice to be heard before any other voices. Such convictions, therefore,
should never be met by reasoning. Prayer and trust
are the only safe attitudes of the soul; and even
these should be but momentary, as it were, lest the
time for action should pass and the blessing be
missed.

If, however, the suggestion does not seem quite
clear enough to act upon, and doubt and perplexity
ensue, especially if it is something about which
one's friends hold a different opinion, then we shall
need to wait for further light. The Scripture rule is,
"Whatsoever is not of faith is sin"; which means
plainly that we must never act in doubt. A clear
conviction of right is the only safe guide. But we
must wait in faith, and in an attitude of entire sur-

render, saying, "Yes," continually to the will of our Lord, whatever it may be. I believe the lack of a will thus surrendered lies at the root of many of our difficulties; and next to this lies the want of faith in any real Divine guidance. God's children are amazingly sceptical here. They read the promises and they feel the need, but somehow they cannot seem to believe the guidance will be given to them; as if God should want us to obey His voice, but did not know how to make us hear and understand Him. It is, therefore, very possible for God to speak, but for the soul not to hear, because it does not believe He is speaking. No earthly parent or master could possibly guide his children or servants, if they should refuse to believe he was speaking, and should not accept his voice as being really the expression of his will.

> "God, who at sundry times and in manners many,
>   Spake to the fathers and is speaking still,
> Eager to see if ever or if any
>   Souls will obey and hearken to His will."

Every moment of our lives our Father is seeking to reveal Himself to us. "I that speak unto thee am He   I that speak in thy heart, I that speak in thy outward circumstances, I that speak in thy losses, I that speak in thy gains, I that speak in thy sorrows or in thy joys, I that speak everywhere and in everything, *I am He.*"

We must, therefore, have perfect confidence that the Lord's voice *is* speaking to us to teach and lead us, and that He will give us the wisdom needed for our right guidance; and when we have asked for light, we must accept our strongest conviction of "oughtness" as being the guidance we have sought. A few rules will help us here.

I.   We must believe that God will guide us.

II.   We must surrender our own will to His guidance.

III.   We must hearken for the Divine voice.

IV.   We must wait for the divine harmony.

V.   When we are sure of the guidance, we must obey without question.

> "God only is the creature's home;
>   Though rough and strait the road,
> Yet nothing less can satisfy
>   The love that longs for God.
>
> "How little of that road, my soul!
>   How little hast thou gone!
> Take heart, and let the thought of God
>   Allure thee further on.
>
> 'The perfect way is hard to flesh;
>   It is not hard to love;
> If thou wert sick for want of God,
>   How swiftly wouldst thou move
>
> "Dole not thy duties out to God,
>   But let thy hand be free;
> Look long at Jesus, His sweet love,
>   How was it dealt to thee?
>
> "And only this perfection needs
>   A heart kept calm all day,
> To catch the words the spirit there
>   From hour to hour may say.

"Then keep thy conscience sensitive,
  No inward token miss :
And go where grace entices thee —
  Perfection lies in this.

"Be docile to thine unseen Guide,
  Love Him as He loves thee;
Time and obedience are enough,
  And thou a saint shalt be."

CHAPTER XII.

CONCERNING TEMPTATION.

CERTAIN very great mistakes are made concerning this matter of temptation, in the practical working out of this life of faith.

First of all, people seem to expect that, after the soul has entered into its rest in God, temptations will cease; and to think that the promised deliverance is not only to be from yielding to temptation, but even also from being tempted. Consequently, when they find the Canaanite still in the land, and see the cities great and walled up to Heaven, they are utterly discouraged, and think they must have gone wrong in some way, and that this cannot be the true land after all.

Then, next they make the mistake of looking upon temptation as sin, and of blaming themselves for what in reality is the fault of the enemy only This brings them into condemnation and discouragement; and discouragement, if continued in, always ends at last in actual sin. The enemy makes an easy prey of a discouraged soul; so that we fall often from the very fear of having fallen.

To meet the first of these difficulties it is only necessary to refer to the Scripture declarations, that the christian life is to be throughout a warfare; and that, especially when seated in heavenly places in Christ Jesus, we are to wrestle against spiritual enemies there, whose power and skill to tempt us must doubtless be far superior to any we have ever heretofore encountered. As a fact, temptations generally increase in strength tenfold after we have entered into the interior life, rather than decrease; and no amount or sort of them must ever for a moment lead us to suppose we have not really found the true abiding place. Strong temptations are generally a sign of great grace, rather than of little grace. When the children of Israel had first left Egypt, the Lord did not lead them through the country of the Philistines, although that was the nearest way; for God said, "lest peradventure the people repent when they see war, and they return to Egypt." But afterwards, when they learned better how to trust Him, He permitted their enemies to attack them. Then also in their wilderness journey they met with but few enemies and fought but few battles, compared to those in the land, where they found seven great nations and thirty-one kings to be conquered, besides walled cities to be taken, and giants to be overcome.

They could not have fought with the Canaanites, and the Hittites, and the Amorites, and the Periztes, and the Hivites, and the Jebusites, until they had gone into the land where these enemies were. And the very power of your temptations, dear christian, therefore, may perhaps be one of the strongest proofs that you really are in the land you have been seeking to enter, because they are temptations peculiar to that land. You must never allow your temptations to cause you to question the fact of your having entered the promised "heavenly places."

The second mistake is not quite so easy to deal with. It seems hardly worth while to say that temptation is not sin, and yet most of the distress about it arises from not understanding this fact. The very suggestion of wrong seems to bring pollution with it, and the evil agency not being recognized, the poor tempted soul begins to feel as if it must be very bad indeed, and very far off from God to have had such thoughts and suggestions. It is as though a burglar should break into a man's house to steal, and, when the master of the house began to resist him and to drive him out, should turn round and accuse the owner of being himself the thief. It is the enemy's grand ruse for entrapping us. He comes and whispers suggestions of evil to us, doubts, blasphemies, jealousies, envyings, and pride; and then turns round and says, "Oh, how wicked you must be to think of such things! It is very plain that you are not trusting the Lord; for if you were, it would have been impossible for these things to have entered your heart." This reasoning sounds so very plausible that the soul often accepts it as true, and at once comes under condemnation, and is filled with discouragement; then it is easy for it to be led on into actual sin. One of the most fatal things in the life of faith is discouragement. One of the most helpful is cheerfulness. A very wise man once said that in overcoming temptations, cheerfulness was the first thing, cheerfulness the second, and cheerfulness the third. We must *expect* to conquer. That is why the Lord said so often to Joshua, " Be strong and of a good courage "; " Be not afraid, neither be thou dismayed "; " Only be thou strong and very courageous." And it is also the reason He says to us, " Let not your heart he troubled, neither let it be afraid." The power of temptation is in the fainting of our own hearts. The enemy knows this well, and always begins his assaults by discouraging us, if it can in any way be accomplished.

Sometimes this discouragement arises from what we think is a righteous grief and disgust at ourselves that such things *could* be any temptation to us ; but which is really a mortification arising from the fact that we have been indulging in a secret self-congratulation that our tastes were too pure, or our separation from the world was too complete for such things to tempt us. We have expected something from ourselves, and have been sorely disappointed not to find that something there, and are discouraged in consequence. This mortification and discouragement are really a far worse condition than the temptation itself, though they present an appearance of true humility, for they are nothing but the results of wounded self-love. True humility can bear to see its own utter weakness and foolishness revealed. because it never expected anything from itself, and knows that its only hope and expectation must be in God. Therefore, instead of discouraging the soul from trusting, it drives it to a deeper and more utter trust. But the counterfeit humility which springs from self, plunges the soul into the depths of a faithless discouragement, and drives it into the very sin at which it is so distressed.

I remember once hearing an allegory that illustrated this to me wonderfully. Satan called together a council of his servants to consult how they might make a good man sin. One evil spirit started up and said, "I will make him sin." "How will you do it?" asked Satan. "I will set before him the pleasures of sin," was the reply; "I will tell him of its delights and the rich rewards it brings." "Ah," said Satan, "that will not do; he has tried. it, and knows better than that." Then another spirit started up and said, "I will make him sin." "What will you do?" asked Satan. "I will tell him of the pains and sorrows of virtue. I will show him that virtue has no delights, and brings no rewards." "Ah, no!" exclaimed Satan, "that will not do at all; for he has tried it, and knows that 'wisdom's ways *are* ways of pleasantness and all her paths are peace.'" "Well," said another imp, starting up, "I will undertake to make him sin." "And what will you do?" asked Satan, again. "I will discourage his soul," was the short reply. "Ah, that will do," cried Satan,—" that will do ! We shall conquer him now." And they did.

An old writer says, " All discouragement is from the devil " ; and I wish every christian would just take this as a pocket-piece, and never forget it. We must fly from discouragement as we would from sin.

But this is impossible if we fail to recognize the true agency in temptation. For if the temptations are our own fault, we cannot help being discouraged. But they are not. The Bible says, "Blessed is the man that endureth temptation"; and we are exhorted to "count it all joy when we fall into divers temptations." Temptation, therefore, cannot be sin ; and the truth is, it is no more a sin to hear these whispers and suggestions of evil in our souls, than it is for us to hear the swearing or wicked talk of bad men as we pass along the street. The sin only comes in either case by our stopping and joining in with them. If, when the wicked suggestions come, we turn from them at once, as we would from wicked talk, and pay no more attention to them, we do not sin. But if we carry them on in our minds, and roll them under our tongues, and dwell on them with a half-consent of our will to them as true, then we sin. We may be enticed by evil a thousand times a day without sin, and we cannot help these enticings. But if the enemy can succeed in making us think that *his* enticings are *our* sin, he has accomplished half the battle, and can hardly fail to gain a complete victory.

A dear lady once came to me under great darkness, simply from not understanding this. She had
been living very happily in the life of faith for some
time, and had been so free from temptation as almost
to begin to think she would never be tempted any
more. But suddenly a very peculiar form of temptation had assailed her, which had horrified her. She
found that the moment she began to pray, dreadful
thoughts of all kinds would rush into her mind.
She had lived a very sheltered, innocent life, and
these thoughts seemed so awful to her, that she felt
she must be one of the most wicked of sinners to be
capable of having them. She began by thinking she
could not possibly have entered into the rest of faith,
and ended by concluding that she had never even
been born again. Her soul was in an agony of distress. I told her that these dreadful thoughts were
altogether the suggestions of the enemy, who came to
her the moment she kneeled in prayer, and poured
them into her mind, and that she herself was not to
blame for them at all ; that she could not help
them any more than she could help hearing if a wicked
man should pour out his blasphemies in her presence.
And I urged her to recognize and treat them as from
the enemy ; not to blame herself or be discouraged,
but to turn at once to Jesus and commit them to
Him. I showed her how great an advantage the enemy
had gained by making her think these thoughts were
originated by herself, and plunging her into condemnation and discouragement on account of them. And
I assured her she would find a speedy victory if she

would pay no attention to them; but, ignoring their presence, would simply turn her back on them and look to the Lord.

She grasped the truth, and the next time these thoughts came she said to the enemy, "I have found you out now. It is you who are suggesting these dreadful thoughts to me, and I hate them, and will have nothing to do with them. The Lord is my Saviour; take them to Him, and settle them in His presence." Immediately the baffled enemy, finding himself discovered, fled in confusion, and her soul was perfectly delivered.

Another thing also. The enemy knows that if a christian recognizes a suggestion of evil as coming from him, he will recoil from it far more quickly than if it seems to be the suggestion of his own mind. If Satan prefaced each temptation with the words, "I am Satan, your relentless enemy; I have come to make you sin," I suppose we would hardly feel any desire at all to yield to his suggestions. He has to hide himself in order to make his baits attractive. And our victory will be far more easily gained if we are not ignorant of his devices, but recognize him at his very first approach.

We also make another great mistake about temptations in thinking that all time spent in combating them is lost. Hours pass, and we seem to have made no progress, because we have been so beset with temptations. But it often happens that we have been serving God far more truly during these hours, than in our times of comparative freedom from temptation. Temptation is really more the devil's wrath against God, than against us. He cannot touch our Saviour, but he can wound our Saviour by conquering us, and our ruin is important to him only as it accomplishes this. We are, therefore, really fighting our Lord's battles when we are fighting temptation, and hours are often worth days to us under these circumstances. We read, "Blessed is the man that *endureth* temptation"; and I am sure this means enduring the continuance of it and its frequent recurrence. Nothing so cultivates the grace of patience as the endurance of temptation, and nothing so drives the soul to an utter dependence upon the Lord Jesus as its continuance. And finally, nothing brings more praise and honor and glory to our dearest Lord Himself, than the trial of our faith which comes through manifold temptations. We are told that it is more precious than gold, though it be tried with fire, and that we, who patiently endure the trial, shall receive for our reward "the crown of life which the Lord hath promised to them that love Him."

We cannot wonder, therefore, any longer at the exhortation with which the Holy Ghost opens the Book of James: "Count it all joy when ye fall into divers temptations, knowing this, that the trying of your faith worketh patience. But let patience have her perfect work, that ye may be perfect and entire, wanting nothing."

Temptation is plainly to be the blessed instrument used by God to complete our perfection, and thus

the enemy's own weapons are turned against himself, and we see how it is that all things, even temptations, can work together for good to them that love
God.

As to the way of victory over temptations, it
seems hardly necessary to say to 'hose whom I am
at this time especially addressing, that it is to be by
faith.   For this is, of course, the foundation upon
which the whole interior life rests.   Our one great
motto is throughout, "We are nothing, Christ is
all."   And always and everywhere we have started
out to stand, and walk, and overcome, and live by
faith.   We have discovered our own utter helplessness, and know that we cannot do anything for ourselves.   Our only way, therefore, is to hand the
temptation over to our Lord, and trust Him to conquer it for us.   But when we put it into His hands
we must *leave* it there.   It must be as real a committing of ourselves to Him for victory, as it was at first
a committing of ourselves to Him for salvation.   He
must do all for us in the one case, as completely as
in the other.   It was faith only then, and it must be
faith only now.

And the victories which the Lord works in conquering the temptations of those who thus trust
Him are nothing short of miracles, as thousands can
testify.

But into this part of the subject I cannot go at
present, as my object has been rather to present
temptation in its true light, than to develop the way
of victory over it.   I want to deliver conscientious

faithful souls from the bondage into which they are sure to be brought, if they fail to understand the true nature and use of temptation, and confound it with sin. I want that they should not be ignorant of the fact that temptations are, after all, an invaluable part of our soul's development; and that, whatever may be their original source, they are used by God to work out in us many blessed graces of character which would otherwise be lacking. Wherever temptation is, there is God also, superintending and controlling its power. "Where wert thou, Lord! while I was being tempted?" cried the saint of the desert. "Close beside thee, my son, all the while," was the tender reply.

Temptations try us; and we are worth nothing if we are not tried. They develop our spiritual strength and courage and knowledge; and our development is the one thing God cares for. How shallow would all our spirituality be if it were not for temptations. "Blessed is the man that endureth temptation: for when he is tried he shall receive the crown of life, which the Lord hath promised to them that love Him." This "crown of life" will be worth all that it has cost of trial and endurance to obtain it; and without these it could not be attained.

An invalid lady procured once the cocoon of a very beautiful butterfly with unusually magnificent wings hoping to have the pleasure of seeing it emerge from its cocoon in her sick-chamber. She watched it eagerly as spring drew on, and finally was delighted to see the butterfly beginning to emerge.

But it seemed to have great difficulty. It pushed, and strained, and struggled, and seemed to make so little headway, that she concluded it must need some help, and with a pair of delicate scissors she finally clipped the tight cord that seemed to bind in the opening of the cocoon. Immediately the cocoon opened wide, and the butterfly escaped without any further struggle. She congratulated herself on the success of her experiment, but found in a moment that something was the matter with the butterfly. It was all out of the cocoon it is true, but its great wings were lifeless and colorless, and dragged after it as a useless burden. For a few days it lived a miserable sickly life, and then died, without having once lifted its powerless wings. The lady was sorely disappointed and could not understand it. But when she related the circumstance to a naturalist, he told her that it had all been her own fault. That it required just that pushing and struggling to send the life fluid into the veins of the wings, and that her mistaken kindness in shortening the struggle, had left the wings lifeless and colorless.

Just so do our spiritual wings need the struggle and effort of our conflict with temptation and trial; and to grant us an escape from it would be to weaken the power of our soul to "mount up with wings as eagles," and would deprive us of the "crown of life" which is promised to those who endure.

CHAPTER XIII.

FAILURES.

THE very title of this chapter may perhaps startle
some. "Failures," they will say; "we thought
there were no failures in this life of faith!"

To this I would answer that there ought not to be,
and need not be; but, as a fact, there sometimes are.
And we have got to deal with facts, and not with
theories. No teacher of this interior life ever says
that it becomes impossible to sin; they only insist
that sin ceases to be a necessity, and that a possibility of uniform victory is opened before us. And
there are very few who do not confess that, as to
their own actual experience, they have at times been
overcome by momentary temptation.

Of course, in speaking of sin here, I mean conscious, known sin. I do not touch on the subject of
sins of ignorance, or what is called the inevitable sin
of our nature, which are all covered by the atonement, and do not disturb our fellowship with God.
I have no desire nor ability to treat of the *doctrines*

concerning sin; these I will leave with the theolo
gians to discuss and settle, while I speak only of the
believer's experience in the matter. And I wish it
to be fully understood that in all I shall say, I have
reference simply to that which comes within the
range of our consciousness.

Misunderstanding, then, on this point of known or
conscious sin, opens the way for great dangers in the
higher christian life. When a believer, who has, as
he trusts, entered upon the highway of holiness,
finds himself surprised into sin, he is tempted either
to be utterly discouraged, and to give everything up
as lost; or else, in order to preserve the doctrine un-
touched, he feels it necessary to cover his sin up,
calling it infirmity, and refusing to be honest and
above-board about it. Either of these courses is
equally fatal to any real growth and progress in the
life of holiness. The only way is to face the sad
fact at once, call the thing by its right name, and
discover, if possible, the reason and the remedy.
This life of union with God requires the utmost honesty with Him and with ourselves. The communion
which the sin itself would only momentarily disturb,
is sure to be lost by any dishonest dealing with it.
A sudden failure is no reason for being discouraged
and giving up all as lost. Neither is the integrity of
our doctrine touched by it. We are not preaching a
state, but a *walk*. The highway of holiness is not a
place, but a way. Sanctification is not a thing to be
picked up at a certain stage of our experience, and
forever after possessed, but it is a life to be lived

day by day, and hour by hour. We may for a moment turn aside from a path, but the path is not obliterated by our wandering, and can be instantly regained. And in this life and walk of faith, there may be momentary failures, which, although very sad and greatly to be deplored, need not, if rightly met, disturb the attitude of the soul as to entire consecration and perfect trust, nor interrupt, for more than the passing moment, its happy communion with its Lord.

The great point is an instant return to God. Our sin is no reason for ceasing to trust, but only an unanswerable argument why we must trust more fully than ever. From whatever cause we have been betrayed into failure, it is very certain that there is no remedy to be found for it in discouragement. As well might a child who is learning to walk, lie down in despair when he has fallen, and refuse to take another step; as a believer, who is seeking to learn how to live and walk by faith, give up in despair because of having fallen into sin. The only way in both cases is to get right up and try again. When the children of Israel had met with that disastrous defeat, soon after their entrance into the land, before the little city of Ai, they were all so utterly discouraged that we read, "Wherefore the hearts of the people melted, and became as water. And Joshua rent his clothes, and fell to the earth upon his face before the ark of the Lord until the eventide, he and the elders of Israel, and put dust upon their heads. And Joshua said, Alas! O Lord God, wherefore hast

Thou at all brought this people over Jordan to deliver us into the hands of the Amorites to destroy us? Would to God we had been content, and dwelt on the other side Jordan! O Lord, what shall I say, when Israel turneth their backs before their enemies? For the Canaanites and all the inhabitants of the land shall hear of it, and shall environ us round and cut off our name from the earth: and what wilt Thou do unto Thy great name?" What a wail of despair this was! And how exactly it is repeated by many a child of God in the present day, whose heart, because of a defeat, melts and becomes as water, and who cries out, "Would to God we had been content and dwelt on the other side Jordan!" and predicts for itself further failures and even utter discomfiture before its enemies. No doubt Joshua thought then, as we are apt to think now, that discouragement and despair were the only proper and safe condit'on after such a failure. But God thought otherwise. "And the Lord said unto Joshua, Get thee up; wherefore liest thou upon thy face?"

The proper thing to do was not to abandon themselves thus to utter discouragement, humble as it might look, but at once to face the evil and get rid of it, and afresh and immediately to "sanctify themselves." "Up, sanctify the people," is always God's command. "Lie down and be discouraged," is always the enemy's temptation. Our feeling is that it is presumptuous, and even almost impertinent, to go at once to the Lord, after having sinned against Him. It seems as if we ought to suffer the consequences of our sin first for a little while, and endure the accusings of our conscience. And we can hardly believe that the Lord *can* be willing at once to receive us back into loving fellowship with Himself.

A little girl once expressed the feeling to me, with a child's outspoken candor. She had asked whether the Lord Jesus always forgave us for our sins as soon as we asked Him, and I had said, "Yes, of course He does." "*Just* as soon?" she repeated, doubtingly. "Yes," I replied, "the very minute we ask, He forgives us." "Well," she said deliberately, "I cannot believe that. I should think He would make us feel sorry for two or three days first. And then I should think He would make us ask Him a great many times, and in a very pretty way too, not just in common talk. And I believe that *is* the way He does, and you need not try to make me think He forgives me right at once, no matter what the Bible says." She only *said* what most christians *think*, and, what is worse, what most christians act on, making their discouragement and their very remorse separate them infinitely further off from God than their sin would have done. Yet it is so totally contrary to the way we like our children to act towards us, that I wonder how we ever could have conceived such an idea of God. How a mother grieves when a naughty child goes off alone in despairing remorse, and doubts her willingness to forgive; and how, on the other hand, her whole heart goes out in welcoming love to the darling who runs to her at once and begs her forgiveness! Surely our God knew this yearning love when He said to us, " Return, ye backsliding children, and I will heal your backslidings."

The fact is, that the same moment which brings the consciousness of having sinned, ought to bring also the consciousness of being forgiven. This is especially essential to an unwavering walk in the highway of holiness, for no separation from God can be tolerated here for an instant.

We can only walk in this path by looking continually unto Jesus, moment by moment ; and if our eyes are taken off of Him to look upon our own sin and our own weakness, we shall leave the path at once. The believer, therefore, who has, as he trusts, entered upon this highway, if he finds himself overcome by sin, must flee with it instantly to the Lord. He must act on 1 John i. 9 : " If we confess our sins, He is faithful and just to forgive us our sins, and to cleanse us from all unrighteousness." He must not hide his sin and seek to salve it over with excuses, or to push it out of his memory by the lapse of time. But he must do as the children of Israel did, rise up "*early* in the morning," and "*run*" to the place where the evil thing is hidden, and take it out of its hiding-place, and lay it " out before the Lord." He must confess his sin. And then he must stone it with stones, and burn it with fire, and utterly put it away from him, and raise over it a great heap of stones, that it may be forever hidden from his sight. And he must believe, then and there, that God *is*, according to His word, faithful and just to forgive him his sin, and that He does do it; and further, that He also cleanses him from all unrighteousness. He must claim an immediate forgiveness and an immediate cleansing by faith, and must go on trusting harder and more absolutely than ever.

As soon as Israel's sin had been brought to light and put away, at once God's word came again in a message of glorious encouragement, "Fear not, neither be thou dismayed. . . . See, I have given into thy hand the king of Ai, and his people, and his city, and his land." Our courage must rise higher than ever, and we must abandon ourselves more completely to the Lord, that His mighty power may the more perfectly work in us all the good pleasure of His will. Moreover, we must forget our sin as soon as it is thus confessed and forgiven. We must not dwell on it, and examine it, and indulge in a luxury of distress and remorse. We must not put .t on a pedestal, and then walk around it and view it on every side, and so magnify it into a mountain that hides our God from our eyes. We must follow the example of Paul, and "forgetting those things which are behind, and reaching forth unto those things which are before," we must "press toward the mark for the prize of the high calling of God in Christ Jesus."

I would like to bring up two contrastive illustrations of these things. One was an earnest christian man, an active worker in the Church, who had been living for several months in the enjoyment of full salvation. He was suddenly overcome by a tempta-

tion to treat a brother unkindly. Not having supposed it possible that he could ever sin again, he
was at once plunged into the deepest discouragement, and concluded he had been altogether mistaken, and had never entered into the life of full
trust at all.   Day by day his discouragement increased, until it became despair, and he concluded he
had never even been born again, and gave himself
up for lost. He spent three years of utter misery,
going further and further away from God, and being
gradually drawn off into one sin after another, until
his life was a curse to himself and to all around
him.   His health failed under the terrible burden,
and fears were entertained for his reason. At the
end of three years he met a christian lady, who
understood the truth about sin that I have been trying to explain.   In a few. moments' conversation
she found out his trouble, and at once said, "You
sinned in that act, there is no doubt about it, and I
do not want you to try and excuse it. But have
you never confessed it to the Lord and asked Him
to forgive you?" "Confessed it!" he exclaimed,
"why it seems to me I have done nothing but confess it, and entreat God to forgive me night and day
for all these three dreadful years."   "And you have
never believed He did forgive you?" asked the lady.
"No," said the poor man, "how could I, for I never
felt as if He did?"   "But suppose He had said He
forgave you, would not that have done as well as
for you to feel it?"   "Oh, yes," replied the man,
"if God said it, of course I would believe it."

" Very well, He does say so," was the lady's answer,
and she turned to the verse we have taken above
(1 John i. 9) and read it aloud. " Now," she continued, "you have been all these three years confessing and confessing your sin, and all the while
God's record has been declaring that He was faithful
and just to forgive it _nd to cleanse you, and yet
you have never once believed it. You have been
'making God a liar' all this while by refusing to
believe His record."

The poor man saw the whole thing, and was dumb
with amazement and consternation; and when the
lady proposed they should kneel down, and that he
should confess his past unbelief and sin, and should
claim, then and there, a present forgiveness and a
present cleansing, he obeyed like one in a maze.
But the result was glorious. In a few moments the
light broke in, and he burst out into praise at the
wonderful deliverance. In three minutes his soul
was enabled to traverse back by faith the whole
long weary journey that he had been three years in
making, and he found himself once more resting in
Jesus, and rejoicing in the fulness of His salvation.

The other illustration was the case of a christian
lady who had been living in the land of premise
about two weeks, and who had had a very bright
and victorious experience. Suddenly, at the end of
that time, she was overcome by a violent burst of
anger. For a moment a flood of discouragement
swept over her soul. The enemy said, " There, now,
that shows it was all a mistake. Of course you

have been deceived about the whole thing, and have never entered into the life of full trust at all. And now you may as well give up altogether, for you never can consecrate yourself any more entirely, nor trust any more fully, than you did this time; so it is very plain this life of holiness is not for you!" These thoughts flashed through her mind in a moment, but she was well taught in the ways of God, and she said at once, "Yes, I have sinned, and it is very sad. But the Bible says that if we confess our sins, God is faithful and just to forgive us our sins and to cleanse us from all unrighteousness, and I believe He will do it." She did not delay a moment, but while still boiling over with anger, she ran, she could not walk, into a room where she could be alone, and kneeling down beside the bed, she said, "Lord, I confess my sin. I have sinned, I am even at this very moment sinning. I hate it, but I cannot get rid of it. I confess it with shame and confusion of face to Thee. And now I believe that, according to Thy word, Thou dost forgive and Thou dost cleanse." She said it out loud, for the inward turmoil was too great for it to be said inside. As the words "Thou dost forgive and Thou dost cleanse" passed her lips, the deliverance came. The Lord said, "Peace, be still," and there was a great calm. A flood of light and joy burst on her soul, the enemy fled, and she was more than conqueror through Him that loved her. The whole thing, the sin and the recovery from it, had occupied not five minutes, and her feet trod on more firmly than ever in the blessed highway of holiness. Thus the valley of Achor became to her a door of hope, and she sang afresh and with deeper meaning her song of deliverance, " I will sing unto the Lord, for He hath triumphed gloriously."

The truth is, the only remedy, after all, in every emergency, is to trust in the Lord.   And if this is all we ought to do, and all we can do, is it not better to do it at once?   I have often been brought up short by the question, "Well, what can I do but trust ? "   And I have realized at once the folly of seeking for deliverance in any other way, by saying to myself, " I shall have to come to simple trusting in the end, and why not come to it at once now in the beginning ? "   It is a life and walk of *faith* we have entered upon, and if we fail in it our only recovery must lie in an increase of faith, not in a lessening of it.

Let every failure, then, if any occur, drive you instantly to the Lord, with a more complete abandonment and a more perfect trust; and you will find that, sad as they are, they will not take you out of the land of rest, nor permanently interrupt your sweet communion with Him.

And now, having shown the way of deliverance from failure, I want to say a little as to the causes of failure in this life of full salvation.   The causes do not lie in the strength of the temptation nor in our own weakness, nor, above all, in any lack in the power or willingness of our Saviour to save us.   The promise to Israel was positive, " There shall not any man be able to stand before thee all the days of thy life." And the promise to us is equally positive. "God is faithful, who will not suffer you to be tempted above that ye are able; but will with the temptation also make a way of escape that ye may be able to bear it."

The men of Ai were "but few," and yet the people who had conquered the mighty Jericho "fled before the men of Ai." It was not the strength of their enemy, neither had God failed them. The cause of their defeat lay somewhere else, and the Lord Himself declares it, "Israel hath sinned, and they have also transgressed my covenant which I commanded them; for they have even taken of the accursed thing, and have also stolen and dissembled also, and they have put it even among their own stuff. Therefore the children of Israel could not stand before their enemies, but turned their backs upon their enemies." It was a hidden evil that conquered them. Deep down under the earth, in an obscure tent in that vast army, was hidden something against which God had a controversy, and this little hidden thing made the whole army helpless before their enemies. "There is an accursed thing in the midst of thee, O Israel; thou canst not stand before thine enemies until ye take away the accursed thing from among you." The teaching here is simply this, that anything allowed in the heart which is contrary to the will of God, let it seem ever so insignificant, or be ever so deeply hidden, will cause us to fall before our enemies. Any root of bitterness cherished

towards another, any self-seeking and harsh judg·
ments indulged in, any slackness in obeying the
voice of the Lord, any doubtful habits or surroundings, any one of these things will effectually cripple
and paralyze our spiritual life. We may have hidden
the evil in the most remote corner of our hearts, and
may have covered it over from our sight, refusing
even to recognize its existence, of which, however,
we cannot help being all the time secretly aware.
We may steadily ignore it, and persist in declarations
of consecration and full trust, we may be more
earnest than ever in our religious duties, and have
the eyes of our understanding opened more and
more to the truth and the beauty of the life and walk
of faith. We may seem to ourselves and to others
to have reached an almost impregnable position of
victory, and yet we may find ourselves suffering bitter defeats. We may wonder, and question, and
despair, and pray; nothing will do any good until
the accursed thing is dug up from its hiding-place,
brought out to the light, and laid before God. And
the moment a believer who is walking in this interior
life meets with a defeat, he must at once seek for
the cause, not in the strength of that particular
enemy, but in something behind, some hidden want
of consecration lying at the very centre of his being.
Just as a headache is not the disease itself, but only a
symptom of a disease situated in some other part of
the body, so the sin in such a christian is only the
symptom of an evil hidden probably in a very differ·
ent part of his being.

Sometimes the evil may be hidden even in that, which at a cursory glance, would look like good. Beneath apparent zeal for the truth, may be hidden a judging spirit, or a subtle leaning to our own understanding. Beneath apparent christian faithfulness, may be hidden an absence of christian love. Beneath an apparently rightful care for our affairs, may be hidden a great want of trust in God. I believe our blessed Guide, the indwelling Holy Spirit, is always secretly discovering these things to us by continual little twinges and pangs of conscience, so that we are left without excuse. But it is very easy to disregard His gentle voice, and insist upon it to ourselves that all is right; and thus the fatal evil will continue hidden in our midst, causing defeat in most unexpected quarters.

A capital illustration of this occurred to me once in my housekeeping. I had moved into a new house and, in looking over it to see if it was all ready for occupancy, I noticed in the cellar a very clean-looking cider-cask headed up at both ends. I debated with myself whether I should have it taken out of the cellar and opened to see what was in it, but concluded, as it seemed empty and looked nice, to leave it undisturbed, especially as it would have been quite a piece of work to get it up the stairs. I did not feel quite easy, but reasoned away my scruples and left it. Every spring and fall, when house-cleaning time came on, I would remember that cask, with a little twinge of my housewifely conscience, feeling that I could not quite rest in the thought of a perfectly cleaned house, while it remained unopened, for how did I know but under its fair exterior it contained some hidden evil. Still I managed to quiet my scruples on the subject, thinking always of the trouble it would involve to investigate it; and for two or three years the innocent-looking cask stood quietly in my cellar. Then, most unaccountably, moths began to fill my house. I used every possible precaution against them, and made every effort to eradicate them, but in vain. They increased rapidly and threatened to ruin everything I had. I suspected my carpets as being the cause, and subjected them to a thorough cleaning. I suspected my furniture, and had it newly upholstered. I suspected all sorts of impossible things. At last the thought of the cask flashed on me. At once I had it brought up out of the cellar and the head knocked in, and I think it is safe to say that thousands of moths poured out. The previous occupant of the house must have headed it up with something in it which bred moths, and this was the cause of all my trouble.

Now I believe that, in the same way, some innocent-looking habit or indulgence, some apparently unimportant and safe thing, about which we yet have now and then little twinges of conscience, something which is not brought out fairly into the light, and investigated under the searching eye of God, lies at the root of most of the failure in this higher life. *All* is not given up. Some secret corner is kept locked against the entrance of the Lord. And therefore we cannot stand before our enemies, but find ourselves smitten down in their presence.

In order to prevent failure, or to discover its cause if we have failed, it is necessary that we should keep continually before us this prayer, "Search me, O God, and know my heart; try me and know my thoughts; and see if there be any evil way in me, and lead me in the way everlasting."

There may be something very deceptive in our sufferings over our failures. We may seem to ourselves to be wholly occupied with the glory of God, and yet in our inmost souls it may be self alone that occasions all our trouble. Our self-love is touched in a tender spot by the discovery that we are not so saintly as we thought we were; and this chagrin is often a greater sin than the original fault itself.

The only safe way to treat our failures is neither to justify nor condemn ourselves on account of them, but to lay them quietly and in simplicity before the Lord, looking at them in peace and in the spirit of love.

All the old mystic writers tell us that our progress is aided far more by a simple, peaceful turning to God, than by all our chagrin and remorse over our lapses from Him. Only be faithful, they say, in turning quietly to Him alone, the moment you perceive what you have done, and His presence will deliver you from the snares which have entrapped you. To look at self plunges you deeper into the slough, for this very slough is after all nothing but self; while the gentlest look towards God will calm and deliver your heart.

Finally, let us never forget for one moment, no

matter how often we may fail, that the Lord Jesus *is* able, according to the declaration concerning Him, to deliver us out of the hands of our enemies, that we may " serve Him without fear, in holiness and righteousness before Him all the days of our life."

Let us then pray, every one of us, day and night, " Lord, keep us from sinning, and make us living witnesses of Thy mighty power to save to the uttermost " ; and let us never be satisfied until we are so pliable in His hands, and have learned so to trust Him, that He will be able to " make us perfect, in every good work to do His will, working in us that which is well-pleasing in His sight, through Jesus Christ ; to whom be glory for ever and ever. Amen."

CHAPTER XIV.

DOUBTS.

A GREAT many christians are slaves to the habit of doubting. No drunkard was ever more utterly bound by the chains of his fatal habit than they are by theirs. Every step of their whole christian life is taken against the fearful odds of an army of doubts, that are forever lying in wait to assail them at each favorable moment. Their lives are made wretched, their usefulness is effectually hindered, and their communion with God is continually broken by their doubts. And althougl he entrance of the soul upon the life of faith, of which this book treats, does in many cases take it altogether out of the region where these doubts live and flourish; yet even here it sometimes happens that the old tyrant will rise up and reassert his sway, and will cause the feet to stumble and the heart to fail, even when he cannot succeed in utterly turning the believer back into the dreary wilderness again.

We all of us remember, doubtless, the childish fas

cination, and yet horror, of that story of Christian's imprisonment in Doubting Castle by the wicked giant Despair, and our exultant sympathy in his escape through those massive gates and from that cruel tyrant. Little did we suspect then that we should ever find ourselves taken prisoner by the same giant, and imprisoned in the same castle. And yet I fear to every member of the Church of Christ there has been at least one such experience. Turn to the account again, if it is not fresh in your minds, and see if you do not see pictured there experiences of your own that have been very grievous to bear at the time, and very sorrowful to look back upon afterwards.

It seems strange that people, whose very name of Believers implies that their one chiefest characteristic is that they believe, should have to confess to such experiences. And yet it is such a universal habit that I feel if the majority of the Church were to be named over again, the only fitting and descriptive name that could be given them would be that of Doubters. In fact, most christians have settled down under their doubts, as to a sort of inevitable malady, from which they suffer acutely, but to which they must try to be resigned as a part of the necessary discipline of this earthly life. And they lament over their doubts as a man might lament over his rheumatism, making themselves out as an "interesting case" of especial and peculiar trial, which requires the tenderest sympathy and the utmost consideration.

And this is too often true of believers, who are earnestly longing to enter upon the life and walk of faith, and who have made perhaps many steps towards it.   They have got rid, it may be, of the old doubts that once tormented them, as to whether their sins are really forgiven, and whether they shall, after all, get safe to Heaven; but they have not got rid of doubting.   They have simply shifted the habit to a higher platform.   They are saying, perhaps, "Yes, I believe my sins *are* forgiven, and I *am* a child of God through faith in Jesus Christ.   I dare not doubt this any more.   But then — " And this "but then" includes an interminable array of doubts concerning every declaration and every promise our Father has made to His children.   One after another they fight with them and refuse to believe them, until they can have some more reliable proof of their being true, than the simple word of their God.   And then they wonder why they are permit- ted to walk in such darkness, and look upon them- selves almost in the light of martyrs, and groan under the peculiar spiritual conflicts they are com- pelled to endure.

Spiritual conflicts!   Far better would they be named did we call them spiritual rebellions !   Our fight is to be a fight of faith, and the moment we doubt, our fight ceases and our rebellion begins.

I desire to put forth, if possible, one vigorous pro- test against this whole thing.

Just as well might I join in with the laments of a drunkard and unite with him in prayer for grace to endure the discipline of his fatal indulgences, as to give way for one instant to the weak complaints of these enslaved souls, and try to console them under their slavery.　To one and to the other I would dare to do nothing else but proclaim the perfect deliverance the Lord Jesus Christ has in store for them, and beseech, entreat, command them, with all the force of my whole nature, to avail themselves of it and be free.　Not for one moment would I listen to their despairing excuses.　You ought to be free, you *can* be free, you MUST be free!

Will you undertake to tell me that it is an inevitable necessity for God to be doubted by His children?　Is it an inevitable necessity for your children to doubt you?　Would you tolerate their doubts a single hour?　Would you pity your son and condole with him, and feel that he was an interesting case, if he should come to you and say, "Father, I cannot believe your word, I cannot trust your love"?

I remember once seeing the indignation of a mother I knew, stirred to its very depths by a little doubting on the part of one of her children.　She had brought two little girls to my house to leave them while she did some errands.　One of them, with the happy confidence of childhood, abandoned herself to all the pleasures she could find in my nursery, and sang and played until her mother's return.　The other one, with the wretched caution and mistrust of maturity, sat down alone in a corner to wonder whether her mother would remember to come back for her, and to fear she would be for

gotten, and to imagine her mother would be glad of
the chance to get rid of her anyhow, because she
was such a naughty girl, and ended with working
herself up into a perfect frenzy of despair.   The
look on that mother's face, when upon her return
the weeping little girl told what was the matter with
her, I shall not easily forget.   Grief, wounded love,
indignation, and pity, all strove together for mastery.
But indignation gained the day, and I doubt if that
little girl was ever so vigorously dealt with before.

A hundred times in my life since has that scene
come up before me with deepest teaching, and has
compelled me, peremptorily, to refuse admittance to
the doubts about my Heavenly Father's love, and
care, and remembrance of me, that have clamored
at the door of my heart for entrance.

I am convinced that to many people doubting is
a real luxury, and to deny themselves from indulging
in it would be to exercise the hardest piece of self-
denial they have ever known.   It is a luxury that,
like the indulgence in all other luxuries, brings very
sorrowful results ; and, perhaps, looking at the sadness and misery it has brought into your own Christian experience, you may be tempted to say, " Alas !
it is no luxury to me, but only a fearful trial."

But pause for a moment.   Try giving it up, and
you will soon find out whether it is a luxury or not.
Do not your doubts come trooping to your door as a
company of sympathizing friends, who appreciate
your hard case, and have come to condole with you?
And is it no luxury to sit down with them and enter

tain them, and listen to their arguments, and join in
with their condolences? Would it be no self-denial
to turn resolutely from them, and refuse to hear a
word they have to say? If you do not know, try it
and see.

Have you never tasted the luxury of indulging in
hard thoughts against those who have, as you think,
injured you? Have you never known what a posi·
tive fascination it is to brood over their unkindnesses,
and to pry into their malice, and to imagine all sorts
of wrong and uncomfortable things about them? It
has made you wretched, of course, but it has been a
fascinating sort of wretchedness. that you could not
easily give up.

And just like this is the luxury of doubting.
Things have gone wrong with you in your experience. Dispensations have been mysterious, temptations have been peculiar, your case has seemed different from that of any one's around you. What more
natural than to conclude that for some reason God
has forsaken you, and does not love you, and is indifferent to your welfare? And how irresistible is the
conviction that you are too wicked for Him to care
for, or too difficult for Him to manage.

You do not mean to blame Him, or accuse Him of
injustice, for you feel that His indifference and rejec-
tion of you are fully deserved because of your unworthiness. And this very subterfuge leaves you at
liberty to indulge in your doubts under the guise of
a just and true appreciation of your own shortcom-
ings. But all the while you are as really indulging

in hard and wrong thoughts of your Lord as ever you did of a human enemy; for He says He came not to save the righteous, but sinners; and your very sinfulness and unworthiness is your chiefest claim upon His love and His care.

As well might the poor little lamb that has wandered from the flock and got lost in the wilderness say, " The shepherd does not love me, nor care for me, nor remember me, because I am lost. He only loves and cares for the lambs that never wander."

As well might the ill man say, " The doctor will not come to see me, nor give me any medicines, because I am ill. He only cares for and visits well people." Jesus says, " They that are whole need not a physician, but they that are sick." And again He says, " What man of you, having an hundred sheep, if he lose one of them, doth not leave the ninety and nine in the wilderness, and go after that which is lost, until he find it ? "

Any thoughts of Him, therefore, which are different from what He says of Himself, are hard thoughts; and to indulge in them is far worse than to indulge in hard thoughts of any earthly friend or foe.

From the beginning to the end of your christian life it is always sinful to indulge in doubts. Doubts are all from the devil, and are always untrue. And the only way to meet them is by a direct and emphatic denial.

And this brings me to the practical part of the

whole subject, as to how to get deliverance from this fatal habit. My answer would be that the deliverance from this can be by no other means than the deliverance from any other sin. It is to be found in the Lord and in Him only. You must hand your doubting over to Him, as you have learned to hand your other temptations. You must do just what you do with your temper, or your pride. You must *give it up* to the Lord. I believe myself the only effectual remedy is to take a pledge against it, as you would urge a drunkard to do against drink trusting in the Lord alone to keep you steadfast.

Like any other sin, the stronghold is in the will and the will to doubt must be surrendered exactly as you surrender the will to yield to any other temptation. God always takes possession of a sur-rendered will. And if we come to the point of saying that we will not doubt, and surrender this central fortress of our nature to Him, His blessed Spirit will begin at once to work in us all the good pleasure of HIS WILL, and we shall find ourselves kept from doubting by His mighty and overcoming power.

The trouble is that in this matter of doubting the soul does not always make a full surrender, but is apt to reserve to itself a little secret liberty to doubt, looking upon it as being sometimes a necessity.

"I do not want to doubt any more," we will say, or, "I hope I shall not"; but it is hard to come to the point of saying, "I will not doubt again." But no surrender is effectual until it reaches the point of saying, "I will not." The liberty to doubt must be

given up forever. And the soul must consent to a
continuous life of inevitable trust. It is often necessary, I think, to make a definite transaction of this
surrender of doubting, and to come to a point about
it. I believe it is quite as necessary in the case of a
doubter as in the case of a drunkard.

It will not do to give it up by degrees. The total-
abstinence principle is the only effectual one here.

Then, the surrender once made, the soul must rest
absolutely upon the Lord for deliverance in each time
of temptation. It must lift up the shield of faith the
moment the assault comes. It must hand the very
first suggestion of doubt over to the Lord, and must
tell the enemy to settle the matter with Him. It must
refuse to listen to the doubt a single moment. Let
it come ever so plausibly, or under whatever guise
of humility, the soul must simply say, "I dare not
doubt; I must trust. The Lord is good, and HE DOES
love me. Jesus saves me; He saves me now."
Those three little words, repeated over and over, —
"Jesus saves me, Jesus saves me," — will put to
flight the greatest army of doubts that ever assaulted
any soul. I have tried it times without number, and
have never known it to fail. Do not stop to argue
the matter out with your doubts, nor try to prove that
they are wrong. Pay no attention to them whatever;
treat them with the utmost contempt. Shut your
door in their faces, and emphatically deny every
word they say to you. Bring up some "It is written," and hurl it after them. Look right at Jesus,
and tell Him you trust Him, and you mean to trust

Him. Let the doubts clamor as they may, they cannot hurt you if you will not let them in.

I know it will look to you sometimes as though you were shutting the door against your best friends, and your heart will long after your doubts more than ever the Israelites longed after the flesh-pots of Egypt. But deny yourself; take up your cross in this matter, and unmercifully refuse ever to listen to a single word.

This very day a perfect army of doubts stood awaiting my awaking, and clamored at my door for admittance. Nothing seemed real, nothing seemed true; and least of all did it seem possible that I — miserable, wretched *I* — could be the object of the Lord's love, or care, or notice. If I only had been at liberty to let these doubts in, and invite them to take seats and make themselves at home, what a luxury I should have felt it to be! But years ago I made a pledge against doubting; and I would as soon think of violating my pledge against intoxicating liquor as to violate this one. I DARED not admit the first doubt. I therefore lifted up my shield of faith the moment I was conscious of these suggestions, and handing the whole army over to my Lord to conquer, I began to say, over and over, "The Lord *does* love me He *is* my present and my perfect Saviour; Jesus saves me, Jesus saves me *now!*" The victory was complete. The enemy had come in like a flood, but the Lord lifted up a standard against him, and he was routed and put to flight; and my soul is singing the song of Moses and the children of

Israel, saying, " I will sing unto the Lord, for He
hath triumphed gloriously: the horse and his rider
hath He thrown in the sea. The Lord is my strength
and my song, and He is become my salvation. The
Lord is a man of war; the Lord is His name."

It will help you to resist the assaults of this temptation to doubt, to see clearly that doubting is sin.
It is certainly a direct disobedience to our Lord,
who commands us, " Let not your heart be troubled,
neither let it be afraid." And all through the Bible
everywhere the commands to trust are imperative,
and admit of no exceptions. Time and room would
fail me to refer to one hundredth part of these, but
no one can read the Psalms without being convinced
that the man who trusts without a question, is the
only man who pleases God and is accepted of Him.
The " provocation " of Israel was that they did not
trust; " anger also came up against Israel, because
they believed not in God, and trusted not in His
salvation." (Psalms lxxviii. 17-22.) And in contrast, we read in Isaiah concerning those who trust,
" Thou wilt keep him in perfect peace whose mind
is stayed on Thee, because he trusteth in Thee."

Nothing grieves or wounds *our* hearts like doubting on the part of a friend, and nothing, I am convinced, grieves the heart of God more than doubting
from us.

One of my children, who is now with the Lord,
said to me one evening as I was tucking her up in
bed, " Well, mother, I have had my first doubt."
" Oh, Ray," I said, " what was it ? " " Why," she

replied, "Satan came to me and told me not to believe the Bible, for it was not a word of it true." "And what did thee say to him?" I asked. "Oh," she replied, triumphantly, "I just said to him, Satan, I *will* believe it. So there!" I was delighted with the child's spiritual intelligence in knowing so well how to meet doubts, and encouraged her with all my heart, explaining to her how all doubts and discouragements are from the enemy, and how he is always a liar and must not be listened to for a moment. The next night, I had forgotten all about it, however, and was surprised and startled when she said, as I was tucking her in bed, "Well, mother, Satan has been at it again." "Oh, Ray darling!" I exclaimed in dismay, "what did he say this time?" "Well," she replied, "he just told me that I was such a naughty little girl that Jesus could not love me, and I was foolish to think He did." "And what did thee say this time?" I asked. "Oh!" she replied, "I just looked at him cross and said, Satan, shut thy mouth!" And then she added, with a smile, "He can't make me unhappy one bit."

A grander battle no soul ever fought than this little child had done, and no greater victory was ever won!

Dear, doubting soul, go and do likewise; and a similar victory shall be thine.

As you lay down this book take up your pen and write out your determination never to doubt again. Make it a real transaction between your soul and the Lord   Give up your liberty to doubt forever.   Put your will in this matter over on the Lord's side, and trust Him to keep you from falling. Tell him all about your utter weakness and your long-encouraged habits of doubt, and how helpless you are before your enemy, and commit the whole battle to Him. Tell Him you will not doubt again; and then henceforward keep your face steadfastly looking unto Jesus, away from yourself and away from your doubts, holding fast the profession of your faith without wavering, because He is faithful who has promised. And as surely as you do thus hold the beginning of your confidence steadfast unto the end, just so surely shall you find yourself in this matter made MORE than conqueror, through Him who loves you.

CHAPTER XV.

PRACTICAL RESULTS IN THE DAILY WALK AND CONVERSATION.

IF all that has been said concerning the life hid with Christ in God be true, its results in the practical daily walk and conversation ought to be very marked, and the people who have entered into the enjoyment of it ought to be, in very truth, a " peculiar people, zealous of good works."

My son at college once wrote to a friend to this effect: that christians are God's witnesses necessarily, because the world will not read the Bible, but they will read our lives; and that upon the report these give will very much depend their belief in the Divine nature of the religion we profess. As we all know, this is an age of facts, and inquiries are being increasingly turned from theories to realities. If our religion is to make any headway now, it must be proved to be more than a theory, and we must present, to the investigation of the critical minds of our age, the grand facts of lives which have been actually and manifestly transformed by the mighty power of God

working in us all the good pleasure of His will. Give
us "forms of life," say the scientists, and we will be
convinced.   And when the Church is able to present
to them in all its members, the form of a holy life,
their last stronghold will be conquered.

I desire, therefore, before closing my book, to
speak very solemnly of what I conceive to be the
necessary fruits of a life of faith, such as I have been
describing, and to press home to the hearts of every
one of my readers their responsibility to walk worthy
of the high calling wherewith they have been called.

And I would speak to some of you, at least, as per
sonal friends, for I feel sure we have not gone thus
far together through this book without there having
grown in your hearts, as there has in mine, a tender
personal interest and longing for one another, that we
may in everything show forth the praises of Him who
has called us out of darkness into His marvellous light.
As a friend, then, to friends, I am sure I may speak
very plainly, and will be pardoned if I go into some
particulars of life and character which are vital to
all true Christian development.

The standard of practical holy living has been so
low among christians that any good degree of real
devotedness of life and walk is looked upon with
surprise, and even often with disapprobation, by a
large portion of the Church.   And, for the most part,
the professed followers of the Lord Jesus Christ are
so little like Him in character or in action, that to
an outside observer there would not seem to be much
harmony between them.

But we, who have heard the call of our God to a life of entire consecration and perfect trust, must do differently from all this. We must come out from the world and be separate, and must not be conformed to it in our characters nor in our purposes. We must no longer share in its spirit or its ways. Our conversation must be in Heaven, and we must seek those things that are above, where Christ sitteth on the right hand of God. We must walk through the world as Christ walked. We must have the mind that was in Him. As pilgrims and strangers we must abstain from fleshly lusts that war against the soul. As good soldiers of Jesus Christ, we must disentangle ourselves from the affairs of this life as far as possible, that we may please Him who hath chosen us to be soldiers. We must abstain from all appearance of evil. We must be kind one to another, tender-hearted, forgiving one another, even as God, for Christ's sake, hath forgiven us. We must not resent injuries or unkindness, but must return good for evil, and turn the other cheek to the hand that smites us. We must take always the lowest place among our fellow-men; and seek not our own honor, but the honor of others. We must be gentle, and meek, and yielding; not standing up for our own rights, but for the rights of others. All that we do must be done for the glory of God. And, to sum it all up, since He which hath called us is holy, so we must be holy in *all manner* of conversation; because it is written, " Be ye holy, for I am holy."

Now, dear friends, this is all exceedingly practical.

and means, surely, a life very different from the lives of most professors around us. It means that we do really and absolutely turn our backs on self, and on self's motives and self's aims. It means that we are a peculiar people, not only in the eyes of God, but in the eyes of the world around us; and that, wherever we go, it will be known from our Christ-like lives and conversation that we are followers of the Lord Jesus Christ; and are not of the world, even as He was not of the world. We shall no longer feel that our money is our own, but the Lord's, to be used in His service. We shall not feel at liberty to use our energies exclusively in the pursuit of worldly means, but, seeking first the kingdom of God and His righteousness, shall have all needful things added unto us. We shall find ourselves forbidden to seek the highest places, or to strain after worldly advantages. We shall not be permitted to be conformed to the world in our ways of thinking or of living. We shall feel no desire to indulge in the world's frivolous pursuits. We shall find our affections set upon heavenly things, rather than upon earthly things. Our days will be spent not in serving ourselves, but in serving our Lord; and all our rightful duties will be more perfectly performed than ever, because whatever we do will be done "not with eye-service as men-pleasers, but as the servants of Christ, doing the will of God from the heart."

Into all these things we shall undoubtedly be led by the blessed Spirit of God, if we give ourselves up to His guidance. But unless we have the right standard of Christian life set before us, we shall be hindered by our ignorance from recognizing His voice; and it is for this reason I desire to be very plain and definite in my statements.

I have noticed that wherever there has been a faithful following of the Lord in a consecrated soul, several things have inevitably followed, sooner or later.

Meekness and quietness of spirit become in time the characteristics of the daily life; a submissive acceptance of the will of God, as it comes in the hourly events of each day; pliability in the hands of God to do or to suffer all the good pleasure of His will; sweetness under provocation; calmness in the midst of turmoil and bustle; yieldingness to the wishes of others, and an insensibility to slights and affronts absence of worry or anxiety; deliverance from care and fear: all these, and many other similar graces are invariably found to be the natural outward development of that inward life which is hid with Christ in God. Then as to the habits of life: we always see such christians sooner or later giving themselves up to some work for God and their fellow-men, willing to spend and be spent in the Master's service. They become indifferent to outward show in the furniture of their houses and the style of their living, and make all personal adornment secondary to the things of God. The voice is dedicated to God, to speak and sing for Him. The purse is placed at His disposal. The pen is dedicated to write for Him, the lips to speak for Him, the hands and the feet to do

His bidding. Year after year such christians are seen to grow more unworldly, more heavenly-minded, more transformed, more like Christ, until even their very faces express so much of the beautiful inward Divine life, that all who look at them cannot but take knowledge of them that they live with God, and are abiding in Him.

I feel sure that to each one of you have come at least some Divine intimations or foreshadowings of the life I here describe. Have you not begun to feel dimly conscious of the voice of God speaking to you in the depths of your soul about these things? Has it not been a pain and a distress to you of late to discover how much there is wrong in your life? Has not your soul been plunged into inward trouble and doubt about certain dispositions and ways, in which you have been formerly accustomed to indulge? Have you not begun to feel uneasy with some of your habits of life, and to wish that you could do differently in these respects? Have not paths of devotedness and of service begun to open out before you, with the longing thought, " Oh, that I could walk in them " ?

All these longings and doubts, and this inward distress, are the voice of the Good Shepherd in your heart seeking to call you out of all that is contrary to His will. Oh! let me entreat of you not to turn away from His gentle pleadings. You little know the sweet paths into which He means to lead you by these very steps, nor the wonderful stores of blessed-ness that lie at their end, or you would spring forward with an eager joy to yield to every one of His requirements. The heights of Christian perfection can only be reached by faithfully following the Guide who is to lead you there, and He reveals your way to you one step at a time in the teachings and providences of your daily lives, asking only on your part that you yield yourselves up to His guidance. If, then, in anything you are convinced of sin, be sure that it is the voice of your Lord, and surrender it at once to His bidding, rejoicing with a great joy that He has begun thus to lead and guide you. Be perfectly pliable in His wise hands, go where He entices you, turn away from all from which He makes you shrink, obey Him perfectly; and He will lead you out swiftly and easily into a wonderful life of conformity to Himself, that will be a testimony to all around you, beyond what you yourself will ever know.

I knew a soul thus given up to follow the Lord whithersoever He might lead her, who in three short months travelled from the depths of darkness and despair into the realization and conscious experience of the most blessed union with the Lord Jesus Christ. Out of the midst of her darkness, she consecrated herself to the Lord, surrendering her will up altogether to Him, that He might work in her to will and to do of His own good pleasure. Immediately He began to speak to her by His Spirit in her heart, suggesting to her some little acts of service for Him, and calling her out of all un-Christ-like dispositions and ways. She recognized His voice, and yielded to Him each thing He asked for, following Him

whithersoever He might lead her, with no fear but
the one fear of disobeying Him.   He led her rapidly
on, day by day conforming her more and more to
His will, and making her life such a testimony to
those around her, that even some who had begun by
opposing and disbelieving, were forced to acknowledge that it was of God, and were won to a similar
surrender.   And, finally, after three short months of
this faithful following, it came to pass, so swiftly had
she gone, that her Lord was able to reveal to her
wondering soul some of the deepest secrets of His
love, and to fulfil to her the marvellous promise of
Acts i. 5, baptizing her with the Holy Ghost.   Think
you she has ever regretted her whole-hearted following of Him?   Or that aught but thankfulness and
joy can ever fill her soul when she reviews the steps
by which her feet had been led to this place of wondrous blessedness, even though some of them may
have seemed at the time hard to take?   Ah! dear
soul, if thou wouldst know a like blessing, abandon
thyself, like her, to the guidance of the Divine Master,
and shrink from no surrender for which He may call.

> "The perfect way is hard to flesh,
>   It is not hard to love;
> If thou wert sick for want of God,
>   How swiftly wouldst thou move."

Surely thou canst trust Him!   And if some things
may be called for which look to thee of but little moment, and not worthy thy Lord's attention, remember that He sees not as man seeth, and that things
small to thee may be in His eyes the key and the

clew to the deepest springs of thy being. In order
to mould thee into entire conformity to His will, He
must have thee pliable in his hands, and this pliability is more quickly reached by yielding in the little
things than even by the greater. Thy one great
desire is to follow Him tully; canst thou not say
then a continual " Yes, Lord ! " to all His sweet commands, whether small or great, and trust Him to lead
thee by the shortest road to thy fullest blessedness?

My dear friend, this, and nothing less than this, is
what thy consecration meant, whether thou knew it or
uot. It meant *inevitable* obedience. It meant that
the will of thy God was henceforth to be thy will
under all circumstances and at all times. It meant
that from that moment thou surrendered thy liberty of
choice, and gave thyself up utterly into the control of
thy Lord. It meant an hourly following of Him
whithersoever He might lead thee, without any dream
of turning back.

And now I appeal to thee to make good thy word.
Let everything else go, that thou mayest live out, in a
practical daily walk and conversation, the Divine life
thou hast dwelling within thee. Thou art united to
thy Lord by a wondrous tie; walk, then, as He walked,
and show to the unbelieving world the blessed reality
of His mighty power to save, by letting Him save *thee*
to the very uttermost. Thou needst not fear to consent
to this, for He is thy Saviour; and His power is to do
it all. He is not asking thee, in thy poor weakness, to
do it thyself; He only asks thee to yield thyself to
Him, that He may work in thee to will and to do by

His own mighty power.   Thy part is to yield thyself,
His part is to work; and never, never will He give
thee any command which is not accompanied by ample
power to obey it.   Take no thought for the morrow in
this matter; but abandon thyself with a generous trust
to thy loving Lord, who has promised never to call His
own sheep out into any path, without Himself going
before them to make the way easy and safe.   Take
each onward step as He makes it plain to thee.   Bring
all thy life in each of its details to Him to regulate
and guide.   Follow gladly and quickly the sweet
suggestions of His Spirit in thy soul.   And day by
day thou wilt find Him bringing thee more and more
into conformity with His will in all things; moulding
thee and fashioning thee, as thou art able to bear it,
into a vessel unto His honor, sanctified and meet for
His use, and fitted to every good work.   So shall be
given to thee the sweet joy of being an epistle of
Christ known and read of all men; and thy light
shall shine so brightly that men seeing, not thee, but
thy good works, shall glorify, not thee, but thy Father
which is in Heaven.

We are predestined to be "conformed to the
image" of God's Son.   This means, of course, not a
likeness of bodily presence, but a likeness of character and nature.   It means a similarity of thought,
of feeling, of desire, of loves, of hates.   It means,
that we are to think and act, according to our measure, as Christ would have thought and acted under
our circumstances.

A little girl was once questioned what it meant to

be a christian.   She replied, "It means to be just
what Christ would be, if He was a little girl and
lived in my house."

The secret of Christ's life was the pouring out of
Himself for others; and if we are like Him, this will
be the secret of our lives also.   He saved others,
but Himself He could not save.   He "pleased not
Himself," and therefore we are "not to please ourselves," but rather our neighbor, when it is for his
good.

A thoughtful Hindoo religionist, who visited England and America lately to examine into christianity,
said, as the result of his observations, " What christians need is a little more of Christ's christianity,
and a little less of man's."

Man's christianity teaches sacrifice to save ourselves ; Christ's christianity teaches sacrifice to save
others.   Man's christianity produces the fruitless
selfishness of too much of our religion.   Christ's
christianity produces the blessed unselfishness of
lives that are poured out for others, as was His.

In short, then, the one practical outcome of all that
our book has been teaching us, is simply this, that we
are to be Christ-like christians.   And all our experiences amount to nothing if they do not produce this
result   For "not every one that saith unto me, Lord,
Lord, shall enter into the kingdom of heaven ; but
he that doeth the will of my Father which is in
heaven."

CHAPTER XVI.

THE JOY OF OBEDIENCE.

I REMEMBER reading once somewhere this sentence, "Perfect obedience would be perfect happiness, if only we had perfect confidence in the power we were obeying." I remember being struck with the saying, as the revelation of a possible, although hitherto undreamed-of way of happiness; and often afterwards, through all the lawlessness and wilfulness of my life, did that saying recur to me as the vision of a rest, and yet of a possible development, that would soothe and at the same time satisfy all my yearnings.

Need I say that this rest has been revealed to me now, not as a vision, but as a reality; and that I have seen in the Lord Jesus, the Master to whom we may all yield up our implicit obedience, and, taking His yoke upon us, may find our perfect rest?

You little know, dear hesitating soul, of the joy you are missing. The Master has revealed Himself to you, and is calling for your complete surrender, and you shrink and hesitate. A measure of surrender you are willing to make, and think indeed it is fit and proper you should. But an *utter* abandonment, without any reserves, seems to you too much to be asked for. You are afraid of it. It involves too much, you think, and is too great a risk. To be measurably obedient you desire; to be perfectly obedient appalls you.

And then, too, you see other souls who seem able to walk with easy consciences, in a far wider path than that which appears to be marked out for you, and you ask yourself why this need be. It seems strange, and perhaps hard to you, that you must do what they need not, and must leave undone what they have liberty to do.

Ah! dear christian, this very difference between you is your privilege, though you do not yet know it. Your Lord says, "He that *hath* my commandments, and keepeth them, he it is that loveth Me; and he that loveth Me shall be loved of my Father, and I will love him, and will manifest Myself to him." You *have* His commandments; those you envy, have them not. *You* know the mind of your Lord about many things, in which, as yet, *they* are walking in darkness. Is not this a privilege? Is it a cause for regret that your soul is brought into such near and intimate relations with your Master, that He is able to tell you things which those who are further off may not know? Do you not realize what a tender degree of intimacy is implied in this?

There are many relations in life which require from the different parties only very moderate degrees of devotion. We may have really pleasant friendships with one another, and yet spend a large part of our lives in separate interests, and widely differing pursuits. When together, we may greatly enjoy one another's society, and find many congenial points; but separation is not any especial distress to us, and other and more intimate friendships do not interfere. There is not enough love between us, to give us either the right or the desire to enter into and share one another's most private affairs. A certain degree of reserve and distance is the suitable thing, we feel. But there are other relations in life where all this is changed. The friendship becomes love. The two hearts give themselves to one another, to be no longer two but one. A union of souls takes place, which makes all that belongs to one the property of the other. Separate interests and separate paths in life are no longer possible. Things which were lawful before become unlawful now, because of the nearness of the tie that binds. The reserve and distance suitable to mere friendship become fatal in love. Love gives all, and must have all in return. The wishes of one become binding obligations to the other, and the deepest desire of each heart is, that it may know every secret wish or longing of the other, in order that it may fly on the wings of the wind to gratify it.

Do such as these chafe under this yoke which love imposes? Do they envy the cool, calm, reasonable friendships they see around them, and regret the near

ness into which their souls are brought to their beloved one, because of the obligations it creates? Do
they not rather glory in these very obligations, and
inwardly pity, with a tender yet exulting joy, the poor
far-off ones who dare not come so near? Is not
every fresh revelation of the mind of one another a
fresh delight and privilege, and is any path found
hard which their love compels them to travel?

Ah! dear souls, if you have ever known this even
for a few hours in any earthly relation; if you have
ever loved a fellow human being enough to find sacrifice and service on their behalf a joy; if a whole-
souled abandonment of your will to the will of another
has ever gleamed across you as a blessed and longed-
for privilege, or as a sweet and precious reality, then,
by all the tender longing love of your heavenly Master, would I entreat you to let it be so towards
God!

He loves you with more than the love of friendship.
As a bridegroom rejoices over his bride, so does He
rejoice over you, and nothing but a full surrender
will satisfy Him. He has given you all, and He asks
for all in return. The slightest reserve will grieve
Him to the heart. He spared not Himself, and how
can you spare yourself? For your sake He poured out
in a lavish abandonment all that He had, and for His
sake you must pour out all that you have without
stint or measure.

Oh, be generous in your self-surrender! Meet His
measureless devotion for you, with a measureless devotion to Him. Be glad and eager to throw yourself

headlong into His dear arms, and to hand over the
reins of government to Him.   Whatever there is of
you, let Him have it all.   Give up forever everything
that is separate from Him.   Consent to resign from
this time forward all liberty of choice; and glory in
the blessed nearness of union which makes this en
thusiasm of devotedness not only possible but necessary.   Have you never longed to lavish your love and
attentions upon some one far off from you in position
or circumstances, with whom you were not intimate
enough for any closer approach?   Have you not felt
a capacity for self-surrender and devotedness, that has
seemed to burn within you like a fire, and yet had no
object upon which it dared to lavish itself?   Have not
your hands been full of alabaster boxes of ointment,
very precious, which you have never been near enough
to any heart to pour out?   If, then, you are hearing
the sweet voice of your Lord calling you into a place
of nearness to Himself, which will require a separa
tion from all else, and which will make this enthu
siasm of devotedness not only possible, but necessary
will you shrink or hesitate ?   Will you think it hard
that He reveals to you more of His mind than He does
to others, and that He will not allow you to be happy
in anything which separates you from Himself?   Do
you *want* to go where He cannot go with you, or to
have pursuits which He cannot share ?

No ! no, a thousand times, no !   You will spring out
to meet His dear will with an eager joy.   Even His
slightest wish will become a binding law to you, which
it would fairly break your heart to disobey.   You will

glory in the very narrowness of the path He marks out for you, and will pity with an infinite pity the poor far-off ones who have missed this precious joy. The obligations of love will be to you its sweetest privileges; and the right you have acquired to lavish the uttermost abandonment of all that you have upon your Lord, will seem to lift you into a region of unspeakable glory. The perfect happiness of perfect obedience will dawn upon your soul, and you will begin to know something of what Jesus meant when He said, " I *delight* to do thy will, O my God."

And do you think the joy in this will be all on your side? Has the Lord no joy in those who have thus surrendered themselves to Him, and who love to obey Him? Ah, my friends, we are not fit to speak of this but surely the Scriptures reveal to us glimpses of the delight, the satisfaction, the joy our Lord has in us, that ravish the soul with their marvellous suggestions of blessedness. That *we* should need Him, is easy to comprehend; that *He* should need us, seems incomprehensible. That our desire should be towards Him, is a matter of course; but that His desire should be towards us, passes the bounds of human belief. And yet, over and over He says it, and what can we do but believe Him? He has made our hearts capable of this supreme, overmastering affection, and has offered Himself as the object of it. It is infinitely precious to Him, and He says, " He that loveth me shall be loved of my Father, and I will love him, and will manifest myself to him." Continually at every heart He is knocking, and asking to be taken in as the supreme object of love. "Wilt thou have me," He says to the believer, "to be thy Beloved? Wilt thou follow me into suffering and loneliness, and endure hardness for my sake, and ask for no reward but my smile of approval, and my word of praise? Wilt thou throw thyself with an utter abandonment into my will? Wilt thou give up to me the absolute control of thyself and all that thou art? Wilt thou be content with pleasing me and me only? May I have my way with thee in all things? Wilt thou come into so close a union with me as to make a separation from the world necessary? Wilt thou accept me for thy only Lord, and leave all others, to cleave only unto ME?"

In a thousand ways He makes this offer of oneness with Himself to every believer. But all do not say "Yes," to Him. Other loves and other interests seem to them too precious to be cast aside. They do not miss of Heaven because of this. But they miss an unspeakable joy.

You, however, are not one of these. From the very first your soul has cried out eagerly and gladly to all His offers, "Yes, Lord; yes!" You are more than ready to pour out upon Him all your richest treasures of love and devotedness. You have brought to Him an enthusiasm of self-surrender that perhaps may disturb and distress the more prudent and moderate christians around you. Your love makes necessary a separation from the world, which a lower love cannot even conceive of. Sacrifices and services are possible and sweet to you, which could not come into the grasp

THE JOY OF OBEDIENCE.

of a more half-hearted devotedness. The life upon which you have entered gives you the right to a lavish outpouring of your *all* upon your beloved One. Services, of which more distant souls know nothing, become now your sweetest privilege. Your Lord claims from you, because of your union with Him, far more than He claims of them. What to them is lawful, love has made unlawful for you. To you He can make known His secrets, and to you He looks for an instant response to every requirement of His love.

Oh, it is wonderful! the glorious, unspeakable privilege upon which you have entered! How little it will matter to you if men shall hate you, or shall separate you from their company, and shall reproach you and cast out your name as evil for His dear sake! You may well "rejoice in that day and leap for joy"; for behold. your reward is great in Heaven, and if you are a partaker of His suffering, you shall be also of His glory.

In you He is seeing of the travail of His soul, and is satisfied. Your love and devotedness are His precious reward for all He has done for you. It is unspeakably sweet to Him. Do not be afraid then to let yourself go in a heart-whole devotedness to your Lord, that can brook *no* reserves. Others may not approve, but He will, and that is enough. Do not stint or measure your obedience or your service. Let your heart and your hand be as free to serve Him, as His heart and hand were to serve you. Let Him have all there is of you, body, soul, and spirit, time, talents, voice

everything. Lay your whole life open before Him
that He may control it. Say to Him each day, "Lord,
how shall I regulate this day so as to please Thee?
Where shall I go? what shall I do? whom shall I
visit? what shall I say?" Give your intellect up into
His control and say, " Lord, tell me how to think so as
to please Thee?" Give Him your reading, your pursuits, your friendships, and say, "Lord, give me the
insight to judge concerning all these things with Thy
wisdom." Do not let there be a day nor an hour
in which you are not intelligently doing His will, and
following Him wholly. And this personal service te
Him will give a halo to your life, and gild the most
monotonous existence with a heavenly glow. Have
you ever grieved that the romance of youth is so
soon lost in the hard realities of the world? Bring
God thus into your life and into all its details, and
a far grander enthusiasm will thrill your soul than
the brightest days of youth could ever know, and
nothing will seem hard or stern again. The meanest life will be glorified by this. Often, as I have
watched a poor woman at her wash-tub, and have
thought of all the disheartening accessories of such
a life, and have been tempted to wonder why such
lives need to be, there has come over me, with a
thrill of joy, the recollection of this possible glorifi-
cation of it, and I have said to myself, Even this life,
lived in Christ, and with Christ, following Him
whithersoever He may lead, would be filled with an
enthusiasm that would make every hour of it glorious. And I have gone on my way comforted to

know that God's most wondrous blessings thus lie in the way of the poorest and the meanest lives. "For," says our Lord Himself, " whosoever," whether they be rich or poor, old or young, bond or free, " whosoever shall do the will of God, the same is my brother, and my sister, and my mother."

Pause a moment over these simple yet amazing words. His brother, and sister, and mother ! What would we not have given to have been one of these ! Oh, let me entreat of you, beloved christian, to come, taste and see for yourself how good the Lord is, and what wonderful things He has in store for those who "keep His commandments, and who do those things that are pleasing in His sight."

" And it shall come to pass, if thou shalt hearken diligently unto the voice of the Lord thy God, to observe and to do all His commandments which I command thee this day, that the Lord thy God will set thee on high, above all nations of the earth; and all these blessings shall come on thee, and overtake thee, if thou shalt hearken unto the voice of the Lord thy God.

" Blessed shalt thou be in the city, and blessed shalt thou be in the field.

" Blessed shall be the fruit of thy body, and the fruit of thy ground, and the fruit of thy cattle, the increase of thy kine, and the flocks of thy sheep.

" Blessed shall be thy basket and thy store.

" Blessed shalt thou be when thou comest in, and blessed shalt thou be when thou goest out.

" The Lord shall cause thine enemies that rise up

against thee to be smitten before thy face; they shall come out against thee one way, and flee before thee seven ways.

"The Lord shall command the blessing upon thee in thy store-houses, and in all that thou settest thine hand unto; and He shall bless thee in the land which the Lord thy God giveth thee.

"The Lord shall establish thee an holy people unto Himself, as He hath sworn unto thee, if thou shalt keep the commandments of the Lord thy God, and walk in His ways.

"And all people of the earth shall see that thou art called by the name of the Lord, and they shall be afraid of thee.

"And the Lord shall make thee plenteous in goods, in the fruit of thy body, and in the fruit of thy cattle, in the fruit of thy ground, in the land which the Lord sware unto thy fathers to give thee.

"And the Lord shall make thee the head, and not the tail; and thou shalt be above only, and thou shalt not be beneath; if that thou hearken unto the commandments of the Lord thy God, which I command thee this day, to observe and to do them."

For the Israelites this was outward and temporal, for us it is inward and spiritual; and, as such, infinitely more glorious. May our surrendered wills leap out to embrace it in all its fulness!

CHAPTER XVII.

ONENESS WITH CHRIST.

ALL the dealings of God with the soul of the believer are in order to bring him into oneness
with Himself, that the prayer of our Lord may be
fulfilled: "That they all may be one; as thou,
Father, art in me and I in thee, that they also may
be one in us." . . . "I in them, and thou in me,
that they may be made perfect in one, and that the
world may know that thou hast sent me, and hast
loved them as thou hast loved me."

This soul-union was the glorious purpose in the
heart of God for His people before the foundation of
the world. It was the mystery hid from ages and generations. It was accomplished in the incarnation of
Christ. It has been made known by the Scriptures.
And it is realized as an actual experience by many
of God's dear children.

But not by all. It is true of all, and God has not
hidden it or made it hard, but the eyes of many a e

too dim and their hearts too unbelieving, and they fail to grasp it. And it is for the very purpose of bringing them into the personal and actual realization of this, that the Lord is stirring up believers everywhere at the present time to abandon themselves to Him, that He may work in them all the good pleasure of His will.

All the previous steps in the christian life lead up to this. The Lord has made us for it; and until we have intelligently apprehended it, and have voluntarily consented to embrace it, the travail of His soul for us is not satisfied, nor have our hearts found their destined and final rest.

The usual course of christian experience is pictured in the history of the disciples. First they were awakened to see their condition and their need, and they came to Christ and gave in their allegiance to Him. Then they followed Him, worked for Him, believed in Him; and yet, how unlike Him! seeking to be set up one above the other; running away from the cross; misunderstanding His mission and His words; forsaking their Lord in time of danger; but still sent out to preach, recognized by Him as His disciples, possessing power to work for Him. They knew Christ only "after the flesh," as outside of them, their Lord and Master, but not yet their Life.

Then came Pentecost, and these disciples came to know Him as inwardly revealed; as one with them in actual union, their very indwelling Life. Henceforth He was to them Christ within, working in them to will and to do of His good pleasure; delivering them by the law of the Spirit of His life from the bondage to the law of sin and death, under which they had been held. No longer was it between themselves and Him, a war of wills and a clashing of interest. One will alone animated them, and that was His will. One interest alone was dear to them, and that was His. They were made ONE with Him.

And surely all can recognize this picture, though perhaps as yet the final stage of it has not been fully reached. You may have left much to follow Christ, dear reader; you may have believed on him, and worked for Him, and loved Him, and yet may not be like Him. Allegiance you know, and confidence you know, but not yet union. There are two wills, two interests, two lives. You have not yet lost your own life that you may live only in His. Once it was I and not Christ; then it was I and Christ; perhaps now it is even Christ and I. But has it come yet to be Christ only, and not I at all?

Perhaps you do not understand what this oneness means. Some people think it consists in a great emotion or a wonderful *feeling* of oneness, and they turn inward to examine their emotions, thinking to decide by the state of these, what is the state of their interior union with God. But nowhere is the mistake of trusting to feelings greater than here.

Oneness with Christ must, in the very nature of things, consist in a Christ-like life and character. It is not what we *feel*, but what we *are* that settles t

question.   No matter how exalted or intense our
emotions on the subject may be, if there is not a
likeness of character with Christ, a unity of aim
and purpose, a similarity of thought and of action,
there can be no real oneness.

This is plain common-sense, and it is Scripture
as well.

We speak of two people being one, and we mean
that their purposes, and actions, and thoughts, and
desires are alike.   A friend may pour out upon us
enthusiastic expressions of love, and unity and oneness, but if that friend's aims, and actions, and ways
of looking at things are exactly opposite to ours, we
cannot feel there is any real oneness between us,
notwithstanding all our affection for one another.
To be truly one with another, we must have the same
likes and dislikes, the same joys and sorrows, the
same hopes and fears.   As some one says, we must
look through one another's eyes, and think with one
another's brains.   This is, as I said above, only
plain common-sense.

And oneness with Christ can be judged by no
other rule.   It is out of the question to be one with
Him in any other way than in the way of nature,
and character, and life.   Unless we are Christ-like in
our thoughts and our ways, we are not one with Him,
no matter how we feel.

I have seen christians, with hardly one Christ-
like attribute in their whole characters, who yet
were so emotional and had such ecstatic feelings of
love for Christ. as to think themselves justified in

claiming the closest oneness with Him. I scarcely know a sadder sight. Surely our Lord meant to reach such cases when He said in Matt. vii. 21, "Not every one that saith unto me, Lord, Lord, shall enter into the kingdom of heaven; but he that doeth the will of my Father which is in heaven." He was not making here any arbitrary statement of God's will, but a simple announcement of the nature of things. Of course it must be so. It is like saying, "No man can enter the ranks of astronomers who is not an astronomer." Emotions will not make a man an astronomer, but life and action. He must *be* one, not merely *feel* that he is one.

There is no escape from this inexorable nature of things, and especially here. Unless we are one with Christ as to character and life and action, we cannot be one with Him in any other way, for there *is* no other way. We must be "partakers of His nature" or we cannot be partakers of His life, for His life and His nature are one.

But emotional souls do not always recognize this. They *feel* so near Christ and so united to Him, that they think it must be real; and overlooking the absolute necessity of Christ-likeness of character and walk, they are building their hopes and their confidence on their delightful emotions and exalted feelings, and think they must be one with Him, or they could not have such rich and holy experiences.

Now it is a psychological fact that these or similar emotions can be produced by other causes than a purely divine influence, and that they are largely dependent upon temperament and physical conditions. It is most dangerous, therefore, to make them a test of our spiritual union with Christ. It may result in just such a grievous self-deception as our Lord warns against in Luke vi. 46–49, "And why call ye me, Lord, Lord, and do not the things which I say?" Our soul delights perhaps in calling Him, Lord, Lord, but are we *doing* the things which He said; for this, He tells us, is the important point, after all.

If, therefore, led by our feelings, we are saying in meetings, or among our friends, or even in our own heart before the Lord, that we are abiding in Him, let us take home to ourselves in solemn consideration these words of the Holy Ghost, "He that saith he abideth in Him, ought himself so to walk, even as He walked."

Unless we are thus walking, we cannot possibly be abiding in Him, no matter how much we may feel as if we were.

If you are really one with Christ you will be sweet to those who are cross to you; you will bear everything and make no complaints; when you are reviled you will not revile again; you will consent to be trampled on, as Christ was, and feel nothing but love in return; you will seek the honor of others rather than your own; you will take the lowest place, and be the servant of all, as Christ was; you will literally and truly love your enemies and do good to them that despitefully use you; you will, in short, live a Christ-like life, and manifest outwardly as well as feel inwardly a Christ-like spirit, and will walk among men as He walked among them. This, dear friends, is what it is to be one with Christ. And if all this is not your life according to your measure, then you are not one with Him, no matter how ecstatic or exalted your feelings may be.

To be one with Christ is too wonderful and solemn and mighty an experience to be reached by any overflow or exaltation of mere feeling. He was holy, and those who are one with Him will be holy also. There is no escape from this simple and obvious fact.

When our Lord tried to make us understand His oneness with God, He expressed it in such words as these, "I do always the things that please Him." "Whatsoever He saith unto me that I do." "The Son can do nothing of Himself, but what He seeth the Father do; for what things soever He doeth, these also doeth the Son likewise." "I can of mine own self do nothing; as I hear I judge, and my judgment is just; because I seek not mine own will, but the will of Him that sent me." "If I do not the works of my Father, believe me not. But if I do, though ye believe not me, believe the works; that ye may know and believe that the Father is in me and I in Him."

The test of oneness then, was the doing of the same works, and it is the test of oneness now. And if our Lord could say of Himself that if He did not the works of his Father, He did not ask to be believed, no matter what professions or claims He might make, surely His disciples must do no less.

It is forever true in the nature of things that "a good tree cannot bring forth evil fruit, neither can a corrupt tree bring forth good fruit." It is not that they will not, but they cannot. And a soul that is one with Christ will just as surely bring forth a Christ-like life, as a grape-vine will bring forth grapes and not thistles.

Not that I would be understood to object to emotions. On the contrary, I believe they are very precious gifts, when they are from God, and are to be greatly rejoiced in. But what I do object to is the making them a test or proof of spiritual states, either in ourselves or others, and depending on them as the foundation of our faith. Let them come or let them go, just as God pleases, and make no account of them either way. But always see to it that the really vital marks of oneness with Christ, the marks of likeness in character, and life, and walk, are ours, and all will be well. For "he that saith I know Him, and keepeth not His commandments, is a liar, and the truth is not in Him. But whoso keepeth His word, in him verily is the love of God perfected: hereby know we that we are in Him."

It may be, my dear reader, that the grief of your life has been the fact that you have so few good feelings. You try your hardest to get up the feelings which you hear others talking about, but they will not come. You pray for them fervently, and are often tempted to upbraid God because He does not grant them to you. And you are filled with an almost unbearable anguish because you think your want of emotion is a sign that there is not any interior union of your soul with Christ. You judge altogether by your feelings, and think there is no other way to judge.

Now my advice to you is to let your feelings go, and pay no regard to them whatever. They really have nothing to do with the matter. They are not the indicators of your spiritual state, but are merely the indicators of your temperament, or of your present physical condition. People in very low states of grace are often the subjects of very powerful emotional experiences. We all know this from the scenes we have heard of or witnessed at camp-meetings and revivals. I myself had a colored servant once who would become unconscious under the power of her wonderful experiences, whenever there was a revival meeting at their church, who yet had hardly a token of any spiritual life about her at other times, and who was, in fact, not even moral. Now surely, if the Bible teaches nothing else, it does teach this, that a Christ-like life and walk must accompany any experience which is really born of His spirit. It could not be otherwise in the very nature of things. But I fear some christians have separated the two things so entirely in their conceptions, as to have exalted their experiences at the expense of their walk, and have come to care far more about their emotions than about their character.

A certain colored congregation in one of the Southern States was a plague to the whole neighbor-

hood by their open disregard of even the ordinary
rules of morality; stealing, and lying, and cheating,
without apparently a single prick of conscience on
the subject.   And yet their nightly meetings were
times of the greatest emotion and "power."   Some
one finally spoke to the preacher about it, and begged
him to preach a sermon on morality, which would
lead his people to see their sins.   "Ah, missus," he
replied, " I knows dey 's bad, but den it always brings
a coldness like over de meetings when I preaches
about dem things."

You are helpless as to your emotions, but character you can have if you will.   You can be so filled
with Christ as to be Christ-like, and if you are Christ-
like, then you are one with Him in the only vital and
essential way, even though your feelings may tell you
that it is an impossibility.

Having thus settled what oneness with Christ
really is, the next point for us to consider is how to
reach it for ourselves.

We must first of all find out what are the *facts* in
the case, and what is our own relation to these facts.

If you read such passages as 1 Cor. iii. 16, " Know
ye not that ye are the temple of God, and that the
Spirit of God dwelleth in you ?" and then look at the
opening of the chapter to see to whom these wonderful words are spoken, even to " babes in Christ," who
were " yet carnal," and walked according to man, you
will see that this soul-union of which I speak, this
unspeakably glorious mystery of an indwelling God,
is the possession of even the weakest and most fai

ing believer in Christ. So that it is not a *new* thing you are to ask for, but only to realize that which you already have. Of every believer in the Lord Jesus it is absolutely true, that his "body is the temple of the Holy Ghost, which is in him, which he has of God."

It seems to me just in this way; as though Christ were living in a house, shut up in a far-off closet, unknown and unnoticed by the dwellers in the house, longing to make Himself known to them and be one with them in all their daily lives, and share in all their interests, but unwilling to force Himself upon their notice; as nothing but a voluntary companionship could meet or satisfy the needs of His love. The days pass by over that favored household, and they remain in ignorance of their marvellous privilege. They come and go about all their daily affairs with no thought of their wonderful Guest. Their plans are laid without reference to Him. His wisdom to guide, and His strength to protect, are all lost to them. Lonely days and weeks are spent in sadness, which might have been full of the sweetness of His presence.

But suddenly the announcement is made, "The Lord is in the house!"

How will its owner receive the intelligence? Will he call out an eager thanksgiving, and throw wide open every door for the entrance of his glorious Guest? Or will he shrink and hesitate, afraid of His presence and seek to reserve some private corner for a refuge from His all-seeing eye?

Dear friend, I make the glad announcement to

thee that the Lord is in thy heart. Since the day of thy conversion He has been dwelling there, but thou hast lived on in ignorance of it. Every moment during all that time might have been passed in the sunshine of His sweet presence, and every step have been taken under His advice. But because thou knew it not, and hast never looked for Him there, thy life has been lonely and full of failure. But now that I make the announcement to thee, how wilt thou receive it? Art thou glad to have Him? Wilt thou throw wide open every door to welcome Him in? Wilt thou joyfully and thankfully give up the government of thy life into His hands? Wilt thou consult Him about everything, and let Him decide each step for thee, and mark out every path? Wilt thou invite Him to thy innermost chambers, and make Him the sharer in thy most hidden life? Wilt thou say, "YES!" to all His longing for union with thee, and with a glad and eager abandonment, hand thyself and all that concerns thee over into His hands? If thou wilt, then shall thy soul begin to know something of the joy of union with Christ.

And yet, after all, this is but a faint picture of the blessed reality. For far more glorious than it would be to have Christ a dweller in the house or in the heart, is it to be brought into such a real and actual union with Him as to be one with Him, one will, one purpose, one interest, one life. Human words cannot express such a glory as this. And yet I *want* to express it. I want to make your souls so unutterably hungry to

realize it, that day or night you cannot rest without it
Do you *understand* the words, one with Christ? Do
you catch the slightest glimpse of their marvellous
meaning? Does not your whole soul begin to ex-
ult over such a wondrous destiny? For it is a real
ity. It means to have no life but His life, to have no
will but His will, to have no interests but His interests,
to share His riches, to enter into His joys, to partake
of His sorrows, to manifest His life, to have the same
mind as He had, to think, and feel, and act, and
walk as He did. Oh, who could have dreamed that
such a destiny could have been ours!

Wilt thou have it, dear soul? Thy Lord will not
force it on thee, for He wants thee as His companion
and His friend, and a forced union would be incompatible with this. It must be voluntary on thy part.

The bride must say a willing " Yes," to her bride
groom, or the joy of their union is utterly wanting.
Canst thou say a willing " Yes," to thy Lord?

It is such a simple transaction, and yet so real?
The steps are but three. First, be convinced that
the Scriptures teach this glorious indwelling of thy
God; then surrender thy whole being to Him to be
possessed by Him; and finally believe that He *has*
taken possession, and is dwelling in thee. Begin to
reckon thyself dead, and to reckon Christ as thy
only life. Maintain this attitude of soul unwaveringly. Say, " I am crucified with Christ, nevertheless I live, yet not I, but Christ liveth in me," over
and over day and night, until it becomes the
habitual breathing of thy soul. Put off thy self-life

by faith and in fact continually, and put on practi
cally the life of Christ.   Let this act become, by its
constant repetition, the attitude of thy whole being.
And as surely as thou dost this day by day, thou shalt
find thyself continually bearing about in thy body
the dying of the Lord Jesus, that the life also of
Jesus may be made manifest in thy mortal flesh.
Thou shalt learn to know what salvation means ;
and shalt have opened out to thy astonished gaze
secrets of the Lord, of which thou hast hitherto hardly
dreamed.

> " How have I erred!   God is my home
>   And God Himself is here.
>   Why have I looked so far for Him,
>   Who is nowhere but near ?

> " Yet God is never so far off
>   As even to be near ;
>   He is within, our spirit is
>   The home He holds most dear

> " So all the while I thought myself
>   Homeless, forlorn, and weary;
>   Missing my joy, I walked the earth,
>   Myself God's sanctuary."

CHAPTER XVIII.

'ALTHOUGH" AND "YET." A LESSON IN THE INTE
RIOR LIFE.

IN many of our store windows at Christmas time
there stands a most significant picture. It is a
dreary, desolate winter scene. There is a dark,
stormy, wintry sky, bare trees, and brown grass and
dead weeds, with patches of snow over them. On
a leafless tree at one side of the picture is an empty
and snow-covered nest, and on a branch near sits
a little bird. All is cold, and dark, and desolate
enough to daunt any bird, and drive it to some
fairer clime, but this bird is sitting there in an attitude of perfect contentment, and has its little head
bravely lifted up towards the sky, while a winter
song is evidently about to burst forth from its tiny
throat.

This picture, which always stands on my shelf, has
preached me many a sermon. And the text is always the same, and finds its expression in the two

words that stand at the head of this article, "Al·
though" and "Yet."

"ALTHOUGH the fig-tree shall not blossom, neither
shall fruit be in the vines : the labor of the olive
shall fail, and the field shall yield no meat; the
flock shall be cut off from the fold, and there shall
be no herd in the stall : YET I will rejoice in the
Lord, I will joy in the God of my salvation."

There come times in many lives, when, like this
bird in the winter, the soul finds itself bereft of
every comfort both outward and inward; when all
seems dark, and all seems wrong, even ; when everything in which we have trusted seems to fail us;
when the promises are apparently unfulfilled, and
our prayers gain no response ; when there seems
nothing left to rest on in earth or Heaven.   And it
is at such times as these that the brave little bird
with its message is needed.   "Although" all is
wrong everywhere, "yet" there is still one thing
left to rejoice in, and that is God; the "God of
our salvation," who changes not, but is the same
good, loving, tender God yesterday, to-day, and forever.   We can joy in *Him* always, whether we have
anything else to rejoice in or not.

By rejoicing in Him, however, I do not mean
rejoicing in ourselves, although I fear most people
think this is really what is meant.   It is *their* feelings or *their* revelations or *their* experiences that
constitute the groundwork of their joy, and if none
of these are satisfactory, they see no possibility of
joy at all.

But the lesson the Lord is trying to teach us all
the time is the lesson of self-effacement. He commands us to look away from self and all self's experiences, to crucify self and count it dead, to cease
to be interested in self, and to know nothing and be
interested in nothing but God.

The reason for this is that God has destined us
for a higher life than the self-life. That just as He
has destined the caterpillar to become the butterfly,
and therefore has appointed the caterpillar life to
die, in order that the butterfly life may take its
place, so He has appointed our self-life to die in order that the divine life may become ours instead.
The caterpillar effaces itself in its grub form, that it
may evolve or develop into its butterfly form. It
dies that it may live. And just so must we.

Therefore, the one most essential thing in this
stage of our existence must be the death to self and
the resurrection to a life only in God. And it is
for this reason that the lesson of joy in the Lord,
and not in self, *must* be learned. Every advancing
soul *must* come sooner or later to the place where it
can trust God, the bare God, if I may be allowed
the expression, simply and only because of what He
is in Himself, and not because of His promises or
His gifts. It must learn to have its joy in Him
alone, and to rejoice in Him when all else in Heaven
and earth shall seem to fail.

The only way in which this place can be reached
I believe, is by the soul being compelled to face in
its own experience the loss of all things both inward

and outward. I do not mean necessarily that all
one's friends must die, or all one's money be lost:
but I do mean that the soul shall find itself, from
either inward or outward causes, desolate, and bereft, and empty of all consolation. It must come to
the end of everything that is not God; and must
have nothing else left to rest on within or without.
It must experience just what the prophet meant when
he wrote that " Although."

It must wade through the slough, and fall off of
the precipice, and be swamped by the ocean, and at
last find in the midst of them, and at the bottom of
them, and behind them, the present, living, loving,
omnipotent God! And then, and not until then,
will it understand the prophet's exulting shout of triumph, and be able to join it: " YET, I will rejoice
in the Lord ; I will joy in the God of my salvation."

And then, also, and not until then, will it know the
full meaning of the verse that follows: " The Lord
God is my strength, and He will make my feet like
hind's feet, and He will make me to walk upon mine
high places."

The soul often walks on what seem high places,
which are, however, largely self-evolved and emotional, and have but little of God in them ; and in
moments of loss and failure and darkness, these high
places become precipices of failure. But the high
places to which the Lord brings the soul that rejoices
only in Him, can be touched by no darkness or loss,
for their very foundations are laid in the midst of an
utter loss and death of all that is not God.

If we want an unwavering experience, therefore, we can find it only in the Lord, apart from all else; apart from His gifts, apart from His blessings, apart from all that can change or be affected by the changing conditions of our earthly life.

The prayer which is answered to-day, may seem to be unanswered to-morrow; the promises once so gloriously fulfilled, may cease to be a reality to us; the spiritual blessing which was at one time such a joy, may be utterly lost; and nothing of all we once trusted to and rested on may be left us, but the hungry and longing memory of it all. But when all else is gone, God is still left. Nothing changes Him. He is the same yesterday, to-day, and forever, and in Him is no variableness, neither shadow of turning. And the soul that finds its joy in Him alone, can suffer no wavering.

It is grand to trust in the promises, but it is grander still to trust in the Promiser. The promises may be misunderstood or misapplied, and at the moment when we are leaning all our weight upon them, they may seem utterly to fail us. But no one ever trusted in the Promiser and was confounded.

The God who is behind His promises and is infinitely greater than His promises, can never fail us in any emergency, and the soul that is stayed on Him cannot know anything but perfect peace.

The little child does not always understand its mother's promises, but it knows its mother, and its childlike trust is founded not on her word, but upon herself. And just so it is with those of us who have

learned the lesson of this "Although" and "Yet."
There may not be a prayer answered or a promise
fulfilled to our own consciousness, but what of that?
Behind the prayers and behind the promises, there
is God, and He is enough. And to such a soul the
simple words, GOD IS, answer every question and
solve every doubt.

To the little trusting child the simple fact of the
mother's existence is the answer to all its needs.
The mother may not make one single promise, or
detail any plan, but *she is*, and that is enough for
the child. The child rejoices in the mother; not in
her promises, but in herself. And to the child, as
to us, there is behind all that changes and can
change, the one unchangeable joy of the mother's
existence. While the mother lives, the child must
be cared for, and the child knows this, instinctively
if not intelligently, and rejoices in knowing it. And
while God lives, His children must be cared for as
well, and His children ought to know this, and rejoice in it as instinctively and far more intelligently
than the child of human parents. For what else
can God do, being what He is? Neglect, indifference, forgetfulness, ignorance, are all impossible to
Him. He knows everything, He cares about everything, He can manage everything; and He loves us;
and what more could we ask? Therefore, come
what may, we will lift our faces to our God, like our
brave little bird teacher, and, in the midst of our
darkest "Althoughs," will sing our glad and triumphant "Yet."

All of God's saints in all ages have done this. Job said, out of the depths of sorrow and trials which few can equal, " *Though* He slay me *yet* will I trust in Him."

David could say in the moment of his keenest anguish, " Yea, *though* 'I walk through the valley of the shadow of death," *yet* " I will fear no evil; for Thou art with me." And again he could say, " God is our refuge and strength, a very present help in trouble. Therefore, will not we fear, *though* the earth be removed, and *though* the mountains be carried into the midst of the sea ; *though* the waters thereof roar and be troubled ; *though* the mountains shake with the swelling thereof. . . . . God is in the midst of her; she shall not be moved; God shall help her, and that right early."

Paul could say in the midst of his sorrows, " We are troubled on every side, *yet* not distressed; we are perplexed, *but* not in despair; persecuted, *but* not forsaken ; cast down, *but* not destroyed. . . . . For which cause we faint not ; but *though* our outward man perish, *yet* the inward man is renewed day by day. For our light affliction, which is but for a moment, worketh for us a far more exceeding and eternal weight of glory ; while we look, not at the things which are seen, but at the things which are not seen ; for the things which are seen are temporal ; but the things which are not seen are eternal."

All this and more can the soul say that has learned this lesson of rejoicing in God alone.

Spiritual joy is not a *thing*, not a lump of joy, so to speak, stored away in one's heart to be looked at and rejoiced over. Joy is only the gladness that comes from the possession of something good, or the knowledge of something pleasant. And the chris-tian's joy is simply his gladness in knowing Christ, and in his possession of such a God and Saviour. We do not on an earthly plane rejoice in our joy, but in the thing that causes our joy. And on the heav-enly plane it is the same. We are to " rejoice in the Lord, and joy in the God of our salvation"; and this joy no man nor devil can take from us, and no earthly sorrows can touch.

A writer on the interior life says, in effect, that our spiritual pathway is divided into three regions, very different from one another, and yet each one a necessary stage in the onward progress. First, there is the region of beginnings, which is a time full of sensible joys and delights, of fervent aspirations, of emotional experiences, and of many secret manifesta-tions of God. Then comes a vast extent of wilder-ness, full of temptation, and trial, and conflict, of the loss of sensible manifestations, of dryness, and of inward and outward darkness and distress. And then, finally, if this desert period is faithfully trav-ersed, there comes on the further side of it a region of mountain heights of uninterrupted union and communion with God, of superhuman detachment from everything earthly, of infinite contentment with the Divine will, and of marvellous transformation into the image of Christ.

Whether this order is true or not, I cannot here discuss, but of one thing I am very sure, that to many souls who have tasted the joy of the " region of beginnings " here set forth, there has come after- wards a period of desert experience at which they have been sorely amazed and perplexed. And I cannot but think such might, perhaps, in this expla- nation, find the answer to their trouble. They are being taught the lesson of detachment from all that is not God, in order that their souls may at last be brought into that interior union and oneness with Him which is set forth in the picture given of the third and last region of mountain heights of blessedness.

The soul's pathway is always through death to life. The caterpillar cannot in the nature of things be- come the butterfly in any other way than by dying to the one life in order to live in the other. And neither can we. Therefore, it may well be that this region of death and desolation must needs be passed through, if we would reach the calm mountain heights beyond. And if we know this, we can walk triumphantly through the darkest experience, sure that all is well, since God is God.

In the lives of many who read this paper there is, I feel sure, at least one of these desert " Althoughs," and in some lives there are many.

Dear friends, is the " Yet " there also? Have you learned the prophet's lesson? Is God enough for you? Can you sing and *mean* it,

> "Thou, O Christ, art all I want,
> More than all in thee I find"?

If not, you need the little bird to speak to you.

And the song that he sings, as he sits on that bare and leafless tree, with the winter storm howling around him, must become your song also.

"Though the rain may fall and the wind be blowing,
　　And cold and chill is the wintry blast;
Though the cloudier sky is still cloudier growing,
　　And the dead leaves tell that summer is passed;
Yet my face I hold to the stormy heaven,
　　My heart is as calm as a summer sea;
Glad to receive what my God hath given,
　　　　Whate'er it be,

"When I feel the cold, I can say, "He sends it,"
　　And His wind blows blessing I surely know;
For I 've never a want but that He attends it;
　　And my heart beats warm, though the winds may blow
The soft sweet summer was warm and glowing,
　　Bright were the blossoms on every bough;
I trusted Him when the roses were blowing,
　　　　I trust Him now.

"Small were my faith should it weakly falter,
　　Now that the roses have ceased to blow;
Frail were the trust that now should alter,
　　Doubting His love when the storm-clouds grow.
If I trust Him once I must trust Him ever,
　　And His way is best, though I stand or fall,
Through wind or storm He will leave me never,
　　　　For He sends all."

CHAPTER XIX.

THE BAPTISM OF THE HOLY GHOST.

THE baptism of the Holy Spirit is the crowning and vital point in all christian experience. And right views concerning it are of very great importance. It seems to be a subject beset with difficulties and errors at the present time, though evidently it was intended to be one of the simplest and most easily understood of all.

In considering it, two questions only, need to be settled: *first*, What or who is the Holy Ghost? and *second*, What is it to be baptized with the Holy Ghost?

The answer to the first question is, that the Holy Ghost or Holy Spirit is simply God's spirit. It is the life and power and nature of God, manifested in a spiritual way to man's spirit. It is in fact God Himself, as a spirit, communicating with the spiritual part of man's nature.

In John xiv. 16–23, we are shown this :—

"And I will pray the Father, and He shall give you another Comforter, that He may abide with you forever; even the Spirit of Truth; whom the world cannot receive, because it seeth Him not, neither knoweth Him: but ye know Him; for He dwelleth with you, and shall be in you. I will not leave you comfortless: I will come to you. Yet a little while, and the world seeth me no more; but ye see me: because I live, ye shall live also. At that day ye shall know that I am in my Father, and ye in me, and I in you. He that hath my commandments, and keepeth them, he it is that loveth me; and he that loveth me shall be loved of my Father, and I will love him, and will manifest myself to him. Judas saith unto Him (not Iscariot), Lord, how is it tha. thou wilt manifest thyself unto us, and not unto the world? Jesus answered and said unto him, If a man love me, he will keep my words: and my Father will love him, and we will come unto him and make our abode with him."

Here Christ speaks of His own coming and the Spirit's coming as interchangeable experiences, as though it were the same thing whether He should say, "I will come," or "the Spirit will come," or "my Father will come." He simply means that He has been with them in bodily presence, but hereafter He will be with them in spiritual presence; or in other words, that God had been manifesting Himself through the Divine Man, Christ Jesus, but hence forth He would manifest Himself in a spiritual way, through the Holy Spirit, *i. e.*, His own spirit. Consequently the Holy Spirit is called by God "my Spirit" all through the Old Testament, and also very frequently in the New Testament "the Spirit of God," and "the Spirit of Christ."

"But ye are not in the flesh, but in the Spirit, if so be that the Spirit of God dwell in you. Now if any man have not the Spirit of Christ, he is none of his. And if Christ be in you, the body is dead because of sin; but the Spirit is life because of righteousness. But if the Spirit of Him that raised up Jesus from the dead dwell in you, He that raised up Christ from the dead shall also quicken your mortal bodies by His Spirit that dwelleth in you."

The different expressions used here all mean, of course, the same thing; "the Spirit"; the "Spirit of Christ"; "Christ in you"; "the Spirit of Him that raised up Jesus"; and all mean evidently the Holy Spirit. If we substitute the words "life" or "nature" for Spirit, we shall perhaps be helped to understand just what the Holy Spirit is. As we read in Rom. viii. 2, "For the law of the Spirit of life in Christ Jesus hath made me free from the law of sin and death."

The Holy Spirit therefore is the "Spirit of life in Christ Jesus," or in other words is the holy *life* or *nature* of Christ, of which we are to be made partakers; as the Scripture expresses it, "partakers of the Divine nature."

And this brings us to our second question as to what it is to be *baptized* with the Holy Ghost.

The word "baptize" means to immerse, to dip into. Baptism with anything, therefore, must mean being immersed, or dipped into, that thing. **To be baptized** with the Holy Ghost means to be immersed into the Spirit of God, as to character or nature. It is variously described as being "partakers of the Divine nature" (2 Pet. i. 4); having "Christ to dwell in the heart by faith" (Eph. iii. 17); being a "temple of the living God" (2 Cor. vi. 16); being a "habitation of God through the Spirit" (Eph. ii. 22). To be filled with the Holy Ghost, therefore, means simply to be filled with God.

The word "baptize" is used in connection with the Holy Spirit eight times. Six of these cases are the announcements concerning Christ's mission as the Head of the new spiritual dispensation, the baptizer with the Holy Ghost (Matt. iii. 11; Mark i. 8; Luke iii. 16; John i. 26–33; Acts i. 5). Once it .s used in describing the conversion of Cornelius and his household (Acts xi. 16), where it was an experience that accompanied their believing the words spoken by Peter. And once it is used to declare the divine process by which every member of Christ is baptized into the one body (1 Cor. xii. 13).

The same word "baptize" is also used in several places to express the same fact, but not with the actual words "Holy Ghost." As, for instance, "baptized into Jesus Christ" (Rom. vi. 3); "baptized into Christ" (Gal. iii. 27); "buried with Him in baptism" (Col. ii. 12), etc., etc.

It is plain, therefore, that the expression "baptism of the Holy Ghost" has no exclusive meaning, but is only one way of describing the fact of our abiding in Christ and His abiding in us; in other words, "the life hid with Christ in God."

We say of an artist that he is baptized with the spirit of the old masters, and we mean, not necessarily that he had at any one time any especial or overwhelming experience, though this might be, but that he is all the time dipped into and permeated by their spirit; that he thinks like them, and paints like them, and has their views and ways. And, simiiarly, when we say of a man that he is baptized with the Spirit of Christ, we ought to mean that he is dipped into and permeated by the Divine Spirit and nature of Christ, as the law of his continual being.

The mistake is too often made of looking upon the "baptism of the Spirit" as an *experience* rather than a *life;* as an outpouring rather than an incoming; as an arbitrary bestowment rather than a necessary vitality. Yet the Scripture plainly teaches that the gift of the Holy Spirit is a universal gift to all believers, one without which they cannot be believers at all. It is impossible to be a child of God without the Spirit, for the new birth is distinctly declared to be a birth of the Spirit. John iii. 5, 6.

Every one, therefore, who is born of God is born of the Spirit, and has the Spirit within him as his new indwelling life. "If any man have not the Spirit of Christ, he is none of His" (Rom. viii. 9) and the converse of this is necessarily true, that if any man belongs to Christ he must have the Spirit of Christ.

In Gal. iv. 6, we read, "because ye are sons God hath sent forth the Spirit of His Son into your hearts." "Because ye are sons"; the very fact of sonship implies in the intrinsic nature of things the possession of the Spirit of God, for it is simply impossible to be born of God and not have God's Spirit get least in measure.

In 1 Cor. xii. 13, we read, "For by one Spirit are we all baptized into one body, whether we be Jews or Gentiles, whether we be bond or free; and have been all made to drink into one Spirit." Notice the "all" twice repeated in this verse. Plainly the teaching is that every one who belongs to the "one body" at all, belongs to it only by right of having been baptized into it by the "one Spirit."

In 1 Cor. iii. 16, 17, we have another most striking declaration of this : —

"Know ye not that ye are the temple of God, and that the Spirit of God dwelleth in you? If any man defile the temple of God, him shall God destroy; for the temple of God is holy, which temple ye are.

If we refer back to the opening of this chapter we shall see that the apostle here was not writing to advanced christians, but to babes in Christ who were "yet carnal," and could not be spoken to as "spiritual," and who were not able to bear anything but the simplest milk of the Gospel (see verses 1–3). And yet to these very christians, who were "yet carnal," and who "walked as men," Paul anounces the fact that even they are the temple of God, and that the Spirit of God dwelleth in them ; not will dwell, but dwelleth now. And on this fact he founds his appeal to them for holiness and purity.

We must believe, therefore, that this unspeakably glorious mystery of an indwelling Holy Ghost is the possession of even the weakest and most failing child of God, whether His presence has ever yet been recognized or not, or His control acknowledged and obeyed. He *is* within each one of us, although He may not yet have been allowed to take full possession. We *are* His temple, although we may not yet have opened every inward chamber of our hearts to His indwelling.

In seeking the baptism of the Holy Spirit, therefore, it is not a new thing you are to ask for, but simply to recognize the presence of that which you already have, and to submit fully to His possession and His control.

No one can doubt that the "well of water springing up into everlasting life," which Christ declared should be *in* the soul that came to Him to drink, is the Holy Ghost; and our Lord plainly declares that this water is already provided, and that all the soul needs is to come and drink.

"In the last day, that great day of the feast, Jesus stood and cried, saying, If any man thirst, let him come unto me and drink. He that believeth on me, as the Scripture hath said, out of his belly shall flow rivers of living water. (But this spake he of the Spirit, which they that believe on him should receive; for the Holy Ghost was not yet given; because that Jesus was not yet glorified.)"

The Holy Spirit is a gift, but the being baptized
or filled with the Spirit is not a gift, but a command.
Water is a gift, but the drinking of water is not a
gift but our duty. The sunlight is a gift, but the letting the sunlight into our houses is our privilege and
our duty. To be baptized with the sunlight, is
merely to get into it and let it shine, and to be baptized with the Spirit is the same.

In Acts iii. 33, we are told that Christ " having
received of the Father the promise of the Holy
Ghost "hath shed forth" this promised gift upon the
church. And in Eph. v. 18, we are commanded to
"be filled with the Spirit."

The Holy Spirit is like the sunlight, which forces
its way into every place where there is the slightest
opening to receive it. The sunlight has been shed
forth upon the world ; and the Holy Ghost, the promise of the Father, *hath been* shed forth upon the
Church. Every man born into the world shares the
world's sunlight, and may have as much or as little
of it as he pleases, and every man born into the
Church, (I mean, of course, the invisible Church of all
believers,)shares the Church's gift of the Holy Ghost,
and may have as little or as much as he pleases.

If I want sunlight in my house, I do not need to
ask God to give me a fresh thing shed down from
the sky, but I need only to open all the doors and
windows of my house to permit the entrance of the
sunlight which has already been given ; and if I
want to be baptized with the sunshine I do not need
to ask for more sunshine, but simply to go out into

the sunshine and be baptized. Similarly, if I want to be filled with the Spirit, I need not ask for more of the Spirit to be given to me, but only that more of myself may be given to the Spirit. I am not to look for any fresh outpouring from God, but for a fresh incoming into me of that Spirit which has already been "shed forth" upon every believer.

The preaching of the Gospel since the coming of Christ is called, in 2 Cor. iii. 8, the "ministration of the Spirit," and, in the common language of christians, we speak of the present age as being the "dispensation of the Holy Ghost." We mean by this, that the vital element of this age is the presence and power of God's Spirit as the controlling life of everything that lives.

This dispensation or "ministration of the Spirit" was prophesied of in the Old Testament in many places. (See Joel ii. 28, 29.) "And it shall come to pass afterward, that I will pour out my Spirit upon all flesh"; and notice the expression "all flesh, showing it was dispensational as well as personal.

Christ reiterated this promise of the coming Spirit, and told His disciples to wait for its fulfilment.

"And being assembled together with them, com manded them that they should not depart from Jeru-salem, but wait for the promise of the Father, which, saith he, ye have heard of me. For John truly baptized with water; but ye shall be baptized with the Holy Ghost not many days hence." (Acts i. 4, 5.) See also Luke xxiv. 49; John xv. 26; John xiv. 16, 17: John xvi. 7–13.

On the day of Pentecost, when the great outpouring came, declaration was made, " This is that
which was spoken by the prophet Joel : and it shall
come to pass in the last days, saith God, I will
pour out of my Spirit upon all flesh." (Acts ii. 1-4,
16-18.)

Evidently the repetition here of the prophetical
expression, " upon all flesh," marks this outpouring
of the Spirit as the introduction of a new dispensation, the formal instalment of the Spirit, set up in
the midst of the kingdom of matter, and thenceforth
to rule over and control it. The disciples were told
to " tarry " and "wait for " the ushering in of this
ministration or dispensation of the Spirit. But after
t had been thus ushered in, there was no command
henceforth to tarry, but always either an immediate
bestowal, or the command to an immediate reception.

In Acts ii. 38, 39, the apostle Peter, in the very
first sermon preached in this new dispensation, announced that whoever believed in Christ should receive the wonderful gift, declaring to the people in
the plainest words that it was their inalienable birthright : " For the promise is unto you and to your
children, and to all that are afar off, even as many
as the Lord our God shall call." It was to be no
special gift to a few, but belonged universally to
every awakened soul. See also on this point, Acts
x. 44-47; Acts xi. 15-17; Acts xv. 8, 9. And yet, in
spite of all this there were christians then as now
who did not receive this filling with the Spirit. " And

It came to pass that while Apollos was at Corinth,
Paul having passed through the upper coasts came
to Ephesus; and finding certain disciples, he said
unto them, Have ye received the Holy Ghost since
ye believed? And they said unto him, We have
not so much as heard whether there be any Holy
Ghost." (Acts xix. 1, 2.)

These christians were like many in the church
now; they had "not so much as heard" of their
glorious possession of the Holy Ghost. The question was not, "Has God given?" but, "Have you
received?" Such christians are like blind men,
who do not know the sun is shining, and do not open
their windows and let it in. These blind believers
in Jesus kneel down in their shut-up hearts and pray
for the baptism of the Spirit, when all the while this
very longed-for Holy Ghost is beating upon every
avenue of their being, seeking for an entrance.

If we compare Acts xviii. 24, 25, with Acts xix. 3,
we shall understand the ignorance of these Ephesian
converts. Apollos, who was their teacher, could not
instruct them in that of which he himself was ignorant, and as he "knew only the baptism of John,"
they also, of course, knew no other. There is much
similar teaching of ignorance in the church to-day;
and what is needed now is the same thing that was
needed then, that some Aquila and Priscilla, or Paul,
shall expound unto all such "the way of God more
perfectly."

There are four different forces of nature used to
describe the work of the Spirit: —

I.   FIRE: Matt. iii. 11.
II.   WATER: John iv. 10, 14.
III. WIND: John iii. 8.
IV.   LIGHT: Eph. v. 8, 9, 10, 13 ; John i. 4-9.

It is characteristic of all these that they force their way into every opening, let it be ever so small, and can only be kept out by erecting barriers against them.   How much more true must this be of that all-pervading immanent presence of the Spirit of God, which these things are declared to typify. Therefore, if only we know it, the Holy Ghost, like the sunlight on a dome, is beating against every human heart, and streams in at the tiniest opening.

Some one has said : " Just as the atmosphere was full of electricity before we adapted the telegraph to it, before we harnessed the lightning to carry our messages, and compelled it to drive our cars, so there is an atmosphere full of spiritual electricity around us of which we have only to take hold in order to secure to ourselves its inherent powers.   The fulness of God, the Spirit of God, surrounds every human soul.   And the soul has only to surrender itself wholly to God, when God will stream through and into that soul with His saving power and heavenly glory."

But there is in the lives of many christians an experience of a wonderful and instantaneous baptism, which makes an epoch in their lives, and which seems to transform their characters.   In the light of the above teaching, what is the explanation of this ?

It is, as we have proved, an incontrovertible fact

that every child of God is and must be indwelt by
the Spirit of God.   But it is equally a fact that not
all are "filled" with this Spirit.   And the definite,
conscious experience, of which so many speak as the
baptism of the Holy Ghost, is simply the moment
when the soul, either consciously or unconsciously,
surrenders itself fully to this divine incoming.   The
command is, "Be filled with the Spirit," and we
obey this command by abandoning our whole selves
to God, and opening every avenue of our being to
His possession.   Like sunlight, or like the wind, He
enters and fills every spot that is opened to Him.
The result of this, when done suddenly, is often a
very emotional and overwhelming sense of His presence.   But this sudden experience does not rise from
the fact that anything *new* has been shed forth from
God, but only that that which has been already shed
forth on the day of Pentecost, eighteen hundred years
ago, is now allowed to enter and take full possession.

It is not more of the Spirit the lifeless christian
needs, but only that the Spirit should have more of
him.   And the conscious baptism is not the *coming*
of the Spirit as of a thing from the outside, but the
full taking possession of the whole being by the indwelling Spirit already within.   "Be filled with the
Spirit," as if to say, "You have the Spirit dwelling
in you, but have not yet realized His full power."
You have been "sealed with that Holy Spirit of
promise"; but there are doors to be unlocked, and
rooms to be occupied. before it can be truly said that
you are "filled with all the fulness of God."

As a late writer has said concerning this: "Let me illustrate: I contract with a painter to paint and decorate my house. He sends a thoroughly competent man, with all necessary materials. The workman takes possession of the house; but the work progresses slowly. Why? Well, I have locked sundry doors, and piled up lumber in the corridors, and the man cannot go on with his work. What is wanted is not that I should ask the contractor to 'send the painter,' or to let me have 'more of the painter'; not more of the painter for the house, but more of the house for the painter. Give the painter a chance. Open the barred doors, clear away the obstructing lumber, and he will carry on the work to a satisfactory completion, according to contract."

Like the treasures of coal under a man's field, which existed there just as really before they were known and utilized by him, as they do afterwards; so does the Holy Spirit dwell in all the children of God, whether they know it or not, waiting for them to recognize His presence and yield to His control.

His operations may be hindered and the manifestations of His presence clouded. He may be grieved and thwarted, but nevertheless it is a simple fact that the Spirit of God dwells in *all* the children of God.

In seeking for the baptism of the Holy Ghost, therefore, it is not God's attitude towards us that needs to be changed, but our attitude towards Him. He is not to give us anything new, but we are to receive in a new and far fuller sense that which He has already given.

The vital importance of this teaching will be real-ized by all who have, either in their own experience, or in dealing with others, known something of the extreme difficulties connected with this subject. Earnest, devoted souls have been brought into great darkness because they have not realized in their own experience the wonderful "baptism" of which others speak. They think they cannot have received the longed-for gift, because their emotions and sen-sations have not been like those described by others. The "fruits of the Spirit" are manifested often to a great degree in their lives, but they are afraid to attribute these fruits to the indwelling power of the Holy Ghost, for fear they may be claiming a blessing which they do not really possess. They blame themselves for not possessing this gift, and they try in every way that is suggested to obtain it; but their darkness and trouble only seem to increase, and nothing seems to come of all their seeking.

Now if it were really true that no one has received the Spirit as an indwelling guest, but those who have had some definite conscious experience of "bap tism" at a certain clearly marked time, how are we to account for the "fruits of the Spirit" so beauti-fully developed in many devoted lives, who have known no such epoch in their experience? Dare we say these fruits have been produced by any other power, or have come from any other source, than the indwelling Spirit of God? Is not a tree to be known by its fruits, and *can* any power but the Holy Spirit produce holiness of heart and life? And on the other hand, dare we characterize all the wild fanaticism, or the many un-Christ-like self-seeking ways of some who have received a "wonderful baptism" as being the genuine fruits of that Spirit, whose essential characteristics are a Christ-like wisdom and a Christ-like spirit of meekness and self-sacrifice?

We can only conclude, therefore, that many *are* baptized with the Spirit of God, who can tell of no wonderful experience, and that many who have been prostrated, perhaps, by a mighty baptism, know little or nothing of the true Holy Spirit.

I have discovered by careful investigation that spiritualists have these wonderful emotional experiences quite as often as christians, and I am convinced there are emotions common to highly exalted mental states, no matter what the cause of this exaltation, whose origin is purely physical or psychical, and has nothing more to do with God's Spirit as such, than with any other source of excitation. It is of the body, and not of the spirit at all, and I fear many are sadly deceived by these experiences into thinking they must necessarily be from God, and *must* be tokens of His especial favor, who as a fact know nothing whatever of the reality of being filled with the Spirit.

To sum up the whole subject, then, we have proved the following facts: —

I.   The Holy Spirit has been shed forth on the

whole church of God, as the sunlight has been shed forth on the world.

II. All who are born into the family of God, receive the Spirit of God.

III. To be "baptized" with the Holy Ghost means simply that the soul has surrendered itself wholly to be taken possession of in every part by this indwelling Spirit.

IV. The "fruits" of this indwelling Spirit may or may not be strong emotions and overpowering manifestations, but they positively *must* be without exception Christ-like lives and characters.

V. By the fruits you shall know the baptism.

VI. We are not to limit the baptism of the Holy Ghost to one single motion on God's part, and one single experience on man's part. It is rather the continuous flow of the all-pervading and controlling spirit and life of God into the human soul, cleansing and consuming the darkness and sin there ; and it cannot be known in its entireness and completeness until nothing is left which needs cleansing, or which the fire can consume.

VII. It is not by believing in the Spirit, apart from God, that we receive the Holy Ghost, but by believing in and receiving God as the Spirit, and surrendering ourselves to His control.

The question next arises, How can I personally as a child of God come unto this baptism and be myself individually " filled with the Spirit " ?

To this I answer that here, as in every other expe-rience in the divine life, the things necessary on our

part are surrender and faith. We must be convinced
first of all that it is a fact that we as the children of
God *are* indwelt by the Spirit of God. Then we
must abandon ourselves wholly, body, soul, and spirit,
for His full possession. We must throw wide open
every chamber in our inward temple, and let the
Heavenly Guest enthrone Himself in all. Then we
must believe that He *does* take full possession, and
that we *are* filled with the Spirit up to the measure
of our capacity to receive, and we must begin from
that time onward to reckon on His presence and power
as a continual fact in our lives and experience. We
must hold here steadfastly, regardless of all seemings,
going quietly forward in a life of simple obedience
to the Spirit now enthroned within, and the result will
be that very soon the fruits of the Spirit will manifest
themselves in a blessed abundance.

The entrance upon this life of full surrender to
the control of the indwelling Holy Ghost may often
be a sudden and perhaps almost overwhelming flood
of emotion. But in other cases it may come, as it
were, without " observation " in a quiet gladness and
confidence, with a continual increasing development
of spiritual power.

But however this may be, the essential *facts* are as
we have seen, and the soul's part is only and always
to recognize the indwelling presence of the Holy
Ghost, and to yield utterly to His control. For this
is the baptism of the Holy Ghost.

We sometimes see a notice up on buildings,
" Room to let with power." This means that there

is somewhere in the building a steam-engine, with a connection in the vacant room, and that when any one rents the room, they rent also the power of the steam-engine with which it is connected Should a man rent such a room and put his machinery into it, he would need, of course, to make the connection between the machine and the power before he could expect his machine to go. He would not put his machinery in the room, and then go off to see the landlord and ask for the power; but he would look carefully for the point of connection with the power already provided. And just so it is with our hearts. The power of the Holy Ghost is already provided, but we need to make the connection, and this connection can only be made on our part by surrender and faith.

Everything is provided on God's side always, and what we want is simply adjustment to his plans.

I once passed through a large linen manufactory on a Sabbath day. There was one vast room full of the most beautiful and complicated machinery, all standing perfectly still and doing no work. Every wheel and spindle and thread was in its right position for use, and all was in perfect order; but nothing could be done because the power was wanting. The connection with the steam-engine had been cut off. And as I recall it I cannot but think how like those great silent rows of looms were to the silent rows of grand christian men and women who are so divinely gifted for the Master's work, but who are useless, because the connection with the mighty power of the Holy Ghost has not been fully made.

In Luke xi. 9–13, we have the strongest expression possible of the utter freedom of this gift : —

" And I say unto you, Ask, and it shall be given you ; seek, and ye shall find ; knock, and it shall be opened unto you.   For every one that asketh receiveth ; and he that seeketh findeth ; and to him that knocketh it shall be opened.   If a son shall ask bread of any of you that is a father, will he give him a stone ? or if he ask a fish, will he for a fish give him a serpent ?   Or if he shall ask an egg, will he offer him a scorpion ?   If ye then, being evil, know how to give good gifts unto your children, how much more shall your heavenly Father give the Holy Spirit to them that ask Him."

We have only to ask, and at once we receive, for asking and receiving go together.   Moreover, what stronger figure could be used than that of the parent and the hungry child.   What parent is there who is not eager to give bread to the child that needs it ? Yet notice the "how much more," in reference to God.

The whole process, then, is summed up in 1 John v. 14, 15 : —

" And this is the confidence that we have in Him, that, if we ask anything according to His will, He heareth us : and if we know that He hear us, whatsoever we ask, we know that we have the petitions that we desired of Him."

Come out then, dear christian, into the full sunlight of this truth we have been teaching concerning the Holy Ghost, and let the wonderful "promise of the

Father " baptize you, as a man is baptized with sunshine who stands in the full blaze of the natural sun. Do not stay shut up in your unbelief and questioning, and cry for the baptism, but open wide every avenue of your being and let the all-environing Spirit of God pour in and flood your surrendered soul.

The world is full of sunlight; but if I shut my plant up in a dark cellar, it will dwindle and die for want of it. In such a case I might pray forever, "O Lord, pour out thy sunlight on my plant," but none would come. In the nature of things, none could come. But if I take the plant out of the cellar and place it in the sunlight, it is flooded at once.

The Holy Ghost is my soul's sunlight, and the world is full of it. I have only to get out of the cellar of my unbelief and put myself "in the light," and I too shall be flooded at once.

CHAPTER XX.

"And when he was demanded of the Pharisees when the kingdom of God should come, he answered them and said, The kingdom of God cometh not with observation: neither shall they say, lo here! or, lo there! for, behold, the kingdom of God is within you."

THE expressions "kingdom of God" and "kingdom of Heaven" are used in Scripture concerning the divine life in the soul. They mean simply the place or condition where God rules, and where His will is done. It is an interior kingdom, not an exterior one. Its thrones are not outward thrones of human pomp and glory, but inward thrones of dominion and supremacy over the things of time and sense. Its kings are not clothed in royal robes of purple and fine linen, but with the interior garments of purity and truth. And its reign is not in outward show, but in inward power Neither is it in one place rather than another, nor in one form of things above another. It is not, lo here, nor lo there, not in this mountain nor yet at Jerusalem, that we are to find Christ, and enter into His kingdom. It is not a matter of place at all, but one of condition. And in every place and under every name, and through every form, all who seek God and work righteousness shall find His kingdom within them.

But this is very little understood. In our childish fashion of literalism we have too much imbibed the idea that a kingdom must necessarily be in a particular place and with outward observation; and have therefore expected that the kingdom of heaven would mean for us an outward victory of heaven over earth in some particular place, or under some especial form; and that to sit on a throne with Christ, would be to have an outward uplifting in power and glory before the face of all around us.

But as the inner sense of Scripture unfolds to us, we see that this would be but a poor and superficial fulfilling of the real meaning of these wonderful symbols. And the vision of their true significance grows and strengthens before the "eyes that see," until at last we know that our Lord's words were truer than ever we had dreamed before, that the "kingdom of God cometh not with observation; neither shall they say, lo here! or, lo there! for, behold, the kingdom of God is within you."

In Daniel ii. 44, we have the announcement of the kingdom, and in Isaiah ix. 6, 7, the announcement of the King : —

"The God of heaven shall set up a kingdom which shall never be destroyed; and the kingdom shall not be left to other people, but it shall break in pieces and consume all these kingdoms, and it shall stand forever."

"For unto us a child·is born, unto us a son is given: and the government shall be upon His shoulder; and His name shall be called Wonderful, Counsellor, the mighty God, the everlasting Father, the Prince of Peace. Of the increase of His government and peace there shall be no end, upon the throne of David, and upon His kingdom, to order it, and to establish it with judgment and with justice from henceforth even forever. The zeal of the Lord of hosts will perform this."

This kingdom is to break in pieces and consume all other kingdoms by right of the law by which the inward always rules the outward. If there is peace within, no outward turmoil can affect the soul; but outward peace can never quiet an inward tempest. A happy heart can walk in triumphant indifference through a sea of external trouble; while internal anguish cannot find happiness in the most favorable surroundings. What a man is within himself, makes or unmakes his joy, and not what he possesses outside of himself.

Some one said to Diogenes, "The king has degraded you." "Yes," replied Diogenes, triumphantly, "but I am not degraded!" No act of kings or emperors can degrade a soul that retains its own dignity; no tyrant can enslave a man who is inwardly free.

Therefore to have this divine kingdom set up within, means that all other powers to conquer or enslave are broken, and the soul reigns triumphant over them all. Men and devils may try to hold such a one in bondage, but they are powerless before the might of this interior kingdom. No longer will fashion, or conventionality, or the fear of man, or the love of ease, or any other of the many tyrants to which christians cringe and bow, rule a soul that has been raised to a throne in this inward kingdom. No sin or temptation can overcome, no sorrow can crush, no discouragement can hinder. Let a man or woman have been bound in ever so tyrannical chains of sinful habits, this kingdom will set them free. Circumstances make men kings in the outward life, but in this hidden life men become kings over circumstances. And the soul that has aforetime been the slave of a thousand outward things, finds itself here utterly independent of them, every one.

For the King in this kingdom is One whom no circumstances can affect or baffle. He it is indeed who makes circumstances. And since the government is upon His shoulders, we cannot doubt that He will order the kingdom with a judgment and justice that will leave nothing for any subject in His kingdom to desire.

In the expression "the government shall be upon His shoulder," we have the whole secret of this wonderful kingdom. Upon *His* shoulder, not upon *ours*. The care is His, the burdens are His, the responsibility belongs to Him, the protection rests

11

upon Him, the planning, and providing, and controlling, and guiding, all are in His hands. No one can
question as to His perfect fulfilment of every requirement of His kingship. Therefore those who are in
His kingdom, are utterly delivered from any need to
be anxious, or burdened, or perplexed, or troubled.
And by this deliverance they become kings. The
government is not upon their shoulders, and they
have no business to interfere with it. Their King
has assumed the whole responsibility, and if He can
but see His subjects happy and prosperous, He is
content Himself to bear all the weight and care of
kingship. How often we speak of the responsibilities of earthly kings, and pity them for the burdens
that kingship imposes. We recognize, even on an
earthly plane, that to be a king means, or ought to
mean, the bearing of the burdens of even the meanest of his subject. And even now, as I write, many
hearts are aching with sympathy for the new Czar,
who has assumed the grievous burden of the mighty
Russian Empire.

From this instinctive sense of every human heart
as to the rightful duties and responsibilities of kingship, we may learn what it means to be in a kingdom over which God is King, and where He has
himself declared all things shall be ordered with
judgment and justice from henceforth and even forever. Surely no care or anxiety can ever enter here,
if the heart but knows its kingdom and its King!

In John xviii. 36, our King tells us the tactics of
His kingdom: "Jesus answered, My kingdom is not

of this world: if my kingdom were of this world, then would my servants fight, that I should not be delivered to the Jews; but now is my kingdom not from hence."

Earthly kings and earthly kingdoms gain and keep their supremacy by outward conflict; God's kingdom conquers by inward power. Earthly kings subdue enemies; God subdues enmity. His victories must be interior before they can be exterior. He does not subjugate, but he conquers. Even we, on our earthly plane, know something of this principle, and do not value any victory over another which only reaches the body and has not subdued the heart. No true mother cares for an outward obedience merely; nothing will satisfy her but the inward surrender. Unless the citadel of the heart is conquered, the conquest seem worthless. And with God how much more will this be the case, since we are told that " He seeth not as man seeth; for man looketh on the outward appearance, but the Lord looketh on the heart." We speak of "subduing hearts," and we mean, not that they are overpowered or forced into an unwilling and compulsory surrender, but that they are conquered by being won, and are willingly yielded up to another's control. And it is after this fashion and no other that God subdues. So that to read that " His kingdom ruleth over all," means that all hearts are won to His service in a glad and willing surrender.

For again I repeat, His reign must be inward before it can be outward. And in truth it is no reign at all, unless it is within. If we think of it a moment we shall see that this must be so in the very nature of things, and that it is impossible to conceive of God reigning in a kingdom where the subduing reaches no further than the outside actions of His subjects. His kingdom is not of this world, but is in a spiritual sphere, where its power is over the souls and not the bodies of men; and therefore only when the soul is conquered, can it be set up.

Understood in this light, how full of love and blessing do all those declarations and prophecies become, which tell us that God is to subdue His enemies under His feet, and is to rule them in righteousness and power! And how glorious with hope does the voice of that great multitude heard by John sound out, saying, "Alleluia! for the Lord God omnipotent reigneth!"

In confirmation of all this we have two passages descriptive of this kingdom, in Rom. xiv. 17, and 1 Cor. iv. 20: "For the kingdom of God is not meat and drink; but righteousness and peace and joy in the Holy Ghost." "For the kingdom of God is not in word, but in power."

Not outward things, but inward. Not what a man eats and drinks, not where he lives, nor what is his nationality, nor the customs of his race, not even what he thinks nor what he says; but what are the inward characteristics of his nature, and the inward power of his spiritual life. For these alone constitute this kingdom of God. Not what I *do*, but what I *am*, is to decide whether I belong to it or not. And only as inward righteousness, and inward peace, and inward joy, and inward power are bestowed and experienced, can this kingdom be set up. Therefore no outward subjugation can accomplish results like these, but only the interior work of the all-subduing spirit of God.

I have been greatly instructed by the story of Ulysses, when he was sailing past the islands of the sirens. These sirens had the power of charming by their songs all who listened to them, and of inducing them to leap into the sea. To avert this danger, Ulysses filled the ears of his crew with wax, that they might not hear the fatal music, and bound himself to the mast with knotted cords; and thus they passed the isle in safety. But when Orpheus was obliged to sail by the same island, he gained a better victory, for he himself made sweeter music than that of the sirens, and enchanted his crew with more alluring songs; so that they passed the dangerous charmers not only with safety, but with disdain. Wax and knotted cords kept Ulysses and his crew from making the fatal leap; but inward delights enabled Orpheus and his crew to reign triumphant over the very source of temptation itself. And just so is it with the kingdom of which we speak. It needs no outward law to bind it, but reigns by right of its inward life. So that it is said of those who have entered it, " Against such there is no law."

For it is a kingdom of kings. The song we shall one day sing, nay, that we ought to be

singing even now and here in this life, declares
this : " Unto Him that loved us, and washed us
from our sins in His own blood, and hath made
us kings and priests unto God and His Father ;
to Him be glory and dominion for ever and ever.
Amen." (Rev. i. 5, 6.)

We who have entered this kingdom, or, rather,
in whom this kingdom is set up, sit upon the throne
with our King and share His dominion. The world
was His footstool, and it becomes our footstool also.
Over the things of time and sense He reigned triumphant by the power of a life lived in a plane
above them and superior to them, and so may we.
We are all of us familiar with the expression that
such or such a person " rises superior to his surroundings," and we mean that there is in that soul
a hidden power that controls its surroundings, in
stead of being controlled by them. Our King es-
sentially rose superior to His surroundings ; and it is
given to us who are reigning with Him to do the
same.

But, just as He was not a king in outward appearance, but only in inward power, so shall we be. He
reigned, not in this, that He had all the treasures
and riches of the world at His command, but that
He had none of them, and could do without them.
And so shall our reigning be. We shall not have all
men bowing down to us, and all things bending to
our will ; but with all men opposing and all things
adverse, we shall walk in a royal triumph of soul
through the midst of them. We shall suffer the

oss of all things, and by that loss be set forever
free from their power to bind. We shall hide ourselves in the impregnable fortress of the will of our
King, and shall reign there in a perpetual kingdom.

All this is contrary to man's thought of kingship.
The only idea the human heart can compass, is, that
outward circumstances must bend and bow to the
soul that is seated on a throne with Christ. Friends
must approve, enemies must be silenced, obstacles
must be overcome, affairs must prosper, or there can
be no reigning. If man had had the ordering of
Daniel's business, or of that matter of the three
Hebrew children in the burning fiery furnace, he
would have said the only way of victory would be
for the minds of the kings to have been so changed
that Daniel should not have been cast into the den
of lions, and the Hebrew children should have been
kept out of the furnace. But God's way was infinitely grander. He suffered Daniel to be cast among
the lions, in order that he might reign triumphant
over them when in their very midst, and He allowed
Shadrach, Meshach, and Abednego to be cast into
the burning, fiery furnace, in order that they might
walk through it without so much as the smell of fire
upon them. He tells us, not that we shall walk in
paths where there are no dragons and adders, but
that we shall walk through the midst of dragons and
adders, and shall " tread them under our feet."

And how much more glorious a kingdom is this
than any outward rule or control could be ! To be
inwardly a king, while outwardly a slave, is one of

the grandest heights of triumph of which our hearts can conceive.   To be destitute, afflicted, tormented, to be stoned and torn asunder, and slain with the sword; to wander in sheep-skins and goat-skins, and in deserts and mountains, and in dens and caves of the earth, and yet to be through it all, kings in interior kingdoms of righteousness, peace and joy in the Holy Ghost, is surely a kingdom that none but God could give, and none but God-like souls receive.

A few such kings we have at some time or other seen or heard of in this world of ours, and all hearts have acknowledged their unconscious sway. One I read of among the brethren of the monastery of St. Cyr.   Because of their piety, these brethren incurred the hatred of the monasteries around them, and the anger of their superiors, and were cast out as evil from their community.   One of them was sent as prisoner to a monastery where his chief enemies dwelt, and was there subjected to the most cruel and degrading treatment.   Although he was of gentle birth, and had been an abbot in the community he had left, he was compelled to do the most menial work, was forced to carry a noisome burden on his back, and was driven out to beg with a placard on his bosom declaring him to be the vilest of the vile.   But through it all the spirit of the saint reigned triumphant, and nothing disturbed his calm, or soured for a moment his Christ-like sweetness.   For his persecutors he never had anything but words of kindness and smiles of

love. And at last by the mighty power of the divine
kingdom in which he lived, he subdued all hearts
around him to himself, and became the trusted
friend and adviser, and the beloved ruler over the
very enemies who had once so delighted to persecute
and revile him. "Blessed are the meek, for they
shall inherit the earth." By his meekness he conquered and became king.

At one time a dangerous criminal was sent to the
monastery for imprisonment. He was so violent that
no bonds sufficed to bind him, and no strength could
control him. At last he was taken to the cell of
this brother from St. Cyr, and they were shut up
together; even the stolid monks themselves recognizing in that divine meekness a power to conquer
that surpassed all the powers with which they were
acquainted. The saint received the violent man as
a beloved brother, and smiled upon him with heavenly kindness. But the criminal returned it with
abuse and violence. He broke the monk's furniture
and destroyed his bed, he kicked him, and beat him,
and tore his hair, and spat upon him. He exhausted
himself in his violence against him. Through it
all the monk made no resistance, and said no word
but words of love; and when at length the criminal,
worn out with his fury, paused to take breath, the
beaten and outraged man looked upon his persecutor
with a smile of ineffable love and tender compas-
sion, as though he would gather him to his bosom
and comfort him for his misery. It was more than
the criminal could bear. Hatred, and revenge, and

anger he could repay in kind, but against love ana meekness like this he had no weapons, and his heart was conquered. He fell at the feet of the saint and washed them with his tears, as he entreated forgiveness for his cruelty, and vowed a lifelong loyalty to his service. And from that moment all trouble with that criminal was over. He followed the saint about like a loving and faithful dog, eager to do or to be anything the other might desire. And when the time of his imprisonment was over, and the gates of his prison were opened for his release, he could no be induced to go, because he could not bear to leave the man who had saved him by love.

Of such a nature is kingship in this kingdom of heaven.

Each soul can make the application for itself, with out need of comment from me.

In Matt. v., vi., and vii., we have the King of this kingdom describing the characteristics of His kingdom and giving the laws for His subjects. "Blessed are the poor in spirit," He says, "for theirs is the kingdom of heaven." Not the rich, or great, or wise, or learned, but the poor in· spirit, the meek, the merciful, the pure in heart, those who mourn, and those who hunger and thirst, those who are persecuted, and reviled, and spoken evil against, all such belong to this kingdom. Gentleness, yieldingness, meekness, charity, are the characteristics of these kings, and they reign in the power of them.

One christian asked another, "How can I make people respect me?" "I would *command*. their respect," was the reply.   And this meant, not that he should stand up and say in tones of authority, "Now I command you all to respect me," but that he should so act, and live, and be, that no one could help respecting him.   Men sometimes win an outward show of respect and submission by an overbearing tyranny, but he who would rule the hearts of his subjects must try other methods.

Our Lord developed this thought to some who wished to share His throne. He called them to Him, and said, "Ye know that they which are accounted to rule over the Gentiles exercise lordship over them; and their great ones exercise authority upon them. But so shall it not be among you: but whosoever will be great among you, shall be your minister: and whosoever of you will be the chiefest, shall be servant of all. For even the Son of man came not to be ministered unto, but to minister, and to give his life a ransom for many."

From the human standpoint, that man alone reigns who is able to exercise lordship over those around him. From the divine standpoint the soul that serves is the soul that reigns. Not he who demands most, receives this inward crowning, but he who gives up most.

What grander kingship can be conceived of than that which Christ sets forth in the sermon on the mount, "But I say unto you, that ye resist not evil; but whosoever shall smite thee on thy right cheek, turn to him the other also. And if any man will sue thee at the law and take away thy coat, let him

have thy cloak also. And whosoever shall compe
thee to go a mile, go with him twain"?

Surely only a soul that is in harmony with God
can mount such a throne of dominion as this!

But this is our destiny. We are made for this
purpose. We are born of a kingly race, and are
heirs to this ineffable kingdom; "heirs of God and
joint heirs with Christ."

Would that we could realize this; and could see
in every act of service or surrender to which we
might find ourselves called, an upward step in the
pathway that leads us to our kingdom and our
throne!

I mean this in a very practical sense. I mean
that the homely services of our daily lives, and the
little sacrifices which each day demands, will be, if
faithfully fulfilled, actual rounds in the ladder by
which we are mounting to our thrones. I mean that
if we are faithful over the "few things" of our
earthly kingdom, we shall be made ruler over the
'many things" of the heavenly kingdom.

He that follows Christ in this ministry of service
and of suffering, will reign with Him in the glory of
supreme self-sacrifice, and will be the "chiefest" in
His divine kingdom of love. Knowing this, who
would hesitate to "turn the other cheek," since by
the turning a kingdom is to be won and a throne is
to be gained?

Joseph was a type of all this. In slavery and in
prison he reigned a king, as truly as when seated
on Pharaoh's throne or riding in Pharaoh's chariot.

(See Gen. xxxix. 6, 22, 23.) He became the greatest by being the least, the chiefest by being servant
of all.

Dear reader, art thou reigning after this fashion,
and in this sort of a kingdom? Art thou the greatest in thy little world of home, or church, or social
circle by being the least, and chiefest by being the
servant of all? If not, thy kingdom is not Christ's
kingdom, and thy throne is not one shared by
Him.

To enter into the secrets of this interior kingdom
and to partake of its heavenly power, is no notional
victory, no fancied supremacy. It is a real and
actual reigning, which will cause thee as a matter of
fact to "rise superior" to the world and the things
of it, and to walk through it independent of its
smiles or frowns, dwelling in a region of heavenly
peace and heavenly triumph which earth can neither
give nor take away. "For the kingdom of God is
not in word but in power." It is not a talk but a
fact; and those who are in it recognize their kingship and prove it by reigning.

But perhaps thou wilt say, "How can I enter into
this kingdom, if I am not already in?" Let our
Lord himself answer thee: "At the same time came
the disciples unto Jesus, saying, Who is the greatest
in the kingdom of heaven? And Jesus called a
little child unto him, and set him in the midst of
them, and said, Verily I say unto you, Except ye
be converted, and become as little children, ye shall
not enter into the kingdom of heaven. Whosoever

therefore shall humble himself as this little child, the same is greatest in the kingdom of heaven."

It is a kingdom of child-like hearts, and only such can enter it.

To be a "little child" means simply to *be* one. I cannot describe it better than this. We all have known little children in our lives, and have delighted ourselves in their simplicity and their trustfulness, their light-hearted carelessness, and their unquestioning obedience to those in authority over them. And to be the greatest in this divine kingdom means to have the most of this guileless, tender, trustful, self-forgetting, obedient heart of the child.

"Not every one that saith unto me, Lord, Lord, shall enter into the kingdom of heaven; but he that doeth the will of my Father which is in heaven."

It is not saying, but doing, that will avail us here. We must be a child, or we cannot sit on the child's throne. And to be a child means to do the Father's will; since the very essence of true childhood is the spirit of obedience united to the spirit of trust.

Become a little child, then, by laying aside all thy greatness, all thy self-assertion, all thy self-dependence, all thy wisdom, and all thy strength, and consenting to die to thy own self-life, be born again into the kingdom of God. The only way out of one life into another is by a death to one and a new birth into the other. It is the old story, therefore, reiterated so often and in so many different ways, of through death to life. Die, then, that you may live.

Lose your own life that you may find Christ's life.
The caterpillar can only enter into the butterfly's
kingdom by dying to its caterpillar life, and emerging
into the resurrection life of the butterfly; and just
so can we also only enter into the kingdom of God by
the way of a death out of the kingdom of self, and
an emergence into the resurrection life of Christ.
Let everything go, then, that belongs to the natural;
all your own notions, and plans, and ways, and
thoughts; and accept in their stead God's plans, and
ways, and thoughts. Do this faithfully and do it
persistently, and you shall come at last to sit on His
throne, and to reign with Him in an interior kingdom
which shall break in pieces and consume all other
kingdoms, and shall stand for ever and ever.

There is no other way. This kingdom cannot be
entered by pomp, and show, and greatness, and
strength; but by littleness, and helplessness, and
childlikeness, and babyhood, and death. He that
humbleth himself, and he only, shall be exalted
here; and to mount the throne with Christ requires
that we shall first have followed Him in the suffering, and loss, and crucifixion. If we suffer with
him, we shall also reign with Him. Not as an
arbitrary reward for our suffering, but as the result
that will follow in the very nature of things. Christ's
loss must necessarily bring Christ's gain, Christ's
death must bring Christ's resurrection; and to
follow Him in the regeneration, will surely and inevitably bring the soul that follows to His crown and
His throne.

In a volume of sermons for children I have found a vivid illustration of this royal kingdom : —

" A little fellow from one of the Refuges in England had risked his life to save one of his comrades, and England's Queen had sent him a medal by the hand of one of England's earls. The little fellow was held forward by his comrades to receive it, for he was shy and nervous and tried to sidle away.

" Look at the noble chairman ; he had driven down from his proper place in the House of Lords, where were gathered earls and dukes, and the men who had done well as lawyers, and judges, and statesmen, and warriors, and the Princes of the royal blood. Yet, all peer though he was, he was moved to the sincerest depths of his being as he murmured, ' I have the honor,' and pinned the life-saving medal on the child's jacket. His heart was full. He paused to swallow down something that would rise in his throat before he could go on.

" There is the ' glory and honor ' of successful statesmen, and warriors, and lawyers, but the glory of self-forgetful saving of life is a glory that excelleth, and that was the wondrous glory won by this boy. He had plunged into the stream and shared a drowning boy's risk, and that little hand, look at it there, steadying him by holding the table, had come out holding the saved.

" Why has self-forgetfulness such mighty power? How was it that a twelve-year-old boy could bow down an audience of grown men before him ? What gave to that brow, with its stubby crown of carroty

hair, a glory and honor more than the lustre of gold
and jewels?　Why was it that that small body in its
little breeches and jacket, wiping its tears on the
rough little sleeve, could grip thousands of hearts
and hold them all, and make them for the time loyal
members of his kingdom?

"Why was all this so?

"It was so because that little boy in his measure
had been like Christ, in the self-forgetful spirit of
sacrifice for others.　He had a bit of the same
beauty we are all made on purpose to worship; the
glory before which angels give a great shout, and all
the company of heaven fall down and adore, saying
with a loud voice, 'Worthy is the Lamb that was
slain!'"

The "Lamb that was slain" is the mightiest King
the world has ever known, and all who partake of His
spirit share in His kingdom.

And since this kingdom is not a *place*, but is *character*, those who have not the character cannot by any
possibility be in it.

We pray daily, "Thy kingdom come."　Do we
know what we are praying for?　Do we comprehend
the change it will make in us if it comes in us?　Are
we willing to be so changed?

What is the kingdom of God but the rule of God?
And what is the rule of God but the will of God?
Therefore when we pray, "Thy will be done on
earth as it is in heaven," we have touched the secret
of it all.

A horde of savages might conquer a civilized

kingdom by sheer brute force; but if they would conquer the civilization of that kingdom, they could only do so by submitting to its control. And just so is it with the kingdom of heaven. It yields its sceptre to none but those who render obedience to its laws.

"To him that overcometh will I give to sit with me in my throne, even as I also overcame and am set down with my Father in his throne."

"He always reigns who sides with God," says an old writer. And again, "He who perfectly accepts the will of God, dwells in a perpetual kingdom."

Art thou reigning after this fashion and in this sort of a kingdom?

Art thou the "chiefest" by being the "servant of all"?

Art thou a king over thy circumstances, or do thy circumstances reign over thee?

Dost thou triumph over thy temptations, or do they triumph over thee?

Canst thou sit on an inward throne in the midst of outward defeat and loss?

Canst thou conquer by yielding, and become the greatest by being the least?

If thou canst answer Yes to all these questions, then thou art come into thy kingdom; and whatever thy outward lot may be, or the estimation in which men may hold thee, thou art in very truth among the number of those concerning whom our Lord declares "the same shall be called great in the kingdom of heaven."

CHAPTER XXI.

THE CHARIOTS OF GOD.

FOUNDATION TEXT. — Psalm lxviii. 17.

CHARIOTS are for conveyance and progress. Earthly chariots carry the bodies of those who ride in them over all intervening distances or obstacles to the place of their destination; and God's chariots carry their souls. No words can express the glorious places to which that soul shall arrive who travels in the chariots of God. And our verse tells us they are "very many." All around us on every side they wait for us; but we, alas! do not always see them. Earth's chariots are always visible, but God's chariots are invisible.

2 Kings vi. 14–17.

The king of Syria came up against the man of God with horses and chariots that were visible to every one, but God had chariots that could be seen by none save the eye of faith. The servant of the prophet could only see the outward and visible, and he cried, as so many have done since, "Alas, my

Master! how shall we do?" But the prophet himself sat calmly within his house without fear, because his eyes were opened to see the invisible. And all that he asked for his servant was, "Lord, I pray thee open his eyes that he may see."

This is the prayer we need to pray for ourselves and for one another, "Lord, open our eyes that we may see." For the world all around us is full of God's horses and chariots, waiting to carry us to places of glorious victory.

But they do not look like chariots. They look instead like enemies, sufferings, trials, defeats, misunderstandings, disappointments, unkindnesses. They look like Juggernaut cars of misery and wretchedness, that are only waiting to roll over us and crush us into the earth; but they really are chariots of triumph in which we may ride to those very heights of victory for which our souls have been longing and praying.

Deut. xxxii. 12, 13.

If we would "ride on the high places of the earth" we must get into the chariots that can take us there; and only the "chariots of God" are equal to such lofty riding as this.

Isa. lviii. 14.

We may make out of each event in our lives either a Juggernaut car to crush us, or a chariot in which to ride to heights of victory. It all depends upon how we take them; whether we lie down under our trials and let them roll over and crush us, or whether we climb up into them as into a chariot, and make them carry us triumphantly onward and upward.

2 Kings ii. 11, 12.

Whenever we mount into God's chariots the same thing happens to us spiritually that happened to Elisha. We shall have a translation. Not into the heavens above us, as Elisha did, but into the heaven within us, which after all is almost a grander translation than his. We shall be carried up away from the low earthly grovelling plane of life, where everything hurts and everything is unhappy, up into the "heavenly places in Christ Jesus," where we shall ride in triumph over all below.

Eph. ii. 6.

These "heavenly places" are interior, not exterior, and the road that leads to them is interior also. But the chariot that carries the soul over this road is generally some outward loss, or trial or disappointment; some chastening that does not indeed seem for the present to be joyous, but grievous; but that nevertheless afterward yieldeth the peaceable fruits of righteousness to them that are exercised thereby.

Heb. xii. 5-11.

Look upon these chastenings, no matter how grievous they may be for the present, as God's chariots sent to carry your souls into the "high places" of spiritual achievement and uplifting, and you will find that they are after all "paved with love."

Canticles iii. 9, 10.

Your own individual chariot may look very unlovely. It may be a cross-grained relative or friend;
it may be the result of human malice, or cruelty, or
neglect; but every chariot sent by God must necessarily be paved with love, since God is love, and God's
love is the sweetest, softest, tenderest thing to rest
one's self upon that was ever found by any soul anywhere. It is His love indeed that sends the chariot.

Hab. iii. 8, 12, 13.

Here the prophet tells us that it was God's dis-
pleasure against the obstacles which beset the path
of His people that made Him come to their rescue,
riding in His "chariots of salvation." Everything
becomes a "chariot of salvation" when God rides
upon it.

Ps. civ. 3; Isa. xix. 1.

The "clouds" that darken our skies and seem to
shut out the shining of the sun of righteousness are,
after all, if we only knew it, His chariots, into which
we may mount with Him, and "ride prosperously"
over all the darkness.

Ps. xlv. 3, 4; Ps. xviii. 10; Deut. xxxiii. 26.

A late writer has said that we cannot, by even the
most vigorous and toilsome efforts, sweep away the
clouds, but we can climb so high above them as to
reach the clear atmosphere overhead; and he who
rides with God rides upon the heavens far above all
earth-born clouds.

Ps. lxviii. 32–34.

This may sound fanciful, but it is really exceedingly practical when we begin to act it out in our
daily lives.

I knew a lady who had a very slow servant. She
was an excellent girl in every other respect, and very
valuable in the household, but her slowness was a
constant source of irritation to her mistress, who
was naturally quick, and who always chafed at slowness. The lady would consequently get out of temper with the girl twenty times a day, and twenty
times a day would repent of her anger, and resolve
to conquer it, but in vain. Her life was made miserable by the conflict. One day it occurred to her
that she had for a long while been praying for patience, and that perhaps this slow servant was the
very chariot the Lord had sent to carry her soul over
into patience. She immediately accepted it as such,
and from that time used the slowness of her servant
as a chariot for her soul. And the result was a victory of patience that no slowness of anybody was
ever after able to disturb.

Another instance : I knew a sister at one of our
conventions who was put to sleep in a room with two
others on account of the crowd. *She* wanted to
sleep, but *they* wanted to talk, and the first night she
was greatly disturbed, and lay there fretting and
fuming long after the others had hushed and she
might have slept. But the next day she heard something about God's chariots, and at night she accepted

these talking sisters as her chariots to carry her over into sweetness and patience, and she lay there feeling peaceful and at rest. When, however, it grew very late, and she knew they all ought to be sleeping, she ventured to say slyly, " Sisters, I am lying here riding in a chariot," and the effect was instantaneous in producing perfect quiet. Her chariot had carried her over to victory, not only inwardly, but at last outwardly as well.

If we would ride in God's chariots, instead of in our own, we should find this to be the case continually.

Isa. xxxi. 1-3; Ps. xx. 7, 8.

Our constant temptation is to trust in the "chariots of Egypt." We can *see* them ; they are tangible and real, and they look so substantial ; while God's chariots are invisible and intangible, and it is hard to believe they are there. Our eyes are not opened to see them.

2 Kings xix. 23.

We try to reach the high places with the " multitude of our chariots." We depend first on one thing, and then on another, to advance our spiritual condition and to gain our spiritual victories. We "go down to Egypt for help." And God is obliged often to destroy all our own chariots before he can bring us to the point of mounting into His.

Micah v. 10; Hag. ii. 22.

We lean too much upon a dear friend to help us onward in the spiritual life, and the Lord is obliged to separate us from that friend. We feel that all our spiritual prosperity depends on our continuance under the ministry of a favorite preacher, and we are mysteriously removed. We look upon our prayer-meeting or our Bible-class as the chief source of our spiritual strength, and we are shut up from attending it. And the "chariot of God," which alone can carry us to the places where we hoped to be taken by the instrumentalities upon which we have been depending, is to be found in the very deprivations we have so mourned over. God must burn up with the fire of His love every chariot of our own that stands in the way of our mounting into His.

Isa. lxvi. 15, 16.

Let us be thankful, then, for every trial that will help to destroy our chariots, and will compel us to take refuge in the chariot of God, which stands ready and waiting beside us.

Ps. lxii. 5–8.

We have to be brought to the place where all other refuges fail us, before we can say, " He only." We say, " He *and* — something else." "He, and my ex-experience," or " He, and my church relationships," or " He, and my Christian work "; and all that comes after the "and " must be taken away from us, or must be proved useless before we can come to the " He only." As long as visible chariots are at hand, the soul will not mount into the *in*visible ones.

Ps. lxviii. 4.

If we want to ride with God "upon the heavens," we have to be brought to an end of all riding upon the earth.

Ps. lxviii. 24.

To see God's "goings," we must get into the "sanctuary" of his presence ; and to share in His "goings" and "go" with Him, we must abandon all earthly "goings."

Prov. xx. 24; Ps. xvii. 5; Ps. xl. 1, 2.

When we mount into God's chariot our goings are "established," for no obstacles can hinder its triumphal course.   All losses therefore are gains that bring us to this.

Phil. iii. 7–9.

Paul understood this, and he gloried in the losses which brought him such unspeakable gain.

2 Cor. xii. 7–10.

Even the "thorn in the flesh," the messenger of Satan sent to buffet him, became only a chariot to his willing soul, that carried him to heights of triumph which he could have reached in no other way. To "take pleasure" in one's trials, what is this but turning them into the grandest of chariots?

Joseph had a revelation of his future triumphs and reigning, but the chariots that carried him there looked to the eye of sense like the bitterest failures and defeats.   It was a strange road to a kingdom, through slavery and a prison, and yet by no other road could Joseph have reached his triumph.

His dream, Gen. xxxvii. 5-10; His chariots, Gen. xxxvii. 19, 20,
   27, 28; xxxix. 19, 20; How he rode in his chariots, Gen.
   xxxix. 1-6, 21-23; His triumph, Gen. xliii. 38-43.

And now a word as to how one is to mount into
these chariots.

My answer would be simply this : Find out where
God is in each one of them, and hide yourself in
Him.   Or, in other words, do what the little child
does when trouble comes, who finds its mother and
hides in her arms.   The real chariot after all that
takes us through triumphantly is the carrying of
God.

Isa. xlvi. 4.

The baby carried in the chariot of its mother's
arms rides triumphantly through the hardest places,
and does not even know they are hard.

Isa. lxiii. 9.

And how much more we, who are carried in the
chariot of the " arms of God " !

Get into your chariot, then.   Take each thing that
is wrong in your lives as God's chariot for you.   No
matter who the builder of the wrong may be, whether
men or devils, by the time it reaches your side it is
God's chariot for you, and is meant to carry you to
a heavenly place of triumph.   Shut out all the second causes, and find the Lord in it.   Say, " Lord,
open my eyes that I may see, not the visible enemy,
but thy unseen chariots of deliverance."

Accept His will in the trial, whatever it may be,
and hide yourself in His arms of love.   Say, " Thy

will be done; Thy will be done!" over and over. Shut out every other thought but the one thought of submission to His will and of trust in His love. Make your trial thus your chariot, and you will find your soul "riding upon the heavens" with God in a way you never dreamed could be.

I have not a shadow of doubt that if all our eyes were opened to-day we would see our homes, and our places of business, and the streets we traverse, filled with the " chariots of God." There is no need for any one of us to walk for lack of chariots. That cross inmate of your household, who has hitherto made life a burden to you, and who has been the Juggernaut car to crush your soul into the dust, may henceforth be a glorious chariot to carry you to the heights of heavenly patience and long-suffering. That misunderstanding, that mortification, that unkindness, that disappointment, that loss, that defeat, all these are chariots waiting to carry you to the very heights of victory you have só longed to reach.

Mount into them, then, with thankful hearts, and lose sight of all second causes in the shining of His love who will "carry you in His arms" safely and triumphantly over it all.

CHAPTER XXII.

"WITHOUT ME YE CAN DO NOTHING."

CONCERNING THE LIFE OF DIVINE UNION IN ITS PRACTICAL ASPECTS.

NOT long ago I was driving with a Quaker preacher through our beautiful Philadelphia Park, when our conversation turned on the apparent fruitlessness of a great deal of the preaching in the church at the present time. We had spoken, of course, of the foundation cause in the absence of the power of the Holy Ghost, but we still felt that this could not account for it all, as we both of us knew many preachers really baptized with the Spirit, who yet seemed to have no fruit to their ministry. And then I suggested that one reason might be in the fact that so many ministers, when preaching or talking on religious subjects, put on a different tone and manner from the one they ordinarily use, and by this very manner remove religion so far from the range of ordinary life, as to fail of gaining any real hold on the hearts of the men and women whose whole lives are lived on the plane of ordinary and homely pleasures and duties. "Now, for instance,"

I said, "if in thy preaching from the Friends' gallery thee could use the same tone and manner as thy present one, how much more effectual and convincing thy preaching would be." "Oh, but I could not do *that*," was the reply, "because the preacher's gallery is so much more solemn a place than this." "But why is it more solemn?" I asked. "Is it not the presence of God only that makes the gallery or the pulpit solemn, and have we not the presence of God equally here? Is it not just as solemn to live in our every-day life as it is to preach, and ought we not to do the one to His glory just as much as the other?" And then I added, as the subject seemed to open out before me, "I verily believe a large part of the difficulty lies in the unscriptural and unnatural divorce that has been brought about between our so-called religious life and our so-called temporal life; as if our religion were something apart from ourselves, a sort of outside garment that was to be put on and off according to our circumstances and purposes. On Sundays, for instance, and in church, our purpose is to seek God, and worship and serve Him, and therefore on Sundays we bring out our religious life and put it on in a suitably solemn manner, and live it with a strained gravity and decorum which deprives it of half its power. But on Mondays our purpose is to seek our own interests and serve them, and so we bring out our temporal life and put it on with a sense of relief, as from an unnatural bondage, and live it with ease and naturalness, and consequently with far more power."

The thoughts thus started remained with me and gathered strength. Not long afterward I was present at a meeting where the leader opened with reading John xv., and the words, "Without me ye can do nothing," struck me with amazement. Hundreds of times before I had read those words, and had thought that I understood them thoroughly. But now it seemed almost as though they must have been newly inserted in the Bible, so ablaze were they with wondrous meaning.

"There it is," I said to myself, "Jesus himself said so, that apart from Him we have no real life of any kind, whether we call it temporal or spiritual, and that, therefore, all living or doing that is without Him is of such a nature that God, who sees into the realities of things, calls it 'nothing.'" And then the question forced itself upon me as to whether any soul really believed this statement to be true; or, if believing it theoretically, whether any one made it practical in their daily walk and life. And I saw, as in a flash almost, that the real secret of divine union lay quite as much in this practical aspect of it as in any interior revealings or experiences. For if I do nothing, literally nothing, apart from Christ, I am of course united to Him in a continual oneness that cannot be questioned or gainsaid; while if I live a large part of my daily life and perform a large part of my daily work apart from Him, I have no real union, no matter how exalted and delightful my emotions concerning it may be.

It is to consider this aspect of the subject, there

fore, that the present paper is written. For I am
very sure that the wide divorce made between things
spiritual and things temporal, of which I have spoken,
has done more than almost anything else to hinder
a realized interior union with God, and to put all
religion so outside of the pale of common life as to
make it an almost unattainable thing to the ordinary
mass of mankind. Moreover it has introduced an
unnatural constraint and stiltedness into the experience of Christians that seems to shut them out from
much of the free, happy, childlike ease that belongs
of right to the children of God.

I feel, therefore, that it is of vital importance for
us to understand the truth of this matter.

And the thought that makes it clearest to me is
this, that the fact of our oneness with Christ contains
the whole thing in a nutshell. If we are one with
Him, then of course in the very nature of things we
can do nothing without Him. For that which is one
cannot act as being two. And if I therefore do anything without Christ, then I am not one with Him
in that thing, and like a branch severed from the
vine I am withered and worthless. It is as if the
branch should recognize its connection with and dependence upon the vine for most of its growth, and
fruit-bearing, and climbing, but should feel a capacity
in itself to grow and climb over a certain fence or
around the trunk of a certain tree, and should therefore sever its connection with the vine for this part
of its living. Of course that which thus sought an
independent life would wither and die in the very

nature of things. And just so is it with us who are branches of Christ the true vine. No independent action, whether small or great, is possible to us without withering and death, any more than to the branch of the natural vine.

This will show us at once how fatal to the realized oneness with Christ, for which our souls hunger, is the divorce I have spoken of. We have all realized, more or less, that without Him we cannot live our religious life, but when it comes to living our so-called temporal life, to keeping house. or transacting business, or making calls, or darning stockings, or sweeping a room, or trimming a bonnet, or entertaining company, who is there that even theoretically thinks such things as these are to be done for Christ, and can only be rightly done as we abide in Him and do them in His strength ?

But if it is Christ working in the Christian who is to lead the prayer-meeting, then, since Christ and the Christian are one, it must be also Christ working in and through the Christian who is to keep the house and make the bargain ; and one duty is therefore in the very essence of things as religious as the other. It is the man that makes the action, not the action the man. And as much solemnity and sweetness will thus be brought into our every-day domestic and social affairs as into the so-called religious occasions of life, if we will only " acknowledge God in all our ways," and do whatever we do, even if it be only eating and drinking, to His glory.

If our religion is really our life, and not merely

something extraneous tacked on to our life, it must necessarily go into everything in which we live ; and no act, however human or natural it may be, can be taken out of its control and guidance.

If God is with us *always*, then He is just as much with us in our business times and our social times as in our religious times, and one moment is as solemn with His presence as another.

If it is a fact that in Him we " live and move and have our being," then it is also a fact, whether we know it or not, that without Him we cannot do anything. And facts are stubborn things, thank God, and do not alter for all our feelings.

In Psalm cxxvii. 1, 2, we have a very striking illustration of this truth. The Psalmist says, " Except the Lord build the house, they labor in vain that build it : except the Lord keep the city, the watchman waketh but in vain. It is vain for you to rise up early, to sit up late, to eat the bread of sorrows; for so He giveth His beloved sleep." The two things here spoken of as being done in vain, unless the Lord is in the doing of them, are purely secular things, so called; simple business matters on the human plane of life. And whatever spiritual lesson they were intended to teach gains its impressiveness only from this, that these statements concerning God's presence in temporal things were statements of patent and incontrovertible facts.

In truth the Bible is full of this fact, and the only wonder is how any believer in the Bible could have overlooked it. From the building of cities down to

the numbering of the hairs of our head and the not-
ing of a sparrow's fall, throughout the whole range
of homely daily living. God is declared to be present
and to be the main-spring of it all. Whatever we do,
even if it be such a purely physical thing as eating and
drinking, we are to do for Him and to His glory;
and we are exhorted to so live and so walk in the
light in everything, as to have it made manifest of
all our works, temporal as well as spiritual, that
" they are wrought in God."

There is unspeakable comfort in this for every
,oving Christian heart, in that it turns all of life into
a sacrament, and makes the kitchen, or the workshop,
or the nursery, or the parlor, as sweet and solemn a
place of service to the Lord, and as real a means of
union with Him, as the prayer-meeting, or the mission board, or the charitable visitation.

A dear young Christian mother and housekeepei
came to me once with a sorely grieved heart, because
of her engrossing temporal life. "There seems,"
she said, "to be nothing spiritual about my life
from one week's end to the other. My large family
of little children are so engrossing that day after
day passes without my having a single moment for
anything but simply attendance on them and on my
necessary household duties, and I go to bed night
after night ᷉sick at heart because I have felt separated from my Lord all day long, and have not been
able to do anything for Him." I told her of what I
have written above, and assured her that all would
be changed if she would only see and acknowledge

God in all these homely duties, and would recognize
her utter dependence upon Him for the doing of
them.   Her heart received the good news with gladness, and months afterward she told me that from
that moment life had become a transformed and
glorified thing, with the abiding presence of the
Lord, and with the sweetness of continual service to
Him.

Another Christian, a young lady in a fashionable
family, came to me also in similar grief that in so
much of her life she was separated from God and
had no sense of His presence.   I told her she ought
never to do anything that could cause such a separation; but she assured me that it was impossible to
avoid it, as the things she meant were none of them
wrong things.   "For instance," she said, "it is plainly
my duty to pay calls with my mother, and yet nothing seems to separate me so much from God as paying calls."   "But how would it be," I asked, "if you
paid the calls as service to the Lord and for His
glory?"   "What!" she exclaimed, "pay calls for
God!   I never heard of such a thing."   "But why
not?" I asked; "if it is right to pay calls at all it
ought to be done for God, for we are commanded
whatsoever we do to do it for His glory, and if it is
not right you ought not to do it.   As a Christian,"
I continued, "you must not do anything that you cannot do for Him."   "I see! I see!" she exclaimed,
after a little pause, "and it makes all life look so
different!   Nothing can separate me from Him that
is not sin, but each act done to His glory, whatever

it may be, will only draw me closer and make His presence more real."

These two instances will illustrate my meaning. And I feel sure there are thousands of other burdened and weary lives that would be similarly transformed if these truths were but realized and acted on.

An old spiritual writer says something to this effect, that in order to become a saint it is not always necessary to change our works, but only to put an interior purpose towards God in them all; that we must begin to do for His glory and in His strength that which before we did for self and in self's capacity; which means, after all, just what our Lord meant when He said, "Without me ye can do nothing."

There is another side of this truth also which is full of comfort, and which the Psalmist develops in the verses I have quoted. "It is vain," he says, "to rise up early, to sit up late, to eat the bread of sorrows." Or, in other words, "What is the use of all this worry and strain? For the work will after all amount to nothing unless God is in it, and if He *is* in it, what folly to fret or be burdened, since He of course, by the very fact of His presence, assumes the care and responsibility of it all."

Ah, it is vain indeed, and I would that all God's children knew it!

We mothers at least ought to know it, for our own ways with our children would teach us something of it every day we live, if we had but the "eyes to see."

How many mothers have risen early, and sat up

late, and eaten the bread of sorrows, just that they might give sleep to their beloved children. And how grieved their hearts would have been if, after all their pains, the children had refused to rest. I can appeal to some mother hearts, I am sure, as thoroughly understanding my meaning. Memories will arise of the flushed and rosy boy coming in at night, tired with his play or his work, with knees out and coat torn, and of the patient, loving toil to patch and mend it all, sitting up late and rising early, that the dearly loved cause of all the mischief might rest undisturbed in childhood's happy sleep. How "vain," and worse than vain, would it have been for that loved and cared-for darling to have himself also sat up late, and risen early, and eaten the bread of sorrows, when all the while his mother was doing it for him just that he might not have it to do.

And if this is true of mothers, how much more true must it be of Him who made the mothers, and who came among us in bodily form to bear our burdens, and carry our sorrows, and do our work, just that we might "enter into His rest."

Beloved, *have* we entered into this rest?

"For he that is entered into his rest, he also hath ceased from his own works as God did from His." That is, he has learned at last the lesson that without Christ or apart from Him he can do nothing, but that he can do all things through Christ strengthening him; and therefore he has laid aside all self-effort, and has abandoned himself to God that He may work in him both to will and to do of His good pleasure. This and this only is the rest that remaineth for the people of God.

Scientific men are seeking to resolve all forces in nature into one primal force. Unity of origin is the present cry of science. Light, heat, sound are all said to be the products of one force differently applied, and that force is motion. All things, say the scientists, can be resolved back to this. Whether they are right or wrong I cannot say; but the Bible reveals to us one grand primal force which is behind motion itself, and that is God-force. God is at the source of everything, God is the origin of everything, God is the explanation of everything. Without Him was not anything made that was made, and without Him is not anything done that is done.

Surely, then, it is not the announcement of any mystery, but the simple statement of a simple fact, when our Lord says, "Without me ye can do nothing."

Even of Himself He said, "I can of mine own self do nothing," and He meant that He and His Father were so one that any independent action was impossible. Surely it is the revelation of a glorious necessity existing between our souls and Christ that He should say we could do nothing without Him; for it means that He has made us so one with Himself that independent action is as impossible with us as towards Him, as it was with Him as towards His Father.

Dear Christian, dost thou not catch a glimpse here of a region of wondrous glory?

Let us believe, then, that without Him we can lit-erally do nothing. We *must* believe it, for it is true. But let us recognize its truth, and act on it from this time forward. Let us make a hearty renunciation of all living apart from Christ, and let us begin from this moment to acknowledge Him in all our ways, and do everything, whatsoever we do, as service to Him and for His glory, depending upon Him alone for wisdom, and strength, and sweetness, and pa-tience, and everything else that is necessary for the right accomplishing of all our living.

As I said before, it is not so much a change of acts that will be necessary, as a change of motive and of dependence. The house will be kept, or the children cared for, or the business transacted, per-haps, just the same as before as to the outward, but inwardly God will be acknowledged, and depended on, and served; and there will be all the difference between a life lived at ease in the glory of His pres-ence, and a life lived painfully and with effort apart from Him. There will result also from this bring-ing of God into our affairs a wonderful accession of divine wisdom in the conduct of them, and a far greater quickness and despatch in their accomplish-ment, a surprising increase in the fertility of resource, an ease in apprehending the true nature and bearing of things, and an elargement on every side that will amaze the hitherto cramped and cabined soul.

I mean this literally. I mean that the house will be kept more nicely and with greater ease, the chil-dren will be trained more wifely, the stockings will be darned more swiftly, the guest will be entertained more comfortably, the servants will be managed more easily, the bargain will be made more satisfactorily, and all life will move with far more sweetness and harmony. For God will be in every moment of it, and where He is all *must* go well.

Moreover the soul itself, in this natural and simple way, will acquire such a holy habit of "abiding in Christ" that at last His presence will become the most real thing in life to our consciousness, and an habitual, silent, and secret conversation with Him will be carried on that will yield a continual joy.

Sometimes the child of God asks eagerly and hungrily, "What is the shortest and quickest way by which I can reach the highest degree of union and communion with God, possible to human beings in this life?" No shorter or quicker way can be found than the one I have been declaring. By the homely path of every-day duties done thus in God and for God, the sublimest heights are reached. Not as a reward, however, but as an inevitable and natural result, for if we thus abide in Him and refuse to leave Him, where He is there shall we also be, and all that He is will be ours.

If, then, thou wouldst know, beloved reader, the interior divine union realized in thy soul, begin from this very day to put it outwardly in practice as I have suggested. Offer each moment of thy living and each act of thy doing to God, and say to Him continually, "Lord, I am doing this in Thee and for Thy glory. Thou art my strength, and my wisdom, and

my all-sufficient supply for every need.   I depend
only upon Thee."   Refuse utterly to live for a single
moment or to perform a single act apart from Him.
Persist in this until it becomes the established habit
of thy soul.   And sooner or later thou shalt surely
know the longings of thy soul satisfied in the abiding
presence of Christ, thy indwelling Life.

CHAPTER XXIII.

"GOD WITH US"; OR, THE ONE HUNDRED AND THIRTY-NINTH PSALM.

"Thus doth thy hospitable greatness lie
    Around us like a boundless sea;
We cannot lose ourselves where all is home,
    Nor drift away from Thee."

VERY few of us understand the full meaning of the words in Matt. i. 23, "They shall call His name Emmanuel; which being interpreted is, God with us." In this short sentence is revealed to us the grandest fact the world can ever know; that God, the Almighty God, the Creator of Heaven and earth, is not a far-off Deity, dwelling in a Heaven of unapproachable glory, but is living with us right here in this world, in the midst of our poor, ignorant, helpless lives, as close to us as we are to ourselves. This seems so incredible to the human heart that we are very slow to believe it; but that the Bible teaches it as a fact, from cover to cover, cannot be denied by any honest mind. In the very beginning of Genesis we read of the " presence of the Lord God amongst

the trees of the garden." And from that time on
He is revealed to us always as in the most familiar
and daily intercourse with His people everywhere.
In Exodus we find Him asking them to make Him a
" sanctuary, that He might dwell among them." He
is recorded as having " walked " with them in the
wilderness, and as "taking up His abode " with them
in the promised land. He taught them to rely on
Him as an ever-present Friend and Helper, to consult Him about all their affairs, and to abandon tne
whole management of their lives to Him. And
finally He came in Christ in bodily form and dwelt
in the world as a man among men, making Himself
bone of our bone and flesh of our flesh, taking upon
Him our nature, and revealing to us, in the most
tangible and real way possible, the grand, and blessed,
and incomprehensible fact that He intended to be
with us always, even unto the end of the world.

Whoever will believe this fact with all their hearts
will find in it the solution of every difficulty of their
lives.

I remember when I was a little girl and found myself in any trouble or perplexity, the coming in of
my father or mother on the scene would always bring
me immediate relief. The moment I heard the voice
of one of them saying, " Daughter, I am here," that
moment every burden dropped off and every anxiety
was stilled. It was their simple presence that did it.
They did not need to promise to relieve me, they
did not need to tell me their plans of relief ; the
simple fact of their presence was all the assurance I

required that everything now would be set straight and all would go well for me, and my only interest after their arrival was simply to see *how* they would do it all. Perhaps they were exceptional parents, to have created such confidence in their children's hearts. I think myself they were. But as our God is certainly an exceptional God, the application has absolute force, and His presence is literally all we need. It would be enough for us, even if we had not a single promise nor a single revelation of His plans. How often in the Bible He has stilled all questions and all fears by the simple announcement, "I will be with thee"; and who can doubt that in these words He meant to assure us that all His wisdom, and love, and omnipotent power would therefore, of course, be engaged on our side? Over and over again in my childhood have the magic words, "Oh, there is mother!" brought me immediate relief and comfort; and over and over again in my later years have almost the same words reverently spoken, "Oh, there is God!" brought me a far more blessed deliverance. With Him present, what could I have to fear? Since He has said, "I will never leave thee nor forsake thee," surely I may boldly say, "The Lord is my helper, and I will not fear what man shall do unto me." I remember to this day the inspiring sense of utter security that used to come to me with my earthly father's presence. I never feared anything when he was by. And surely with my Heavenly Father by, there can be no possible room for fear.

It is because of its practical help and comfort,

therefore, that I desire to make this wonderful fact
of "Emmanuel, God with us," clear and definite, for
I am very sure but few, even of God's own children,
really believe it.   They may say they do, they may
repeat a thousand times in the conventional, pious
tone considered suitable to such a sentiment, "Oh,
yes, we know that God is always present with us,
but — "   And in this "but" the whole story is told.
There are no "buts" in the vocabulary of the soul
that accepts His presence as a literal fact.   Such a
soul is joyously triumphant over every suggestion of
fear or of doubt.   It has God, and that is enough
for it.   His presence is its certain security and supply,
always, and for everything.

Let me, then, beg my readers to turn with me for
a while to the 139th Psalm, where we shall find a most
blessed revelation of this truth.

The central thought of the Psalm is to be found in
verses 7 to 12, "Whither shall I go from thy Spirit?
or whither shall I flee from thy presence?   If I
ascend up into heaven, thou art there: if I make my
bed in hell, behold, thou art there.   If I take the
wings of the morning, and dwell in the uttermost
parts of the sea; even there shall thy hand lead me,
and thy right hand shall hold me.   If I say, Surely
the darkness shall cover me; even the night shall be
light about me.   Yea, the darkness hideth not from
thee; but the night shineth as the day: the darkness
and the light are both alike to thee.   For thou hast
possessed my reins: thou hast covered me in my
mother's womb."

I cannot conceive of a more definite or sweeping declaration of His continual presence with us, wherever we may be or whatever we may do, than is contained in this passage. People talk about seeking to get into the presence of the Lord, but here we see that they cannot get out of it; that there is no place in the whole universe where He is not present; neither heaven, nor hell, nor the uttermost parts of the sea; and no darkness so great as to hide for one moment from Him. And the reason of this is, that He "has possessed our reins," which means that He is not only with us, but within us, and consequently must accompany us wherever we ourselves go.

We must accept it as true, therefore, that the words of our Lord, "Lo, I am with you alway, even unto the end of the world," were the expression, not of a beautiful sentiment merely, but of an incontrovertible fact. He *is* with us, and we cannot get away from Him.

We may be in such thick darkness as to be utterly unable to see Him, and may think, probably often have thought, that, therefore, He does not see us. But our Psalm assures us that the darkness hideth not from Him, and that, in fact, darkness and light are both alike to Him. We are as present to His view and as plainly seen when our own souls are in the depths of spiritual darkness, as when they are basking in the brightest light. The darkness may hide Him from us, but it does not hide us from Him. Neither does any apparent spiritual distance or wan-

dering take us out of His presence ; not even if we
go into the depths of sin in our wandering. In the
uttermost parts of the sea, or wherever we may be,
He is ever present to hold and to lead us. There is
not a moment nor a place where we can be left without His care.

There are times in our lives when delirium makes
us utterly unaware of the presence of our most
careful and tender nurses. A child in delirium will
cry out in anguish for its mother, and will harrow her
heart by its piteous lamentations and appeals, when
all the while she is holding its fevered hand, and
bathing its aching head, and caring for it with all the
untold tenderness of a mother's love. The darkness
of disease has hidden the mother from the child, but
has not hidden the child from the mother.

And just so it is with our God and us. The darkness of our doubts or our fears, of our sorrows or
our despair, or even of our sins, cannot hide us from
Him, although it may, and often does, hide Him
from us. He has told us that the darkness and the
light are both alike to Him; and if our faith will
only lay hold of this as a fact, we will be enabled to
pass through the darkest seasons in quiet trust, sure
that all the while, though we cannot see nor feel
Him, our God *is* caring for us, and will never leave
nor forsake us.

Whether, however, this abiding presence of our
God will be a joy to us or a sorrow, will depend
upon what we know about Him. If we think of
Him as a stern tyrant, intent only on His own glory,

we shall be afraid of His continual presence. If we think of Him as a tender, loving Father, intent only on our blessing and happiness, we shall be glad and thankful to have Him thus ever with us. For the presence and the care of love can never mean anything but good to the one beloved.

The Psalm we are considering shows us that the presence of our God is the presence of love, and that it brings us an infinitude of comfort and rest. He says in verses 1 to 5, "O Lord, thou hast searched me, and known me. Thou knowest my downsitting and mine uprising; thou understandest my thought afar off. Thou compassest my path and my lying down, and art acquainted with all my ways. For there is not a word in my tongue, but lo, O Lord, thou knowest it altogether. Thou hast beset me behind and before, and laid thine hand upon me."

Our God knows us and understands us, and is acquainted with all our ways. No one else in all the world understands us. Our actions are misinterpreted, it may be, and our motives misjudged. Our natural characteristics are not taken into account, nor our inherited tendencies considered. No one makes allowances for our ill health; no one realizes how much we have to contend with. But our Father knows it all. He *understands* us, and His judgment of us takes into account every element, conscious or unconscious, that goes to make up our character and to control our actions. Only an all-comprehending love can be just, and our God is just. No wonder Faber can say : —.

> "There is no place where earth's sorrows
> Are more felt than up in Heaven;
> There is no place where earth's failings
> Have such kindly judgment given."

Some of you have been afraid of His justice, per
haps, because you thought it would be against you.
But do you not see now that it is all on your side,
just as a mother's justice is, because "He knoweth
our frame and remembereth that we are dust"?   No
human judge can ever do this; and to me this comprehension of God is one of my most blessed comforts.   Often I do not understand myself; all within
looks confused and hopelessly tangled.   But then I
remember that He has searched me, and that He
knows me and understands the thoughts which so
perplex me, and that, therefore, I may just leave the
whole miserable tangle to Him to unravel.   And my
soul sinks down at once, as on downy pillows, into a
place of the most blissful rest.

Then further, because of this complete knowledge
and understanding of our needs, what comfort it is
to be told that He knows our downsitting and our
uprising; that He compasses our path, and takes note
of our lying down.   Just what a mother does for her
foolish, careless, ignorant, but dearly loved little ones,
this very thing does our God for us.   When a mother
is with her children she thinks of their comfort and
well-being always before her own.   *They* must have
comfortable seats where no draught can reach them,
no matter what amount of discomfort she may herself be compelled to endure.   Their beds must be

soft and their blankets warm, let hers be what they may. Their paths must be smooth and safe, even though she is obliged herself to walk in rough and dangerous ways. Her own comfort, as compared with that of her children, is of no account in a loving mother's eyes. And surely our God has not made the mothers in this world more capable of a self-sacrificing love than He is Himself. He *must* be better and greater on the line of love and self-sacrifice than any mother He ever made. Then, since He has assured us that He knows our downsitting and our uprising, that He compasses our path and our lying down, we may be perfectly and blessedly sure that in even these little details of our lives we get the very best that His love, and wisdom, and power can compass. I mean this in a very literal sense. I mean that He cares for our literal seats and our literal beds, and sees that we, each one, have just that sort of a seat or that sort of a bed which is best for us and for our highest development. And just on this last point is where He is so much better than any mother can be. His love is a wise love, that sees the outcome of things, and cares more for our highest good than for that which is lower. So that, while a mother's weak love cannot see beyond the child's present comfort, and cannot bear to inflict or allow any discomfort, the strong, wise love of our God can bear to permit the present discomfort, for the sake of the future glory that is to result therefrom.

At home and abroad, therefore, let us commit the

choosing of our seats, and of our beds, and of all
the other little homely circumstances of our daily
lives and surroundings, to the God who has thus
assured us that He knows all about every one of
them.

For we are told in our Psalm that He "besets"
our path.   We have some of us known what it was
to be "beset" by unwelcome and unpleasant people
or things.   But we never have thought, perhaps, that
we were beset by God, that He loves us so that He
cannot leave us alone, and that no coldness nor re-
buffs on our parts can drive Him away.   Yet it is
gloriously true !   And, moreover, He besets us "be·
hind" as well as before.   Just as a mother does.
She goes after her children and picks up all they
have dropped, and clears away all the rubbish they
have left behind them.   We mothers begin this in
the nursery with the blocks and playthings, and we
go on with it all our lives long; seeking continually
to set straight that which our children have left
crooked behind them ; often at the cost of much toil
and trouble, but always with a love that makes the
toil and trouble nothing in comparison to caring for
the children we love.   What good mother ever turned
away the poor little tearful darling who came with a
tangled knot for her unravelling, or refused to help
the eager rosy boy to unwind his kite-strings ?   Suppose it *has* been their own fault that the knots and
tangles have come, still her love can sympathize with
and pity the very faults themselves, and all the more
does she seek to atone for them.

All this and more does our God do for us from our earliest infancy, long even before we know enough to be conscious of it, until the very end of our earthly lives. We have seen Him *before* us perhaps, but we have never thought of Him as *behind* us as well. Yet it is a blessed fact that He is behind us all the time, longing to make crooked things straight, to untangle our tangled skeins, and to atone continually for the wrong we have done and the mistakes we have made. If any of us, therefore, have that in our past which has caused us anxiety or remorse, let us lift up our heads in a happy confidence from henceforth, that the God who is behind us will set it all straight somehow, if we will but commit it to Him, and can even make our very mistakes and misdoings work together for good. Ah! it is a grand thing to be "beset" by God.

Then again what depths of comfort there are in verses 14 to 16: "I will praise thee; for I am fearfully and wonderfully made: marvellous are Thy works; and that my soul knoweth right well. My substance was not hid from thee, when I was made in secret, and curiously wrought in the lowest parts of the earth. Thine eyes did see my substance, yet being unperfect; and in thy book all my members were written, which in continuance were fashioned, when as yet there was none of them."

One of the things which often troubles us more than we care to confess, is our dislike of the way we have been put together. Our mental or moral "make-up" does not suit us. We think if we had only been created with less of this or more of that, if we were less impulsive or more enthusiastic, if we had been made more like some one else whom we admire, that then our chances of success would have been far greater; that we could have served God far more acceptably; and could have been more satisfactory in every way to ourselves and to Him. And we are tempted sometimes to think that with our miserable make-up, it is hopeless to expect to please Him.

If we really realized that God Himself had made us, we should see the folly of all this at once, but we secretly feel as if somehow He had not had much hand in the matter, but as if we had been put together in a haphazard sort of way, that had left our characters very much to chance. We believe in creation in the general, but not in the particular, when it comes to ourselves. But in this Psalm we see that God has presided over the creation of each one of us, superintending the smallest details; even, to speak figuratively, writing down what each "member" was to be, when as yet there was none of them. Therefore we, just as we are naturally, with just the characteristics that inhere in us by birth, are precisely what God would have us to be, and were planned out by His own hand to do the especial work that He has prepared for our doing. I mean, of course, our natural characteristics, not the perversion of them by sin on our parts.

There is something very glorifying to the Creator in this way of looking at it. Genius always seeks expression, and seeks, too, to express itself in as great a variety of forms and ways as possible. No true artist repeats himself, but each picture he paints, or statue he carves, is a new expression of his creative power. When we go to an exhibition of pictures, we should feel it a lowering of art if two were exactly alike; and just so is it with us who are "God's workmanship." His creative power is expressed differently in each one of us. And in the individual "make-up" which sometimes so troubles us, there is a manifestation of this power different from every other, and without which the day of exhibition, when we are, each one, to be to the praise of His glory, would be incomplete. All He asks of us is that, as He has had the making of us, so He may also have the managing, since He alone understands us, and is, therefore, the only one who can do it. The man who makes an intricate machine is the best one to manage it and repair it; any one else who meddles with it is apt to spoil it. And when we think of the intricacy of our inward machinery and the continual failure of our own management of it, we may well be thankful to hand it all over to the One who created it, and to leave it in His hands. We may be sure He will then make the best out of us that can be made, and that we, even *we*, with our "peculiar temperaments," and our apparently unfortunate characteristics, will be made vessels unto honor, sanctified and meet for the Master's use, and fitted to every good work.

I met once with a saying in an old Quaker writer

which I have never forgotten: "Be content to be just what thy God has made thee." It has helped me to understand the point upon which I am dwelling; and I feel sure contentment with our own "make-up" is as essential a part of our submission to God as contentment with any other of the circumstances of our daily life. If we did not each one of us exist just as we are by nature, then one expression of God's creative power would be missing, and one part of His work would be left undone. And besides, to complain of ourselves is to complain of the One who has made us, and cannot but grieve Him. Let us be content, then, and only see to it that we let the Divine Potter make out of us the very best He can, and use us according to His own good pleasure.

Verses 17 and 18 bring out another view of God's continual presence with us, and that is, that He is always thinking about us, and that His thoughts are kind and loving thoughts, for the Psalmist calls them precious. "How precious also are thy thoughts unto me, O God! How great is the sum of them! If I should count them, they are more in number than the sand: when I awake, I am still with thee."

So many people are tempted to think that God is not paying any attention to them. They think that their interests and their affairs are altogether beneath His notice, and that they are too unworthy to hope for His attention. But they wrong Him grievously by such thoughts. A mother pays as much attention to her smallest infant as to her oldest children, and is as much interested in its little needs and pleasures as in theirs. I am not sure but she is more. Her thoughts dwell around the one who needs them most; and He who made the mother's heart will not Himself be less attentive to the needs and pleasures of the meanest and most helpless of His creatures. He even hears the young lions when they cry, and not a sparrow can fall to the ground without Him; therefore, we, who are of more value than many sparrows, need not be afraid of a moment's neglect.

In fact, the responsibilities of creating anything require an unintermitting care of it on the part of the Creator; and it is the glory of omnipotence that it can attend at once to the smallest details and to the grandest operations as well.

> 'For greatness which is infinite makes room
> For all things in its lap to lie;
> We should be crushed by a magnificence
> Short of infinity."

I do not know why it is that we consider a man or woman weak who attends to large affairs to the neglect of little details, and then turn around and accuse our God of doing this very thing. But if any of my readers have hitherto been guilty of this folly, let it end now and here, and let each one from hence-forth believe, without any questioning, that always and everywhere the "Lord thinketh upon me."

The remainder of the Psalm develops the perfect accord of thought between the soul and God, where this life of simple faith has been entered upon. Having learned the transforming fact of God's continual presence and unceasing care, the soul is

brought into so profound a union with Him as to
love what He loves, and hate what He hates; and
eagerly appeals to Him to search it, and try it, that
there may be no spot left anywhere in all its being
which is out of harmony with Him.

In the sunlight of His presence darkness must
flee, and the heart will soon feel that it cannot endure to have any corner shut away from His shining;
for in His presence is "fulness of joy," and at His
right hand "there are pleasures forevermore."

An old woman, living in a rather desolate part of
England, made considerable money by selling ale
and beer to chance travellers who passed her lonely
cottage.   But her conscience troubled her about it.
She wanted to be a Christian and to go to Heaven
when she died, but she had an inward feeling that
if she did become a Christian she would have to give
up her profitable business, and this she thought would
be more than she could do; so that between the two
things she was brought into great conflict.

But one night, at the meeting she attended, a
preacher from a distance told about the sweet and
blessed fact of God's continual presence with us, and
of the joy this was sure to bring when it was known.
Her soul was enraptured at the thought of such a
possibility for her, and forgetting all about the beer,
she began at once with a very simple faith to claim
it as a blessed reality.   Over and over again she
exclaimed in her heart, as the preacher went on
with his sermon, "Why, Lord Jesus, I didn't know
as thee wast always with me !   Why, Lord, how good

it is to know that I have got thee all the time to live with me and take care of me! Why, Lord, I sha'n't never be lonely no more!" And when the meeting closed and she took her way home across the moors, all the time the happy refrain went on, "Ah, Lord Jesus, thee art going home with me to-night. Never mind, Lord Jesus, old Betty won't never let thee go again now, I knows I have got thee!"

As her faith thus laid hold of the fact of His presence she began to rejoice in it more and more, until finally, when she had reached her cottage door, her soul was full of delight. As she opened the door, the first object her eyes rested upon was a great pot of ale on the table ready for selling. At once it flashed into her mind, "The Lord will not like to have that ale in the house where He lives," and her whole heart responded eagerly, "That ale shall go." She knew the pot was heavy, and she kneeled beside it saying, "Lord, thee hast come home with me, and thee art going to live with me always in this cottage, and I know thee don't like this ale. Please give me strength to tip it over into the road." Strength was given, and the ale was soon running down the lane. Then the old woman came back into her cottage, and kneeling down again thanked the Lord for the strength given, and added, "Now, Lord, if there is anything else in this cottage that thee does not like, show it to me, and it shall be tipped out too."

Is not this a perfect illustration of the close of our Psalm? "Do not I hate them, O Lord, that hate thee? and am not I grieved with those that rise up against thee? I hate them with a perfect hatred; I count them mine enemies. Search me, O God, and know my heart; try me, and know my thoughts; and see if there be any wicked way in me, and lead me in the way everlasting."

Just as light drives out darkness, so does the realized presence of God drive out sin, and the soul that by faith abides in His presence knows a very real and wonderful deliverance.

And now I trust that some will ask, "How can I find this presence to be real to myself?" I will close, therefore, with a few practical directions.

First, convince yourself from the Scriptures that it is a fact. Facts must always be the foundation of our experiences, or the experiences are worthless. It is not the feeling that causes the fact, but the fact that produces the feeling. And what every soul needs in this case first of all, is to be convinced beyond question, from God's own words about it, that His continual presence with us is an unalterable *fact*.

Then, this point having been settled, the next thing to do is to make it real to ourselves by "practising His presence," as an old writer expresses it, always and everywhere, and in everything.* This means simply that you are to obey the Scripture command, and "in all your ways acknowledge Him," by saying over each hour and moment, "The Lord is here," and by doing everything you do, even if only

* "The Practice of the Presence of God." Willard Tract Repository. A little book I would strongly recommend.

eating and drinking, in His presence and for Him. Literally, "whether, therefore, ye eat or drink, or *whatsoever* ye do, do all to the glory of God."

By this continual "practice of His presence," the soul at last acquires a *habit* of faith; and it becomes, finally, as difficult to doubt His presence as it was at first to believe it.

No great effort is required for this, but simply an unwavering faith. It is not studied reasonings or elaborate meditations that will help you here. The soul must recognize, by an act of simple faith, that God *is* present, and must then accustom itself to a continual conversation with Him about all its affairs, in freedom and simplicity. He does not require great things of us. A little remembrance of His presence, a few words of love and confidence, a momentary lifting of the heart to Him from time to time as we go about our daily affairs, a constant appeal to Him in everything as to a present and loving friend and helper, an endeavor to live in a continual sense of His presence, and a letting of our hearts "dwell at ease" because of it,—this is all He asks; the least little remembrance is welcome to Him, and helps to make His presence real to us.

Whoever will be faithful in this exercise will soon be led into a blessed realization of all I have been trying to tell in this book, and of far more that I cannot tell; and will understand in a way beyond telling, those wonderful words concerning our Lord, "They shall call His name Emmanuel, which being interpreted is, God with us."

TITLES in THIS SERIES

geles, 1925), *AROUND THE WORLD BY FAITH, WITH SIX WEEKS IN THE HOLY LAND* (Los Angeles, n. d.), *TWO YEARS MISSION WORK IN EUROPE JUST BEFORE THE WORLD WAR, 1912-14* (Los Angeles, [1926])

6. Boardman, W. E., *THE HIGHER CHRISTIAN LIFE* (Boston, 1858)

7. Girvin, E. A., *PHINEAS F. BRESEE: A PRINCE IN ISRAEL* (Kansas City, Mo., [1916])

8. Brooks, John P., *THE DIVINE CHURCH* (Columbia, Mo., 1891)

9. RUSSELL KELSO CARTER ON "FAITH HEALING." R. Kelso Carter, *THE ATONEMENT FOR SIN AND SICKNESS* (Boston, 1884) *"FAITH HEALING" REVIEWED AFTER TWENTY YEARS* (Boston, 1897)

10. Daniels, W. H., *DR. CULLIS AND HIS WORK* (Boston, [1885])

11. HOLINESS TRACTS DEFENDING THE MINISTRY OF WOMEN. Luther Lee, *"WOMAN'S RIGHT TO PREACH THE GOSPEL; A SERMON, AT THE ORDINATION OF REV. MISS ANTOINETTE L. BROWN, AT SOUTH BUTLER, WAYNE COUNTY, N. Y., SEPT. 15, 1853"* (Syracuse, 1853) *bound with* B. T. Roberts, *ORDAINING WOMEN* (Rochester, 1891) *bound with* Catherine (Mumford) Booth, *"FEMALE MINISTRY; OR, WOMAN'S RIGHT TO PREACH THE GOSPEL . . ."* (London, n. d.) *bound with* Fannie (McDowell) Hunter, *WOMEN PREACHERS* (Dallas, 1905)

12. LATE NINETEENTH CENTURY REVIVALIST TEACHINGS ON THE HOLY SPIRIT. D. L. Moody, *SECRET POWER OR THE SECRET OF SUCCESS IN CHRISTIAN LIFE AND*

WORK (New York, [1881]) *bound with* J. Wilbur Chapman, *RECEIVED YE THE HOLY GHOST?* (New York, [1894]) *bound with* R. A. Torrey, *THE BAPTISM WITH THE HOLY SPIRIT* (New York, 1895 & 1897)

13. SEVEN "JESUS ONLY" TRACTS. Andrew D. Urshan, *THE DOCTRINE OF THE NEW BIRTH, OR, THE PERFECT WAY TO ETERNAL LIFE* (Cochrane, Wis., 1921) *bound with* Andrew Urshan, *THE ALMIGHTY GOD IN THE LORD JESUS CHRIST* (Los Angeles, 1919) *bound with* Frank J. Ewart, *THE REVELATION OF JESUS CHRIST* (St. Louis, n. d.) *bound with* G. T. Haywood, *THE BIRTH OF THE SPIRIT IN THE DAYS OF THE APOSTLES* (Indianapolis, n. d.) *DIVINE NAMES AND TITLES OF JEHOVAH* (Indianapolis, n. d.) *THE FINEST OF THE WHEAT* (Indianapolis, n. d.) *THE VICTIM OF THE FLAMING SWORD* (Indianapolis, n. d.)

14. THREE EARLY PENTECOSTAL TRACTS. D. Wesley Myland, *THE LATTER RAIN COVENANT AND PENTECOSTAL POWER* (Chicago, 1910) *bound with* G. F. Taylor, *THE SPIRIT AND THE BRIDE* (n. p., [1907?]) *bound with* B. F. Laurence, *THE APOSTOLIC FAITH RESTORED* (St. Louis, 1916)

15. Fairchild, James H., *OBERLIN: THE COLONY AND THE COLLEGE, 1833-1883* (Oberlin, 1883)

16. Figgis, John B., *KESWICK FROM WITHIN* (London, [1914])

17. Finney, Charles G., *LECTURES TO PROFESSING CHRISTIANS* (New York, 1837)

18. Fleisch, Paul, *DIE MODERNE GEMEINSCHAFTSBEWEGUNG IN DEUTSCHLAND* (Leipzig, 1912)

19.   SIX TRACTS BY W. B. GODBEY. *SPIRITUAL GIFTS AND GRACES* (Cincinnati, [1895]) *THE RETURN OF JESUS* (Cincinnati, [1899?]) *WORK OF THE HOLY SPIRIT* (Louisville, [1902]) *CHURCH—BRIDE—KINGDOM* (Cincinnati, [1905]) *DIVINE HEALING* (Greensboro, [1909]) *TONGUE MOVEMENT, SATANIC* (Zarephath, N. J., 1918)

20.   Gordon, Earnest B., *ADONIRAM JUDSON GORDON* (New York, [1896])

21.   Hills, A. M., *HOLINESS AND POWER FOR THE CHURCH AND THE MINISTRY* (Cincinnati, [1897])

22.   Horner, Ralph C., *FROM THE ALTAR TO THE UPPER ROOM* (Toronto, [1891])

23.   McDonald, William and John E. Searles, *THE LIFE OF REV. JOHN S. INSKIP* (Boston, [1885])

24.   LaBerge, Agnes N. O., *WHAT GOD HATH WROUGHT* (Chicago, n. d.)

25.   Lee, Luther, *AUTOBIOGRAPHY OF THE REV. LUTHER LEE* (New York, 1882)

26.   McLean, A. and J. W. Easton, *PENUEL; OR, FACE TO FACE WITH GOD* (New York, 1869)

27.   McPherson, Aimee Semple, *THIS IS THAT: PERSONAL EXPERIENCES SERMONS AND WRITINGS* (Los Angeles, [1919])

28.   Mahan, Asa, *OUT OF DARKNESS INTO LIGHT* (London, 1877)

29.   THE LIFE AND TEACHING OF CARRIE JUDD MONTGOMERY Carrie Judd Montgomery, *"UNDER HIS WINGS": THE STORY OF MY LIFE* (Oakland,

[1936]) Carrie F. Judd, *THE PRAYER OF FAITH* (New York, 1880)

30. THE DEVOTIONAL WRITINGS OF PHOEBE PALMER Phoebe Palmer, *THE WAY OF HOLINESS* (52nd ed., New York, 1867) *FAITH AND ITS EFFECTS* (27th ed., New York, n. d., orig. pub. 1854)

31. Wheatley, Richard, *THE LIFE AND LETTERS OF MRS. PHOEBE PALMER* (New York, 1881)

32. Palmer, Phoebe, ed., *PIONEER EXPERIENCES* (New York, 1868)

33. Palmer, Phoebe, *THE PROMISE OF THE FATHER* (Boston, 1859)

34. Pardington, G. P., *TWENTY-FIVE WONDERFUL YEARS, 1889-1914: A POPULAR SKETCH OF THE CHRISTIAN AND MISSIONARY ALLIANCE* (New York, [1914])

35. Parham, Sarah E., *THE LIFE OF CHARLES F. PARHAM, FOUNDER OF THE APOSTOLIC FAITH MOVEMENT* (Joplin, [1930])

36. THE SERMONS OF CHARLES F. PARHAM. Charles F. Parham, *A VOICE CRYING IN THE WILDERNESS* (4th ed., Baxter Springs, Kan., 1944, orig. pub. 1902) *THE EVERLASTING GOSPEL* (n.p., n.d., orig. pub. 1911)

37. Pierson, Arthur Tappan, *FORWARD MOVEMENTS OF THE LAST HALF CENTURY* (New York, 1905)

38. *PROCEEDINGS OF HOLINESS CONFERENCES, HELD AT CINCINNATI, NOVEMBER 26TH, 1877, AND AT NEW YORK, DECEMBER 17TH, 1877* (Philadelphia, 1878)

39. *RECORD OF THE CONVENTION FOR THE PROMOTION OF*

Scriptural Holiness Held at Brighton, May 29th, to June 7th, 1875 (Brighton, [1896?])

40. Rees, Seth Cook, *Miracles in the Slums* (Chicago, [1905?])

41. Roberts, B. T., *Why Another Sect* (Rochester, 1879)

42. Shaw, S. B., ed., *Echoes of the General Holiness Assembly* (Chicago, [1901])

43. *The Devotional Writings of Robert Pearsall Smith and Hannah Whitall Smith*. [R]obert [P]earsall [S]mith, *Holiness Through Faith: Light on the Way of Holiness* (New York, [1870]) [H]annah [W]hitall [S]mith, *The Christian's Secret of a Happy Life*, (Boston and Chicago, [1885])

44. [S]mith, [H]annah [W]hitall, *The Unselfishness of God and How I Discovered It* (New York, [1903])

45. Steele, Daniel, *A Substitute for Holiness; or, Antinomianism Revived* (Chicago and Boston, [1899])

46. Tomlinson, A. J., *The Last Great Conflict* (Cleveland, 1913)

47. Upham, Thomas C., *The Life of Faith* (Boston, 1845)

48. Washburn, Josephine M., *History and Reminiscences of the Holiness Church Work in Southern California and Arizona* (South Pasadena, [1912?])